A. Neuberg

NLB

Armed Insurrection

Formerly published as
Der bewaffnete Aufstand in 1928
and *L'insurrection armée* in 1931
This edition first published 1970
Translated from the French and German by Quintin Hoare
© NLB, 1970

NLB, 7 Carlisle Street, London W1

Designed by Gerald Cinamon
Maps and Diagrams drawn by Paul White
Typeset in Monotype Ehrhardt
and printed by Western Printing Services Ltd, Bristol
SBN 902308 31 9

Translator's Note: *This translation has been made from the French edition of 1931, and extensively checked against the 1928 German edition. For ease of reading, titles of books have been given in English, even where no English edition in fact exists; this follows the practice of the French edition with respect to works in German, Russian, etc. References from Marx and Engels are to the two-volume* Selected Works (*Moscow, 1958*), *and to the* Selected Correspondence (*Moscow, 1953*). *References from Lenin are to the three-volume* Selected Works (*Moscow, 1967*) *or to the current English edition of the* Collected Works (*translated from the Russian Fourth Edition*). *References from the Sixth World Congress of the Communist International are to the* Proceedings *and the* Theses and Resolutions *as published in* Inprecorr. *In all the above cases, quotations are given in the existing translation; in other cases, and in the case of short quotations from Marx, Engels or Lenin where no precise reference is given, the quotations have been translated from the French version given by Neuberg. For Chinese proper names I have used the Wade-Giles system of transliteration, except for names more familiar in another form – e.g. Canton, Soochow. Wollenberg's introduction has been translated from the German. The footnotes are all Neuberg's, but references have in some cases been made more precise. Square brackets have been used for interpolations by the translator, e.g. Reval [Tallin], N[eumann].*

How we wrote *Armed Insurrection*

by Erich Wollenberg

I. BACKGROUND

In the spring of 1928 Piatnitsky,[1] the Organizing Secretary of the Comintern, called me into his office. I was at that time on the technical staff of the Marx-Engels Institute in Moscow, in charge of its military bureau, and taught in the military schools in which German communists were trained as specialists in insurrection.

Among those who took part in the discussion, in addition to Piatnitsky, were: General Unschlicht,[2] second-in-command to the People's Commissar for Defence and in charge of liaison between the General Staff of the Red Army and the Comintern; 'Ercoli', i.e. Togliatti, head of the Agitprop (agitation and propaganda) division of the Comintern; two or three high-ranking Soviet officers who taught as I did in the military schools for German communists; and a number of other Comintern functionaries.

Piatnitsky explained the aim of our discussion. He said that Alfred Langer's *The Road to Victory: the Art of Armed Insurrection*[3] was an outstanding manual for functionaries with a Marxist-Leninist training. A new, revised and expanded edition must be prepared. In addition, now was the right moment to publish a popular work on armed insurrection, aimed at a wider public of communists and sympathisers. For this purpose the teaching material which the Red Army Staff had devised for the German communist military schools was exceptionally suitable.

[1] An Old Bolshevik who was liquidated during the Stalinist purges (1936–8).

[2] Old Bolshevik, liquidated like Piatnitsky.

[3] This book, published secretly in Germany (in German) in 1928 and reprinted in an illegal second edition in 1931, was the work of a team of German communist military specialists in Moscow, under the direction of 'Alfred' (pseudonym of Ture Lehen, an officer first in the Finnish and later in the Soviet Army). 'Alfred' was assigned to the Comintern (Piatnitsky) by the Red Army Staff. At first the names of all the co-authors were to be given on the title-page (my pseudonym was 'Walter'). However, since this made a terribly long ('*langer*') name for a relatively small book, we banded together under the name 'Alfred Langer'.

The various individual sections of the new book were to be provided by the Red Army Staff and handed over to comrade Ercoli (Togliatti), who was responsible for putting the work together and publishing it as quickly as possible. The new book, partly to distinguish it from the 'Langer' book, was to be called simply *Armed Insurrection*. In order to avoid the suspicion of Soviet interference in the internal affairs of other countries, it would have to leave aside the important experiences of the 1919 armed insurrections in Hungary and Bavaria, which had led to the creation of Red Armies and the seizure of power by the proletariat.[4]

Piatnitsky also said that the new book must carry an 'author's' name, and naturally this could not be either a Russian name or that of any existing communist functionary. Since it was to be published first in German, and since it was a *new* book on the subject of armed insurrection, we chose the name '*Neu*berg'. We added an 'A' before this surname; a 'B' would have served equally well.

It may seem astonishing that an illegal communist book should have to have an 'author's name' and a 'publisher'. The German edition, which also had the subtitle: 'Attempt at a Theoretical Presentation', carried the imprint: '1928 – Otto Meyer, Printer and Publisher – Zurich'. These particulars would allow any comrade found in possession of the 'treasonable' book to claim that he had bought it at a meeting or legal demonstration, from an unknown seller, in the innocent belief that it was a legal publication. 'Look, here is the name of the author, and the Swiss publisher!'

In these notes on 'Neuberg's' book I have set myself the following task: 1. to indicate the political background to the various insurrections; 2. to reveal certain distortions which were made in the presentation of the revolutionary events, 'in the interests of the Soviet State, the Comintern, and the current leadership of the communist parties concerned'.

In addition, I have put names to such authors of the individual sections as are known to me.

The first two sections ('The Second International and Insurrection'; 'Bolshevism and Insurrection') were both written by the Old Bolshevik, O. Piatnitsky, who lived for several years in Germany before the First World War. I have nothing to add to what he says here.

[4] These experiences were dealt with in a book by a Hungarian communist, and in my *The Struggle of the Bavarian Red Army*, which had been brought out in Russian by the State military publishing house in 1928 (with a second edition in 1931).

2. THE REVAL INSURRECTION

The study of the Reval insurrection (Chapter 3) was written by a team under the direction of General Unschlicht. It was based partly on the eye-witness accounts of Estonian communists who had fled to the Soviet Union after the crushing of the insurrection.

The way in which the organization and execution of the Reval rising was presented corresponds by and large to historical truth. However, the account given of its origins passes over in silence the so-called 'Zinoviev conspiracy'. What was this?

After Lenin's death (21 January 1924), as is well known, Zinoviev, Stalin and Kamenev formed the so-called 'troika'. This troika of Old Bolsheviks aimed to prevent the 'New Bolshevik' Trotsky from becoming Lenin's heir. When it turned out after a few months that the 'Trotsky danger' did not exist, or at least no longer existed, the 'troika' broke up. A struggle for power began between Stalin and Zinoviev.

Stalin relied on the all-powerful and omnipresent party apparatus; Zinoviev on the Comintern, which after the defeat of the 'German October', i.e. after the German Communist Party's struggle to win state power in the revolutionary year of 1923 had foundered, had increasingly lost its moral and political weight.

In this situation Zinoviev hoped to strengthen his position *vis-à-vis* Stalin by a victorious armed insurrection in Reval. His dream was that a victory of the communist revolution in Estonia would set off a chain reaction in other countries. In secret discussions, which Zinoviev had carried on in Moscow and Leningrad behind the Party's back and without the knowledge of his Comintern colleagues, the insurrection in Reval was agreed on and its date fixed.

From a purely military point of view, the Estonian communists performed superlatively. They fought with exemplary heroism. But the objective and subjective conditions enumerated by Lenin, and before him by Friedrich Engels, for armed insurrection and the decisive assault by the proletariat on state power – these conditions did not exist in Estonia. Only the vanguard of the revolutionary proletariat was fighting in Reval. In this, the Estonian Communist Party and Zinoviev 'were guilty not simply of a blunder, but of a crime' (Lenin in 1921, in *Left-wing Communism: an Infantile Disorder*).

The Reval insurrection with its thousands upon thousands of victims – dead, maimed or captured – not only delivered Estonia over for many years to white terror and the darkest reaction; it also accelerated the fall of Zinoviev and the rise to power of Stalin.

3. THE HAMBURG INSURRECTION

Hans Kippenberger[5] the organizer and military leader of the Hamburg insurrection, wrote the account of it (Chapter 4) immediately after his arrival in Moscow at the beginning of May 1924. I wrote the chapter's introduction ('The General Situation in Germany') and the 'summing up'. We were working at that time in a special military academy in Moscow, in which the leaders of a future German Red Army were to be formed.

The Hamburg insurrection was essentially confined to the Barmbek district of the city, where Kippenberger, a twenty-five-year-old student from Leipzig, was living.

Kippenberger in his account refers to himself in the third person. He says that he was 'formerly military leader of Barmbek, but . . . a few months previously had been dismissed from this post'. It was only during the evening of Monday, 22 October that the local leadership of the Party in Barmbek literally dragged him out of bed and appointed him military commander of the communist units in Barmbek-Uhlenhorst. He was to commence hostilities at all costs by the following morning, Tuesday, 23 October.

Kippenberger thus found himself 'in a difficult situation from his point of view: he did not know the men, and in addition there was a total lack of information about the state of the Party's fighting organization, about the state of the enemy, etc.' There were also no arms. The 'nineteen rifles and twenty-seven revolvers', as he told me, had been stored badly and were rusty; nothing could be done until they had been thoroughly cleaned and oiled. In addition, there was no overall conception of the general situation in Germany, or even in the other districts of Hamburg.

[5] Kippenberger, a member of the Central Committee of the German Communist Party and one-time communist deputy in the Reichstag, was arrested on 5 November 1936 in Moscow at Ulbricht's request. On the basis of slanderous accusations made by a then intimate associate of Ulbricht's, Kippenberger was condemned to death on 3 October by the GPU (NKVD) directorate and shot. On 30 April 1958 he was 'rehabilitated' by a Soviet military tribunal. The GPU informer had accused him, among other things, of having arranged 'behind Ulbricht's back' for the assassination of two police-officers (Lenk and Anlauf) on 9 August 1931 in front of the Karl-Liebknecht House in Berlin – whereas in reality Ulbricht himself had given the order for this act of individual terror.

Kippenberger suppresses the reason for his dismissal. In August 1923 a three-day general strike had broken out – quite spontaneously and unaided by the German Communist Party – throughout Germany, and had overthrown the ultra-reactionary government of Chancellor Cuno. This was replaced by the Stresemann government, which included leading social democrats in its cabinet. It was then, or as we should stress *then for the first time*, and not even as late as May 1923 – when a general strike had broken out in the Ruhr following the French occupation, and had escalated in Bochum into an armed insurrection[6] – it was then for the first time, in August 1923, that the Kremlin gave the order to prepare for armed insurrection in Germany with the aim of a proletarian seizure of power.

These preparations for revolution included the creation of 'Proletarian Hundreds' in factories, at labour exchanges and in residential blocks. According to Brandler's 'revolutionary theory' – 'In the framework of the Weimar constitution, towards the workers' government of all Germany!' – these Proletarian Hundreds were to be armed only with sticks and clubs. Their 'training' was limited to drilling in factory grounds and on open spaces. Kippenberger, however, had procured a few weapons for the Hundreds which he led in Barmbek, and had organized rifle practice in the wooded areas around Hamburg. As a result, the Greater Hamburg district leadership of the German Communist Party had relieved him of his functions, 'on account of this provocative conduct, which might have led to the banning of the Hundreds', and the Proletarian Hundreds in Barmbek were dissolved. All this had occurred several months before. Yet up to 22 October no new Hundreds had been formed in Barmbek.

The Greater Hamburg district secretary who had directed the

---

[6] In Bochum, under the name 'Walter', I directed an armed rising which broke out spontaneously in May 1923 in connection with a general strike in the Ruhr. The Communist Party *Zentrale* (Heinrich Brandler as leader of the Party, and Ruth Fischer as leader of the Left opposition) condemned the rising; they demanded that the insurgents should disarm, and got their way on the strength of a Party decision. They saw the rising as 'objectively a provocation to the German bourgeoisie', who wished to lay upon the working class and the communists 'the responsibility for their capitulation before the imperialist aggression by Poincaré and his accomplices'. It was after this that I received my first reprimand from the Party. During the insurrection in Bochum, there was fraternization with the soldiers of the French occupation force; the latter greeted our armed Hundreds (see below) with applause, and shouted: '*A bas Poincaré! A bas Stinnes!*' (Stinnes was at that time the most powerful capitalist in the Weimar Republic). It was in May 1923 that the great opportunity for the German Revolution was missed.

proceedings against Kippenberger was Ernst Thälmann, who later entered Comintern mythology as the 'historic leader of the German Communist Party and military commander of the Hamburg insurrection'.

As far as the exemplary organization and conduct of the struggle in Barmbek-Uhlenhorst was concerned, nothing needs to be added to what Kippenberger has recorded with such modesty and reticence. His account need only be supplemented by a summary of the political background which led up to the Hamburg insurrection. We are referring to the conference of Saxony workers' organizations which met in Chemnitz on Sunday, 21 October.

The agenda for this conference had been arranged at a previous session which had taken place before the catastrophic consequences of the French and Belgian invasion of the Ruhr. It was to deal exclusively with social questions: wages and prices, assistance for the unemployed, etc. Because of the Reichswehr's entry into Saxony and Thuringia, the 'Standing Commission' of the conference had moved it forward to Sunday, 21 October, at the request of its communist members.

At the Chemnitz conference then were: 140 factory councillors, 120 trade-union delegates, 79 representatives of control-commissions,[7] 26 high officials of the consumer co-operative society, 15 functionaries of anti-fascist action committees, and 26 leading officials of the trade-union bureaucracy. In no sense was this conference representative of the German working class as a whole.

At the beginning of the session, a delegation from the Central Committee of the Communist Party proposed that the conference should give priority consideration to the question of the Reichswehr intervention, and should proclaim a general strike throughout Germany as a counter-measure. Thereupon the left social democrat Graupe, a minister in the Social Democrat/Communist coalition government of Saxony, explained that he would at once quit the conference hall at the head of all the social democrat delegates if there was any deviation from the fixed agenda (social questions), and if the question of a general strike against the Reichswehr intervention was discussed.

What was to be done?

The Central Committee of the Communist Party, led by Heinrich Brandler, did not want to take upon itself the responsibility for a general

[7] Something resembling organs of 'co-partnership', but without any legal basis.

strike, without the 'Left Social Democrats'. In addition there was the fact that the slogan 'General Strike' was the cue for the 'Military-Political' organizations (see below) which had been created throughout the country since August 1923 to unleash an armed insurrection. The Left opposition of the Communist Party, led by Ruth Fischer, was in agreement with Brandler.

After long debates, the following decision was finally taken: in some single town, a 'spontaneous rising' would be mounted. If this rising unleashed genuinely spontaneous mass movements in the main industrial centres, and if armed insurrections ensued in various parts of the country, then this would be a sure indication of the existence of an acute revolutionary situation. In that case the Communist Party Central Committee could, without isolating itself from the masses, proclaim a general strike throughout Germany and thus unleash an armed insurrection with the aim of seizing power. If, however, the local armed action did not spark off the people's pent-up anger then this would furnish clear proof that the subjective preconditions for the decisive battle still did not exist. The local insurrection would then be a spontaneous action, for which the Central Committee of the Communist Party would not have to bear the responsibility or the consequences.

On the proposal of a member of the *Zentrale*, whose identity could not subsequently be discovered, it was decided unanimously to allow the 'spontaneous rising' to break out in Kiel, whose mutinous sailors had given the signal for the German revolution in November 1918.

Hermann Remmele,[8] however, whose task it was to transmit the order for insurrection on behalf of the Communist Party Central Committee in Chemnitz, decided on his own initiative to go not to Kiel but to Hamburg. Hamburg was the site of the political and

---

[8] A social democrat before the First World War, after 1915 a member of the German Independent Social Democratic Party. The Independent Social Democrats split off from the Social Democrat Party in 1915 because of the latter's policy towards the war. At the Halle Conference of October 1920, where Zinoviev spoke as the Comintern's representative, the left wing of the Independent Social Democrats, under the leadership of Ernst Thälmann and Hermann Remmele, joined the Communist Party. A member of the politburo, Remmele was elected to the 'Troika' – the supreme body – together with Thälmann and Heinz Neumann at the Wedding Congress (Wedding is a proletarian area in the north of Berlin). In 1930–31 Remmele and Neumann moved into opposition to the 'general Line' advocated by Thälmann and Ulbricht, i.e. that the 'main enemy' to be combated was not the Nazis but the 'social fascists', in other words the Social Democrats. Both were liquidated during the Stalin purges.

Military Political 'Seaboard' headquarters, also known as the 'North-West' command, which covered the Communist Party organizations in Greater Hamburg, Schleswig-Holstein with its capital Kiel, Oldenburg, and other towns in the area.[9]

The 'Military-Political Commands' had been created by the German Communist Party Central Committee after the decision had been taken to prepare for armed insurrection in Germany. Six commands – Berlin, North-West, West, South-West, Centre (Saxony, Thuringia) and East – were to correspond to the six infantry divisions of the Reichswehr; their function was to ensure the dislocation of the latter. Hermann Remmele was responsible both for liaison between the Central Committee and the National Command, and for liaison between the West, North-West and South-West political and Military Political leaderships. The political secretary of the North-West was Hugo Urbahns,[10] the Military Political commander was Albert Schreiner,[11] the 'Soviet general' assigned to him was Stern;[12] in the South-West the political secretary was Ernst Meyer, I was Military Political commander, my 'Soviet general' was Alexei N. Stetzky – later a CPSU Central Committee member; the political secretary of the West was Arthur Ewert, the Military Political commander was Wilhelm Zaisser (see p. 19 below), his 'Soviet general', whose name escapes me, was known to the Red Army staff as 'the man with the chin', because of his unusually prominent and jutting chin. In 1927, 'the man with the chin' was head of Red Army Intelligence in Europe with its headquarters in Paris.

[9] The 'Seaboard' or North-West political region was not a part of the Hamburg Party organization, as the Comintern Agitprop worker who assembled and passed on the various sections of the Neuberg as they were entrusted to him believed. 'Seaboard' included all the Prussian provinces on the North Sea or the west coast of the Baltic, including the free Hanseatic cities of Hamburg, Bremen and Lübeck, and the Prussian provinces of Schleswig-Holstein and Oldenburg. Thus, in the Party hierarchy, the political secretary of 'Seaboard', Hugo Urbahns, was the superior of Ernst Thälmann, the district secretary of Greater Hamburg. The North-West Military Political command, in addition to the above-mentioned free cities and provinces, also covered further Prussian provinces.

[10] Urbahns emigrated to Sweden after Hitler's seizure of power, and lived there until his death in 1946.

[11] Political Commissar of an International Brigade in the Spanish Civil War. He has lived since 1945 in the GDR.

[12] During the First World War, Stern, as an ensign or lieutenant in the Austro-Hungarian army, was taken prisoner by the Russians. During the Spanish Civil War, under the name of 'Kléber' and posing as a Canadian, he commanded an International Brigade; his political commissar was Albert Schreiner. He was liquidated during the Stalin purges.

Urbahns was away, at the head of a delegation in Chemnitz, when Remmele arrived in Hamburg to see Schreiner on the morning of 22 October. Urbahns reached Chemnitz several hours after the conference had ended, and after Remmele had set off, as it was thought, for Kiel. Great excitement and confusion reigned in the Communist Party Central Committee. Karl Radek had brought new directives from Moscow: the order for insurrection was to be annulled. A courier was sent off post-haste to Kiel, but nobody there knew anything about Remmele. The next morning, on 23 October, the Central Committee was startled by the news that an insurrection had broken out in Hamburg. What had happened?

In Hamburg, Schreiner and Stern had explained to Remmele that an insurrection in Kiel was impossible. In 1918 Kiel had been the home base of the imperial navy, with some 40,000 mutinous sailors. Now only a couple of thousand sailors were stationed there, regulars on twelve-year service, who for the most part sympathized with the parties of the Right or the extreme Right. The Communist Party in Kiel was very weak. Schreiner did not even know if the Proletarian Hundreds existed there.

According to the information which Remmele had brought with him from Chemnitz, it was absolutely imperative for hostilities to break out in some German town on 23 October, i.e. the next day. In this lay the last chance for the two workers' governments of Saxony and Thuringia to save themselves from liquidation by the Reichswehr. Thereupon Stern made the proposal to start an insurrection in Hamburg. Schreiner hesitantly acquiesced. Thälmann, political secretary for Great Hamburg, was informed. John Schehr, the head of the Hamburg Military Political organization could not be found; indeed he was not seen during the two or three days that the insurrection lasted. Thälmann passed on the order for insurrection to the political leaders of a number of city districts. He was not able to reach all of them.

Remmele set off during the night of 23 October to return to Chemnitz. Reichswehr units already stood at the gates of the city. In the main industrial centres – the Ruhr, Berlin, Upper Silesia – the news of the Hamburg insurrection provoked no action on the part of the workers. The Military Political apparatus – I am speaking in the first instance of the areas 'West' (the Ruhr, Rhineland, etc., under Wilhelm Zaisser) and 'South West' (Württemberg, Baden, Hessen, under my leadership) – stood with arms grounded and waited for the password

'General Strike' as the signal for an all-German uprising. We had not been informed about the events in Chemnitz and the background to the Hamburg insurrection.

Remmele made his report to the Central Committee in the absence of Karl Radek. After a short discussion, a commission was set up consisting of leading members of the Central Committee and of the Military Political national command. This commission, which also included Urbahns, set off for Hamburg. Its mission: to stop the insurrection.

The sequel can be found in Kippenberger's account below.

One further word about the distortions which were made in Kippenberger's account and my introduction in order to compromise Hugo Urbahns as 'the man responsible for the failure of the Hamburg insurrection'.

Urbahns stood trial alone for all the leading comrades of the 'Seaboard' party organization. He assumed full political responsibility for the insurrection and for all the insurgents' actions. He was condemned to a long term in prison. His heroic bearing before the tribunal was celebrated in the communist world. Stalin sent him a personal note of appreciation. He was first calumniated and spattered with mud when he emerged after his liberation as the leader of a left oppositional group associated with Trotsky. He was expelled from the Party in 1926.

4. CANTON AND SHANGHAI

As for the chapters (5 and 6) on the Canton and Shanghai insurrections, I can now say with certainty that they were composed in the High Command of the Red Army. Since my work in both the military schools for German 'insurrection specialists' and, from 1928, in the International Lenin School in Moscow, did not include giving instruction about China, I did not concern myself especially with the teaching material on the Chinese civil war.

However, I was in close contact with comrades who carried out military or political missions in China on behalf of the General Staff of the Red Army (and of the Comintern). Among these were high-ranking Russian officers, like the later Soviet Marshal Blücher,[13]

[13] A Russian metalworker whose real name was Medvediev. In the Russian Civil War and as a Red Army commander he was known under the name of 'Blücher'. When the name

German comrades like Wilhelm Zaisser,[14] and a graceful, kind and lovable Indo-Chinese who under the name of Ho Chi Minh was destined

---

'Blücher' first cropped up in the world press as one of the Red Army generals, the Quai d'Orsay (referring to the clauses of the dictated treaty of Versailles) protested to the German government: personnel of the German Army were not allowed to enter service in foreign armies. The German government and the head of the Prussian branch of the noble family of Blücher swore that the Soviet general could be no member of that old Prussian noble and officer family. They then pointed out that the surname 'von Blücher' could also be found in the Baltic States, which until 1917 had been part of the Russian Empire.

Blücher was for many years Soviet military adviser to the Chinese Generalissimo Chiang Kai Shek, under the name 'General Galen'. 'General Galen' was organizer and commander of the Chinese Southern Army in its lightning advance from Canton to Shanghai (1926–27). After Chiang's betrayal of the Chinese revolution and the bloodbath of communists in Shanghai, the Generalissimo offered 'General Galen' the highest position and honours if he would continue to serve as his military adviser. Against Stalin's orders, Blücher left China. In Vladivostok he was at first put under house-arrest. Stalin wanted to try him 'for insubordination and desertion'. But when Chiang did not confine himself to slaughtering Chinese communists but also assumed a hostile attitude towards the Soviet Union, Blücher was allowed to return to Moscow as a relatively free man in Spring 1927. When I asked him how he had hit upon the name 'Blücher', he laughed and replied: 'That is a close state secret which I am not at liberty to reveal.'

We used naturally to converse in Russian. Blücher was then banished to a sanatorium in Southern Russia. There he studied German assiduously, but with little success. When the Generalissimo's armies attacked Soviet territory across the Amur and Ussuri rivers, Stalin appointed General Blücher as commander-in-chief of the newly-created Far Eastern military region, and Chiang suffered a crushing defeat at the hands of his former military adviser.

In 1938, when Stalin liquidated the entire top command of the Red Army, among them Marshal of the Soviet Union Tukhachevsky, Blücher was at his headquarters in Khabarovsk. It was there that the news reached him that the Marshal Tukha he revered had been executed; the press report added that he, Blücher, had been a member of the Military Tribunal which had pronounced the death sentence. This lie was a moral sentence of death upon Blücher, and the physical one was to follow hard on its heels.

[14] A teacher who fought in the 1914–18 war and by the end was a lieutenant in the reserves. After 1919 Zaisser became a member of the German Communist Party. In the civil strife of 1919–21 he was in the Ruhr as military leader of the Red Guards ('The Red General of the Ruhr'). In August 1923 he was appointed head of the Military Political organization of the 'West' (Ruhr, Rhineland, etc.). In 1924 he attended a course at the Moscow Military Academy, after which he was sent by the Red Army Staff on a secret mission to China. In the Spanish Civil War he commanded the International Brigades under the name of 'General Gómez'. On his return to Moscow, he was disgraced, thrown out of the army, and became an editor in the Foreign Workers' Publishing House. After Hitler attacked the Soviet Union Zaisser was rehabilitated and played a leading part in the National Committee of German officer Prisoners-of-war in the Soviet Union. In 1945 he went back to Germany, to the GDR, where he became Minister for State Security. During the workers' rising in Central Germany (17 June 1953), Zaisser refused to obey Ulbricht's order to open fire on the demonstrating workers. He was dismissed from his post as minister, and expelled from the Party. Up to his death a few years ago he lived in provincial exile, as military instructor in an officer-training school of the Volksarmee.

to make world history. To my knowledge, Blücher and Ho – like other equally high-ranking members of the Staff of the Red Army, among them Tukhachevsky – opposed the official Party line on China; they disapproved of the Chinese Party's entry into the Kuomintang, and saw the Canton insurrection as an undertaking which inevitably contained the seeds of defeat. This viewpoint is put forward unambiguously in the chapter on the Canton insurrection; a critical judgement is similarly expressed on the policy of the Chinese Party, of the Comintern, and of Stalin with respect to the insurrection in Shanghai.

Basing himself on the decisions of the Comintern, the 'editor', i.e. somebody from the bureau of Piatnitsky or of Ercoli-Togliatti, administered a sharp reproof to 'A. Neuberg' for this in the Preface (see the postscript to this edition).

5. TUKHACHEVSKY: 'FIELD-REGULATIONS FOR ARMED INSURRECTION'

In Chapters 7–11, concrete instructions were given on how to organize and carry out armed insurrections in all those countries in which the communist parties faced the 'historic task' of carrying through the bourgeois-democratic or the socialist revolution. In the years in which the 'Neuberg book' appeared, it was aimed at the communists of all countries outside the Soviet Union.

Chapters 7, 8, and 9 deal mainly with the political side of preparation for armed insurrection. Today I can no longer say with certainty whether they were written by Ercoli-Togliatti or by Unschlicht, or perhaps by a team under their direction. I had no share in their composition. Chapters 10 and 11, however, were written by Mikhail N. Tukhachevsky.

When I first met 'Tuka' in the spring of 1924, he was still deputy Chief of Staff of the Red Army, commander of the War Academy, and the president of a commission whose task it was to draw up the 'Provisional Field-Regulations of the Red Army'. After the death of Frunze (31 November 1925), who had succeeded Trotsky, Voroshilov became People's Commissar for the Army (War Minister). His first act was to remove Tukhachevsky from all his functions on the Staff of the Red Army and send him 'into the wilderness', first to Leningrad and then to Minsk. But the new War Minister was not able to fulfil his real wish, to remove him from the army altogether. At the beginning of the thirties, in view of the increasingly critical situation in the Far East and the Kremlin's fear of a Japanese war of aggression, he even had to take him back as his deputy. The liquidation of Tukhachevsky in 1938 during the great Stalinist purges was a final triumph for his rival Voroshilov.[15]

Tukhachevsky had remained president of the 'Commission for the Provisional Field-regulations' in 1925, since all the other members of the Commission had explained that the work in progress could not be brought to a conclusion without him.

Tukhachevsky told me that he saw his contribution to this book as a kind of 'Field-Regulations for Armed Insurrection'. Both chapters: 'The Character of Military Action at the Beginning of the Insurrection', and 'The Character of the Insurgents' Operations during the Insurrection', are larded with quotations from the 'Provisional Field-Regulations of the Red Army', which should really have been called: 'Field-Regulations of the Red Army *and* of Armed Insurrection'.

In 1921–2 Tukhachevsky had pushed for the creation of an 'International Communist General Staff'. As he did not carry this proposal within the Staff of the Red Army, he published a series of articles in Soviet military journals under the pseudonym 'Solomin', in which he beat the drum for his idea. Trotsky had rejected Tukhachevsky-Solomin's proposal on the doubtless correct grounds that the non-Soviet members of this General Staff would be nothing but puppets as long as the proletariat had not seized power in their countries and created Red Armies of their own. Nevertheless, despite certain military and political differences of opinion, both personal and working relations between Trotsky and Tukhachevsky remained the best imaginable. Even under moral pressure from the Party, Tukha never published a derogatory or even a critical statement about Trotsky. In private, he spoke of the first leader of the Red Army with the highest respect.

[15] The most absurd legends were put about to explain the background to Tukhachevsky's liquidation, and indeed are still believed to this day. 'Diabolical intrigue by SS General Heidrich who smuggled forged documents into the hands of Beneš in order to weaken the Soviet army by having it decapitated of its commanders'; 'Conspiracy between General Fritsch and Tukhachevsky to overthrow Hitler and Stalin'; 'The "anti-semite" from the Russian élite sympathized with Hitler'; etc., etc. Marshal of the Soviet Union 'Tukha' was liquidated by Stalin as a member of an oppositional group whose best-known members included the Old Bolsheviks Bukharin and Rykov, and in the army the 'Jew' Gamarnik, political commissar, and the 'Jew' and army general Yakir! 'Tukha' was denounced by Radek, who in his own trial hoped to save his skin by mentioning the name of the Marshal of the Soviet Union in connection with the soviet democratic opposition.

In his contribution to the Neuberg, Tukhachevsky did not shrink from quoting one of Trotsky's orders of the day, ascribing it to him by name; it is almost incredible that the editors of the 1928 edition (first German edition) and of that of 1931 did not extirpate with fire and brimstone the name of the 'watchdog of fascism and agent of world imperialism'.

6. HO CHI MINH: PEASANT INSURRECTION

The author of Chapter 12, 'The Party's Military Work among the Peasants', was the friendly, unassuming Indochinese revolutionary who subsequently entered the history of the great national and social liberation struggles of our epoch under the name of Ho Chi Minh.

When I arrived in Moscow in May 1924, Ho (his name of that period is of no importance) was working in the Agitprop division of the Comintern. His appointed field: colonial and peasant questions. In addition, Ho was vice-president of a 'Peasant International' founded by a non-Party Pole called Dombal. This organization had links with various peasant parties and associations, e.g. in Poland, in the Balkans, in France and Italy, in South America and in Asia. In the Comintern, Dombal and his 'Peasant International' (which was put ironically in inverted commas) was not taken seriously. Much merriment was indulged in at the expense of the amiable 'peasant-visionary', as Bukharin termed him in conversation with me.[16]

In Moscow, as earlier in Paris, Ho had to struggle against the prejudices of the Comintern parties from industrial countries, who denied the revolutionary role of the peasantry in the proletarian liberation struggle. He laughingly alluded to his activity as that of 'a voice crying in the wilderness'.

In 1924, the Red Army Staff sent Ho on a secret mission to China. As silently as he had disappeared from Moscow, he would surface from time to time in the streets of the Soviet capital, with his brilliant eyes and dazzling smile. One day, I think it was in 1927, he told me that he was working on an essay on party work among the peasants, which *inter alia* was intended for the German communists' military school in Moscow. It is this essay which makes up the last chapter of this volume.

[16] After Ho's departure (on a mission to China), Heinrich Brandler became vice-president of the 'Peasant International'.

What Ho wrote over forty years ago still has an almost breathtaking actuality. Introducing his essay, Ho writes: 'The victory of the proletarian revolution in agricultural and semi-agricultural countries is unthinkable without active support from the decisive peasant masses for the revolutionary proletariat. This remains incontrovertibly true, for the bourgeois-democratic as much as for the proletarian revolution.'

Among the 'semi-agricultural countries', Ho included Italy and France. This 'unequivocal conclusion' has only very recently begun to make ground haltingly in France.

On guerrilla tactics in the struggle against an organized army of the ruling class, we find: 'The strength of the guerrillas does not lie in defence, but in their daring and sudden offensive actions. Guerrilla fighters . . . must in all places and at all times be intent on manoeuvring: deal rapid and unexpected blows at the enemy . . . withdraw quickly and avoid a decisive encounter . . . so as to surprise the foe in another quarter.'

This passage could have occurred in one of Ho's orders of the day in recent years.

Armed Insurrection is an exceptionally important document of the military policies of the Comintern, indispensable for the historian. 'But,' one might ask, 'the distortions and falsifications which were made to historical truth in the so-called interests of the Soviet State, of the Comintern and of its sections . . . do these not cancel the historical value of the book?' Absolutely not! These distortions, these falsifications, the suppression of the political background (of the Reval and Hamburg insurrections), these too are part of the military politics of the Comintern and the Kremlin. It is only necessary to know the historical truth, and one can counter the legend. I hope that these introductory remarks have contributed to this.

Hamburg, 1970

For the proletariat, armed insurrection is the highest form of political struggle.

There is one essential precondition for victory. Decisive elements of the proletariat must be prepared to wage an implacable armed struggle to overthrow the political power of the ruling classes. A second precondition is the existence of a large communist party, with a high degree of ideological and organic coherence, armed with Leninist theory and capable of leading the struggle of the masses.

When an elemental, irresistible will to fight inspires the masses, and when millions of men have realized 'the impossibility of going on living in the old way' and are ready for any sacrifice, the duty of the Communist Party is clear. It must lead them skilfully to the key fighting positions; it must choose the correct moment to launch the attack on the old régime; and it must direct the fighting during the insurrection itself, both politically and militarily.

'Insurrection is an art just as war is, and like the other arts it is subject to certain rules; if these are forgotten, the consequence will be defeat for the party which has failed to observe them.' The history of armed struggles waged by the proletariat shows that – despite the lessons of the October Revolution and the remarkable works of Marx, Engels and Lenin on insurrection – all communist parties have not yet learnt the art of insurrection.

The tactics of armed insurrection is an extremely difficult subject to master. The party will only be able to direct the armed struggle of the masses properly if each of its members grasps the basic principles of those tactics.

The tactics of insurrection must be studied on the basis of historical experience, in particular the experience of the armed struggles which the proletariat has waged during the last decades. Only a complete, worldwide study of all the insurrections which have taken place in recent times will allow us to isolate the main factors governing this new field of military art. Only a study of the rich experience provided by the armed struggles of the proletariat will allow us to discover the essential principles of insurrectionary tactics and strategy, and to avoid errors in the future.

Many sections of the Third International, it would appear, have not paid sufficient attention to the study of proletarian insurrections and the tactics of insurrections in general. In our view, even the study of Lenin's works on this question has not been tackled properly. And yet, on every strategic and tactical problem involved in the proletariat's armed struggle to seize power, they contain the entire, concentrated experience of three Russian revolutions – together with an extensive experience of the revolutionary conflicts which have occurred in the West. Lenin gives answers to all the most important questions concerning the preparation and organization of the proletarian revolution.

It is impossible to study the experience of past insurrections or the tactics of armed struggle in general without a good knowledge of the works of Lenin. For Lenin is the supreme strategist and tactician of the proletarian armed struggle, and he has left to posterity a rich experience of that struggle, systematically analysed.

Not only does the bourgeoisie, with the assistance of social democracy, daily wage a bitter political struggle against the revolutionary proletariat, against its vanguard, the Communist Party, and against the proletarian or semi-proletarian (peasant) organizations under the latter's influence. In addition to this, the ruling classes everywhere make immense endeavours to put the experience of proletarian armed struggle, and of reprisals enacted against proletarian insurrections, to their own use. Every bourgeois government today (and not only bourgeois ones) has a stock of ready-made precepts based upon that experience, has resources and plans of action ready for the eventuality of armed intervention by the working class. So that it can pool its experiences in the struggle against the revolutionary proletariat, the bourgeoisie convokes international congresses (the Washington police congress of 1925, etc.). Masses of books and official manuals are published to teach the police and the army how to fight against the insurgents. Diabolical plans are drawn up which propose using the entire arsenal of modern weaponry (including chemical devices) against the revolutionary proletariat in the event of the latter rising in arms against the existing social order.

Since it reckons that the permanent army and the police are unreliable weapons against the proletariat in an immediately revolutionary situation, the bourgeoisie of every country is busy forming a regular counter-revolutionary army (volunteer organizations, student military associations, fascist units, all kinds of defence leagues, military groups in factories, etc.) to defend the existing order.

In order to remove the police from the influence of a populace with revolutionary leanings, certain countries (e.g. Germany) build police compounds at public expense on the fringes of the big industrial towns, and instal the police and their families in these. Some of them are even housed in barracks, put on a military footing, equipped with the most modern weaponry (armoured cars, tanks, aeroplanes, machine-guns, artillery, gas, etc.). All these measures of militarization are aimed at making the police as reliable a force as possible in the struggle against the revolutionary workers.

As far as the army is concerned, the ruling classes have an entire system worked out for maintaining the discipline which alone can ensure its effectiveness in use against the rebels.

The ruling classes are preparing feverishly for the approaching decisive class struggles. To this end, they make use of the experience of past struggles in every possible way. The proletariat, and especially its vanguard the Communist Party, must not lose sight of this fact for an instant.

We live in the epoch of imperialist wars and proletarian revolutions. On the one hand the international imperialist bourgeoisie is launching a systematic war of extermination against the revolutionary proletariat. It is making furious preparations for new acts of banditry as it carves up the world; and it is preaching a crusade against the USSR, the only proletarian state in the universe. International social democracy gives it all the help it can. On the other hand the revolutionary proletariat, in alliance with the toiling peasantry and with the millions of colonial slaves who have joined the revolutionary struggle against imperialism and local reaction, is now increasingly putting all its energy and efforts into preparing the revolutionary landmine which will blow the old world apart. Humanity is entering a period of mighty social convulsions.

The maturing of conditions for the decisive revolutionary conflicts runs parallel to the growth of antagonisms among the various capitalist groups, and of the antagonism between all of these and the USSR, heart of the world proletarian revolution.

Despite the temporary stabilization of capitalism (or rather thanks to that stabilization) it is possible and indeed likely that open civil war (the beginning of the revolution) will start in certain countries before the next world imperialist war, and before the imperialist war against the country of the dictatorship of the proletariat. But the imperialist war and the war against the USSR make the revolution *inevitable* in most states.

The influence of the military factor in revolution is immense. 'Only force can resolve the great problems of history, and *organized force*, in the struggles of today, means military organization.'

Every communist during the revolution is a soldier in the civil war and a leader of the armed struggle of the masses. By preparing the revolutionary mobilization of the workers intensively and meticulously day by day, and by educating them to overthrow the domination of imperialism, communists of all countries must – even today, in a situation which is not immediately revolutionary – prepare themselves seriously for their role as leaders of the future insurrection of the proletariat. It is the task of every communist party to study the art of war, and in particular the experience of the armed struggles of the proletariat in other countries; to study the military problems of insurrection; to propagandize the idea of armed insurrection among the mass of workers. The importance of these tasks cannot be too highly stressed. This is especially true in the age in which we live, when a new upsurge of the revolutionary movement of the proletariat and of the oppressed peoples of the East is imminent.

'Let us remember that the time of mass struggle is at hand. It will be armed insurrection. The party of the politically conscious proletariat must carry out its duty in this great battle!'

The Second International
and Insurrection

Armed insurrection, as one of the forms taken by the class struggle of the proletariat, is central to the system of Marx and Engels. The utilization of this form by the proletariat, at a determinate historical stage in the evolution of the class struggle in any given country, is an absolute, an inexorable necessity. This necessity derives immediately from the entire Marxist conception of the development of Society; of the revolutionary role of violence in history; of the role of the State, as the instrument of a single class's domination; and finally of the dictatorship of the proletariat. *Denial of the inexorable necessity for armed insurrection or, more generally, for armed struggle against the ruling classes on the part of the proletariat, means automatically denial of the class struggle as a whole. It means denial of the very foundations of revolutionary Marxism and its reduction to an odious doctrine of non-resistance.*

Refusal to recognize the dictatorship of the proletariat as the only possible transition from capitalism to socialism amounts in practice to a refusal to accept proletarian revolution in general. All the other conceptions which strive to prove the possibility, and necessity, of a different path – non-violent, i.e. non-revolutionary – from capitalism to socialism deny the historic role of the proletariat as the vanguard of society; they confine the proletariat to a subordinate position *vis-à-vis* the other classes.

Basing himself on the doctrine of Marx and Engels, Lenin wrote works of genius (in particular his remarkable *State and Revolution*) which proved the unshakeable truth of these key propositions of revolutionary Marxism: propositions which have been systematically ignored, distorted and rendered unrecognizable by the opportunists. On the other hand, the history and the shameful ideological collapse of the Second International, and most notably of German social democracy, together with the latter's stance on those basic questions of scientific socialism (the State, dictatorship of the proletariat, insurrection), have confirmed categorically and in practice the propositions of Marx and Engels: propositions defended and supplemented on the basis of new historical facts by Lenin.

As is well-known, German social democracy played the principal role in propagating opportunistic deformations of Marxism on the following key issues: dictatorship of the proletariat; the armed struggle for power; destruction of the bourgeois State and establishment upon its ruins of a proletarian government apparatus – just as it did on every other issue of principle in revolutionary Marxism. For Marx, 'Force, throughout history, has always served as midwife for the old order pregnant with a new order'; 'Between capitalist and communist society lies the period of the revolutionary transformation of the one into the other . . . in which the State can be nothing but the revolutionary dictatorship of the proletariat';[1] 'The revolution is an act in which one part of the population imposes its will upon the other part with the help of rifles, bayonets and cannons . . . and in which the victorious party is of necessity obliged to maintain its dominance through the fear which its weapons inspire in the reactionaries.'[2] According to Marx, 'the violent overthrow of the bourgeoisie lays the foundation for the sway of the proletariat',[3] and 'One thing especially was proved by the Commune, viz. that the working class cannot simply lay hold of the ready-made State machinery, and wield it for its own purposes',[4] but must 'smash it, and this is the preliminary condition for every real people's revolution on the continent'.[5] In contrast, German social democracy, now as always, defends the following proposition: that the passage from the capitalist order to the socialist order will be achieved by pacific means, without bloodshed, without destruction of the bourgeois governmental apparatus, without installing the dictatorship of the proletariat.

In 1875, German social democracy, in its draft programme on the question of the State, ignored the experience of the Paris Commune and the judgement delivered upon it by Marx. It advocated not the dictatorship of the proletariat (and the need for a violent overthrow of

[1] Marx/Engels, *Selected Works*, vol. II, p. 32, in *Critique of the Gotha Programme* (Marx).
[2] Marx/Engels, *Selected Works*, vol. I, p. 639, in *On Authority* (Engels).
[3] Marx/Engels, *Selected Works*, vol. I, p. 45, in *The Communist Manifesto*.
[4] Marx/Engels, *Selected Works*, vol. I, p. 22, in the Preface to the 1872 edition of *The Communist Manifesto*.
[5] Marx/Engels, *Selected Works*, vol. II, p. 463, in Marx's letter to Kugelmann, 12 April 1871.

the old state machine of the bourgeoisie), but 'a free people's State which must replace the existing Prussian State based on class domination'. It is well known that Marx and above all Engels poured scorn on this article of the Gotha programme. They called it 'chatter', 'to be rejected, especially after the Paris Commune', and added that to speak of a free people's State was 'pure nonsense'.[6]

Naturally, with so radically false a conception of the nature of the State, the Gotha programme avoided posing the questions of proletarian dictatorship and of armed struggle to install that dictatorship.

These problems were not posed either in the Second International's gospel, the Erfurt programme of 1891. Nor is there a word in it about the dictatorship of the proletariat, nor even about the democratic republic, that 'last governmental form of bourgeois society, under which the final struggle will unfold' (Marx.)

In 1892 Kautsky, that apostle of the Second International, in what was the official commentary on the Erfurt programme, tried to pose the problem of the transition from one social order to another. But he resolved it in a profoundly opportunist spirit:

This revolution (i.e. the seizure of political power by the proletariat) may take the most diverse forms, depending on the conditions in which it occurs. *It is in no way inseparable from violence and bloodshed.*

We have already seen cases, in the history of the world, of ruling classes who were intelligent enough, weak enough or cowardly enough to surrender voluntarily in the face of necessity.[7]

The opportunist position of German social democracy on the question of how power would pass from the bourgeoisie to the proletariat can here be seen emerging clearly. Kautsky, and social democracy in general, do not at all conceive that transition as the result of a class struggle, which at a certain juncture is transformed into a bitter armed struggle of the oppressed classes against the bourgeoisie and the ruling classes. They do not at all conceive it as the dictatorship of the proletariat. They conceive it as the culmination of a peaceful and orderly evolution, of a voluntary surrender of its social positions by the bourgeoisie.

As to which concrete cases in world history Kautsky is speaking of, that is something nobody knows. He himself does not tell us, and could not do so, since he knows very well that world history has seen

---

[6] Marx/Engels, *Selected Works*, vol. II, p. 42, in Engels's letter to Bebel, 18–28 March 1875.
[7] Kautsky, *The Erfurt Programme*. Neuberg's emphasis.

no case of a ruling class voluntarily surrendering to necessity. Experience teaches us the contrary: no social order, and no class embodying such an order, has ever voluntarily given way to a new ascendant class, or abandoned the arena of history without a bitter struggle.

A characteristic statement of this opportunistic viewpoint was made by Wilhelm Liebknecht, at the Erfurt congress: 'What is revolutionary is not the means, but the ends. Violence has always, since the beginning of time, been a reactionary factor.'[8]

In his new book *The Materialist Conception of History* Kautsky writes on the subject of armed struggle and strikes:

When you have a democratic State (the existing bourgeois State), a consolidated democracy, armed struggle no longer plays any role in the solution of social conflicts. These conflicts are resolved by peaceful means, by propaganda and the vote. Even the mass strike, as a means of pressure by the working class, is of decreasing utility.

So this is Kautsky's 'road to power'! So this is his thinking on the armed struggle of the proletariat against the bourgeoisie, and on strikes as a form of the class struggle and a means of solving social conflicts in the modern capitalist states! It is the opposite of Marx's principles on the same question.

But Kautsky does not confine himself to denying the need for the proletariat to use violence against its class enemies. He confidently asserts that the bourgeoisie itself will not resort to armed struggle against the proletariat:

With the rapid development of industry, it is not military means but economic processes which, increasingly, become decisive in the affairs of the State.

The capitalists do not dominate the masses as the feudalists used to, through their military superiority. . . . They have kept power until now thanks to their wealth and the importance of the economic functions in the existing productive process. They will keep it so long as the masses who are oppressed and exploited by them do not understand the need to replace the capitalists and the organizations which depend on them by other organizations belonging to the working class and fulfilling the same functions equally well, if not better.

Economic necessity, and military superiority, is the weapon used by the capitalists in their struggle against a democratic régime of the toiling classes.[9]

After this 'theoretical' statement on the source of the bourgeoisie's power, Kautsky asserts that the bourgeoisie will not put up any armed

[8] Quoted from the article *Souvenirs d'Engels*, by Charles Rappoport, in *Annales du marxisme*.
[9] *The Materialist Conception of History*.

resistance at the moment in which the means of production pass from its own hands into those of democracy.

The Heidelberg programme, adopted by German social democracy in 1925, sanctions the *de facto* stance of social democracy with respect to the State – the stance *vis-à-vis* the bourgeois republic which has characterized it ever since the revolution of November 1918, and which it still maintains. Social democracy sees the republican régime of today (in Germany and in many other countries – Austria, Switzerland, etc.) as a transitional stage leading to socialism; it therefore categorically takes up the defence of this régime. The experience of the war and of the post-war period has shown only too clearly that the leaders of German social democracy are prepared to make literally any sacrifice in defending the bourgeois republic against the revolutionary proletariat. They accept the role of watch-dog with enthusiasm and fill it with the greatest zeal.

The arguments on violence used by Kautsky in 1892 and 1926 or Liebknecht in 1891, and those used by the other social democratic theoreticians (like T. Haubach today) are as alike as two peas. Haubach declares gravely:

There is a connection between the end and the means, as Jesuit wisdom claims. Every means is at the same time an end, said Hegel, and the wisdom of nations holds that it is impossible to use the devil to drive out the devil. Hence the problem of violence, in each phase of evolution, depends on the idea one has of the final goal of socialism. If one believes that this final goal, socialism, involves the absence of violence as its absolute condition, then, in all cases, one will be obliged to observe the principle of non-violence . . . in order to attain this final goal.[10]

Today, you will no longer find a single social democract theoretician, even among the so-called left social democrats, who does not align himself with the above-quoted formulae of Kautsky and the other social democratic leaders.

Even if certain social democrats – like Julius Deutsch[11] in Austria, the left social democrat Bruno Kalninsch in Lithuania[12] and others – in

[10] Theodor Haubach, 'Socialism and the Armament Question' in *Die Gesellschaft*, no. 2, vol. III, p. 122.

[11] See Julius Deutsch: *Armed force and Social-democracy*. Deutsch points out that, in certain cases, the bourgeoisie employs brutal force against the proletariat. In such cases, the proletariat 'if it does not want to be defeated without a struggle, must not cravenly surrender its future; it will have no choice but to resort to the supreme weapon of the class struggle, and answer force by force'.

[12] Bruno Kalninsch, *The War Policy of Social-democracy*, Riga, 1928. The author writes: 'The social democratic working-class International at its 1928 Brussels congress adopted a

the course of their theoretical works sometimes arrive at the conclusion that, under certain conditions, the proletariat may have recourse
to methods of constraint against the bourgeoisie, this changes nothing
of substance. Kautsky and his like will not reproach them with any
violation of social democratic principles. The strong words of the left
social democrats about the possibility of using violence against the
bourgeoisie are necessary; they serve to keep in their ideological
captivity those proletarian elements who still persist in considering
international social democracy as a working-class party. It is nevertheless clear to everyone that so long as social democracy remains
faithful to its conception of the State, denies the dictatorship of the
proletariat, and sees the bourgeois republic of today as a working-class

---

military programme which, on the subject of limiting armaments, demands: i) a ban on
chemical and bacteriological warfare; ii) limited quotas for heavy artillery, tanks, aeroplanes and naval forces; iii) reductions in war budgets; iv) international control of the
manufacture and sale of arms; v) the suppression of penalties for publishing information
on secret weapons. These decisions to be enacted by means of international agreements
between all countries. Control of them to be entrusted to the League of Nations.

'The International considers that "the campaign for international limitation of armaments will only be successful to the extent that we are able to achieve solutions to international conflicts by peaceful means." To this end, the International demands *"that all
international conflicts be referred to arbitration tribunals"*. The League of Nations must
work out an arbitration treaty which will apply equally to all, and to which *all* governments
will rally.

'The International requires all socialist parties to obtain *a law forbidding any declaration
of mobilization* before the conflict in question has been submitted to the League of Nations
for peaceful resolution. Against governments which refused to submit international
conflicts to the arbitration tribunals and resorted to war, the International recommends
using the most categorical means "without excluding even the use of violent struggle and
of revolutionary methods".'

This then is the attitude of the Second International on the question of war and disarmament. It is not against war, but merely against chemical and bacteriological warfare;
it is not for general disarmament, but merely for the limitation of armaments. War in
general is permissible and possible, if it is authorized by the League of the imperialist
nations. As for the threats of Kalninsch and Deutsch about the utilization of revolutionary
methods against bourgeois governments, these are simply a joke. The notorious resolutions
of the congresses of Stuttgart and Basle in 1907 and 1912 were more revolutionary than the
present grand gestures of social democracy; nevertheless they turned out to be no more
than a scrap of paper at the outbreak of the 1914–18 imperialist war. Let us remember the
wars in Morocco and Syria, the imperialist interventions in the USSR and in China, that
of the United States in Latin America. Let us remember too the many proletarian insurrections which have occurred in numerous countries, the workers' strikes, and the role
and behaviour of social democracy in these events; then we shall see the hypocrisy of the
left leaders on the questions of war, disarmament and revolutionary struggle against the
bourgeoisie.

conquest, to be defended against enemies both within (the revolutionary proletariat) and without, *there can be no question for social democracy of ever in fact calling the toiling masses to arms to overthrow the bourgeoisie.*

The authors of scientific socialism did not betray their principles on the role of violence or on that of proletarian insurrection. It is a legend that Engels, in the preface to Marx's *Civil War in France* which he wrote just before he died in 1895, betrayed his former ideas on insurrection, renounced the methods of 1848 and 1871 and advocated peaceful evolution. This legend has been put about by the reformists of German social democracy for thirty years. But now that Ryazanov has succeeded in obtaining from Bernstein the authentic Engels text, it will no longer deceive anybody.

It is now known that the Social Democratic Party Central Committee editors, when they published Engels's preface, cut out all passages alluding either to the historic goals of German revolutionaries towards 1895 (mobilization and revolutionary education of the masses, organization and education of the Party, etc.), or to the need in the future to utilize armed struggle for the conquest of power.

Engels's true ideas on the use of violence are to be found in a passage of a letter he wrote to Lafargue on 3 April 1895, in which he protests vigorously against the distortion of his preface to Marx's book. This is what he wrote:

Liebknecht has just played me a nice trick. He has taken from my *Introduction* to Marx's articles on France of 1848-50 everything that could serve him to defend the tactics of *peace at any price and of opposition to force and violence*, which it has pleased him for some time now to preach, especially at present when coercive laws are being prepared in Berlin. But I am preaching these tactics only *for the Germany of today*, and even then *with an important proviso*. In France, Belgium, Italy and Austria these tactics could not be followed in their entirety and in Germany they may become inapplicable tomorrow.[13]

Engels' preface - as we know today thanks to the endeavours of Ryazanov - was stripped, for instance, of the following paragraph, which typifies the author's ideas on street combat:

Does that mean that in the future street fighting will no longer play any role? Certainly not. It only means that the conditions since 1848 have become far more unfavourable for civilian fighters and far more favourable for the military. In future, street fighting can, therefore, be victorious only if this disadvantageous situation is compensated by other factors. Accordingly, it will occur more seldom

[13] Marx/Engels, *Selected Correspondence*, p. 568. Engels's emphasis.

in the beginning of a great revolution than in its further progress, and will have to be undertaken with greater forces. *These, however, may then well prefer, as in the whole great French Revolution or on September 4 and October 31 1870, in Paris, the open attack to the passive barricade tactics.*[14]

This passage from Engels's preface, cut out by Bernstein before publication, together with the extract quoted above from the letter to Lafargue, constitute a crushing indictment of the entire ruling faction of German social democracy, and above all of Bernstein who intended in this way to present Engels, in the eyes of the Party and the entire proletariat, as a petty bourgeois revolutionary repenting the revolutionary sins of his youth.

On this subject, it is interesting to quote another little-known passage in Marx, which highlights his ideas on violence and dictatorship only two years before his death. In a letter to the Dutch social democrat Domela Nieuwenhuis, Marx wrote on 22 February 1881:

A socialist government does not come into power in a country unless conditions are so developed that it can immediately take the necessary measures for intimidating the mass of the bourgeoisie sufficiently to gain time – the first desideratum – for permanent action.[15]

The idea that it is possible to scare the bourgeoisie by other means than violence is an illusion which can only assist counter-revolution.

However, German social democracy thinks otherwise. The idea of scaring the bourgeoisie in any way at all never occurs to it. Here is what an authority of that social democracy and of the entire Second International, R. Hilferding, says:

The definition given by Marx (the State as means of constraint in the hands of the ruling classes) is not a theory of the State, in the first place because it refers to all political formations since the very beginning of society. . . .

We socialists, for our part, must understand that the organization is made up of members, of leaders and of an apparatus – in other words, that the State, from the political point of view, is nothing other than the government, directive apparatus and citizens who make up the State. . . .

On the other hand, it follows that the essential element of every modern State is the parties, for an individual can only demonstrate his will through the intermediary of a party. Hence the parties, taken together, are as indispensable an element of the State as the government and the administrative apparatus.[16]

[14] Marx/Engels, *Selected Works*, vol. I, p. 133, in Engels's Preface to Marx's *Class Struggles in France, 1848–1850*. Neuberg's emphasis.
[15] Marx/Engels, *Selected Correspondence*, p. 410.
[16] Hilferding, *The Social Democratic Congress at Kiel in 1927*.

Such is the definition of the State given by the author of *Finance Capital*. Naturally, once the State is not the instrument of one class's domination, but 'the government, directive apparatus, citizens and parties' (so that e.g. the German Communist Party is 'an indispensable element' of the bourgeois State), it follows that in Germany and elsewhere power belongs not to the bourgeoisie, but to all classes and all parties; that it belongs to all the citizens who make up the State. But if this is how matters stand, there can be no question of combating the State; on the contrary, the aim must be to occupy a suitable niche within it. In practice, this means coalition governments in which social democracy collaborates with bourgeois parties. It means a bitter struggle against the revolutionary proletariat and its vanguard, the Communist Party, which is fighting simultaneously against the bourgeoisie and the social democrat leaders to install the dictatorship of the proletariat. This is the theoretical basis of Kautsky's counter-revolutionary thesis on armed struggle and the solution of social conflict, which we quoted earlier. It means that German social democracy (nor is it alone) believes that it has already achieved the dream it was cherishing in 1875 of a free people's State, and that all that remains to be done today is to democratize that State more fully, democratize the League of Nations, and pass peacefully, without revolution, dictatorship or bloodshed, into socialism.

Kautsky justifies this thesis even more explicitly. This is what he says about the State in his previously mentioned book, *The Materialist Conception of History*:

Since the last declarations of Engels on the State, more than a generation has passed, and this period has not left the character of the modern State unchanged. Whether the characterization of the State given by Marx and Engels, which was absolutely accurate in their day, is still of the same importance today, is something which needs to be studied.

In subsequent passages Kautsky, with breathtaking plausibility, strives to prove that the State in the epoch of finance has an entirely different character than that discussed by Marx and Engels. It is no longer an instrument of class constraint. Further on in his book he writes:

The modern democratic State differs from preceding types in that utilization of the government apparatus by the exploiting classes is no longer an essential feature of it, no longer inseparable from it. On the contrary, the democratic State tends not to be the organ of a minority, as was the case in previous régimes, but rather that of the majority of the population, in other words of the toiling classes. Where it is, however, the organ of a minority of exploiters, the reason for this does not lie in its own nature; it is rather that the toiling classes themselves lack unity, knowledge, independence or fighting ability – all qualities which in their turn are a result of the conditions in which they live.

Democracy offers the possibility of cancelling the political power of the exploiters, and today, with the constant increase in the number of workers, this in fact happens more and more frequently.

The more this is the case, the more the democratic State ceases to be a simple instrument in the hands of the exploiting classes. The government apparatus is already beginning, in certain conditions, to turn against the latter – in other words to work in the opposite direction to that in which it used to work in the past. From being an instrument of oppression, it is beginning to change into an instrument of emancipation for the workers.

Any comment would be superfluous here. The government of cartel capitalism is not an instrument in the hands of the owning classes: it is the State leading the proletariat to its emancipation!

If one adds to this the shameless attacks on the Union of Soviets in which Kautsky indulges at various junctures in his work; his dithyrambs in honour of the League of Nations, instrument of peace and defender of democracy; his assurances that the ruling classes will not use arms against democracy; if, finally, one recalls the conduct of German social democracy in the post-war period, especially in 1918, 1919, 1920, 1921 and 1923; then one will see very clearly why Kautksy was obliged to revise the doctrine of Marx and Engels on the State in such a crude fashion.

When he discusses the military and economic power of the modern State, Kautsky comes to the following conclusion:

The international standing which the German Republic has now recovered shows that the strength of a nation is determined to an infinitely greater extent by its cultural and economic progress than by the size of its army. In fact, today, in the full swing of democracy's development, a State surrounded by democracies and pursuing no aggressive aims has almost no need of an army to defend itself, once the League of Nations is rationally organized. If Russia possessed a democratic régime and entered the League of Nations, one of the principal obstacles to general disarmament would be eliminated.

The League of Nations, instrument of peace! The USSR instrument of war! The audacity of this could really not be bettered.

The falsification of Engels's preface, the distortion of Marxism in every essential point – all this was necessary so that the reformists could accomplish their dirty opportunist work under cover of Engels's name. The entire practice of social democracy during these last fifteen years, on which this is not the place to dwell (social democracy has long had its allotted place in the defence-system of the bourgeois order), is a manifest proof of this. Today, everyone can see that social democracy, in practice as in theory, is *against* the proletariat's violence against the bourgeoisie, but *for* the bourgeoisie's violence against the proletariat.

From what has just been said it can be concluded that German social democracy and in its wake the entire Second International, on all the fundamental problems of Marxism, *have never been genuinely and fully Marxist. The genesis of reformism, the shameful ideological decline of German social democracy, started right back in the period of Gotha and Erfurt; it started with the falsification of the works of Marx and Engels on dictatorship, on the armed struggle of the proletariat and on the class struggle in general – decisive problems which form the dividing-line between genuine revolutionaries and all that is alien to the revolution.* It is on this subject that Lenin said:

It is often said and written that the main point in Marx's theory is the class struggle. But this is wrong. And this wrong notion very often results in an opportunist distortion of Marxism and its falsification in a spirit acceptable to the bourgeoisie. For the theory of the class struggle was created *not* by Marx, *but* by the bourgeoisie *before* Marx, and, generally speaking, it is *acceptable* to the bourgeoisie. Those who recognize *only* the class struggle are not yet Marxists; they may be found to be still within the bounds of bourgeois thinking and bourgeois politics. To confine Marxism to the theory of the class struggle means curtailing Marxism, distorting it, reducing it to something acceptable to the bourgeoisie.

Only he is a Marxist who *extends* the recognition of the class struggle to the recognition of the *dictatorship of the proletariat*. This is what constitutes the most profound distinction between the Marxist and the ordinary petty (as well as big) bourgeois. This is the touchstone on which the *real* understanding and recognition of Marxism should be tested. And it is not surprising that when the history of Europe brought the working class face to face with this question as a *practical* issue, not only all the opportunists and reformists, but all the Kautskyites (people who vacillate between reformism and Marxism) proved to be miserable philistines and petty-bourgeois democrats *repudiating* the dictatorship of the proletariat. ... Opportunism *does not extend* recognition of the class struggle to the cardinal point, to the period of *transition* from capitalism to communism, of the *overthrow* and the complete *abolition* of the bourgeoisie. In reality, this period inevitably is a period of an unprecedentedly violent class struggle in unprecedentedly acute forms, and, consequently, during this period the state must evitably be a state that is democratic *in a new way* (for the proletariat and the propertyless in general) and dictatorial *in a new way* (against the bourgeoisie).[17]

[17] Lenin, *Selected Works*, vol. II, p. 291, in *State and Revolution*.

Since they reject the principles of Marx and Engels on the dictatorship of the proletariat and the role of the State, the German social democrats have *never been able to pose adequately in theory the question of armed insurrection* (let alone resolve it in practice).

If we have dwelt so much on German social democracy, it is because it has always been and still is the moral leader of the Second International. Everything that has been said about it applies equally to all the other parties in that International.

2

Bolshevism and Insurrection

Lenin not only restored the Marxist theory of the State (see his *State and Revolution*), he also studied and posed in practice the problem of proletarian dictatorship, and made this into the fighting slogan of the entire international proletariat. Lenin enriched Marxism by his discovery of the concrete force of that dictatorship: the soviet system.

As for insurrection, Lenin was already emphasizing by 1902 (see *What is to be Done?*) the need to prepare for imminent armed insurrection. In 1905, when the circumstances had ripened, he exerted all his authority to show that only armed insurrection – the sharpest and most decisive form of combat in a time of revolution – can lead the proletariat to final victory.

In his post-mortem on the Moscow insurrection of December 1905, Lenin vigorously attacked Plekhanov's famous phrase – parroted by every opportunist: 'They should not have taken to arms.' Lenin's criticism was an object-lesson to our Party and to the entire proletariat; it ran as follows:

We should have taken to arms more resolutely, energetically and aggressively; we should have explained to the masses that it was impossible to confine things to a peaceful strike and that a fearless and relentless armed fight was necessary. And now we must at last openly and publicly admit that political strikes are inadequate; we must carry on the widest agitation among the masses in favour of an armed uprising and make no attempt to obscure this question by talk about 'preliminary stages', or to befog it in any way. We would be deceiving both ourselves and the people if we concealed from the masses the necessity of a desperate, bloody war of extermination, as the immediate task of the coming revolutionary action.[1]

During the October revolution, as we know, Lenin was the heart and soul of the insurrection, the heart and soul of the revolution.

Those professional falsifiers of Marxism, the Mensheviks and Social-Revolutionaries, in unison with the Cadets and other monarchist and bourgeois parties, accused the Bolsheviks of Blanquism;[2] in his reply

---

[1] Lenin, *Selected Works*, vol. I, p. 579, in 'Lessons of the Moscow Uprising'.
[2] Blanquism is a revolutionary doctrine derived from the French revolutionary communist

(in 1917), Lenin provided the classic formulation of the problem of armed insurrection and the conditions for its success:

To be successful, insurrection must rely not upon conspiracy and not upon a party, but upon the advanced class. That is the first point. Insurrection must rely upon a *revolutionary upsurge of the people*. That is the second point. Insurrection must rely upon that *turning-point* in the history of the growing revolution when the activity of the advanced ranks of the people is at its height, and when the *vacillations* in the ranks of the enemy and *in the ranks of the weak, half-hearted and irresolute friends of the revolution are strongest. That is the third point*. And these three conditions for raising the question of insurrection distinguish *Marxism from Blanquism.*

Lenin at once adds:

Once these conditions exist, however, to refuse to treat insurrection as an art [i.e.

Auguste Blanqui (1805–81). Blanqui's doctrine, on many key social and political issues, is very close to modern Marxism, and is the latter's direct precursor. Blanqui was a communist and a materialist, but not a dialectician. He was openly committed to the class struggle and to the dictatorship of a centralized proletarian party. Blanqui believed firmly in the creative role of violence in the historical process.

Blanqui was 'a revolutionary of the old generation', says Engels. Paul Frölich (see his brilliant article on Blanquism in the review '*L'Internationale Communiste*', no. 12, 1925) demonstrates the accuracy of this definition, and adds: 'He was the most vivid expression, the classic representative of that epoch of revolutions which formed the transition between the bourgeois epoch and the proletarian epoch; for in that transitional epoch the conscious spokesman of the revolution was still the bourgeoisie, but was already also the proletariat. As a representative of that epoch both by origin and by activity, he constitutes an intermediate link between Jacobinism and modern communism.' Frölich is absolutely right.

Blanqui's tactic consisted in carrying out the revolution – piercing a breach in the bourgeois order and seizing power at the right moment – with the help of a secret, strongly organized and centralized, armed organization; the proletariat would be drawn in afterwards. Blanqui did not understand and could not understand that certain conditions were required before the insurrection could succeed. The attempted insurrections staged by him and by his disciples all failed. The proletariat, represented by Blanqui, had not yet become entirely aware of itself as a class, had not yet sufficiently crystallized, was still linked to the petty bourgeoisie. Immature social relations produced an immature theory

Marxism-Leninism has inherited from Blanquism the need to organize and prepare the revolution, the ineluctable need for an implacable armed struggle against the existing order. But Marxism-Leninism has not been able to accept the ideas of the 'revolutionary of the old generation' on the tactic of conspiracy. Besides the systematic preparation of revolution, Marx and Lenin highlight the necessity of economic and social preconditions for insurrections (a powerful revolutionary upsurge on the part of the proletariat), in the absence of which victory is inconceivable.

Bernstein, in his time, accused Marx of Blanquism. Today it is the entire Second International which accuses the Communist International of Blanquism, and equates Blanquism with communism. In slandering the communists in this way, the social democrats represent Blanqui, the committed revolutionary of the past, as a petty-bourgeois fanatic.

to prepare it politically and militarily: A. N.] is a betrayal of Marxism and a betrayal of the revolution.[3]

This passage, in a concise and general form, says all that is essential about the preconditions for a victorious insurrection. Nevertheless, Lenin, in that same year of 1917, in his 'Letter to comrades', returns in a more concrete and detailed fashion to the difference between Marxism and Blanquism on the issue of insurrection. At the same time, he underlines the conditions in which the latter can be victorious:

Military conspiracy is Blanquism, *if* it is organized not by a party of a definite class, *if* its organizers have not analysed the political moment in general and the international situation in particular, *if* the party has not on its side the sympathy of the majority of the people, as proved by objective facts, *if* the development of revolutionary events has not brought about a practical refutation of the conciliatory illusions of the petty bourgeoisie, *if* the majority of the Soviet-type organs of revolutionary struggle that have been recognized as authoritative or have shown themselves to be such in practice have not been won over, *if* there has not matured a sentiment in the army (if in war-time) against the government that protracts the unjust war against the will of the whole people, *if* the slogans of the uprising (like 'All power to the Soviets', 'Land to the peasants', or 'Immediate offer of a democratic peace to all the belligerent nations, with an immediate abrogation of all secret treaties and secret diplomacy', etc.) have not become widely known and popular, *if* the advanced workers are not sure of the desperate situation of the masses and of the support of the countryside, a support proved by a serious peasant movement or by an uprising against the landowners and the government that defends the landowners, *if* the country's economic situation inspires earnest hopes for a favourable solution of the crisis by peaceable and parliamentary means.[4]

In his 1915 pamphlet *The Collapse of the Second International*, Lenin wrote on the same subject as follows:

To a Marxist it is indisputable that a revolution is impossible without a revolutionary situation; furthermore, it is not every revolutionary situation that leads to revolution. What, generally speaking, are the symptoms of a revolutionary situation? We shall certainly not be mistaken if we indicate the following three major symptoms: (1) when it is impossible for the ruling classes to maintain their rule without any change; when there is a crisis, in one form or another, among the 'upper classes', a crisis in the policy of the ruling class, leading to a fissure through which the discontent and indignation of the oppressed classes burst forth. For a revolution to take place, it is usually insufficient for 'the lower classes not to want' to live in the old way; it is also necessary that 'the upper classes should be unable' to live in the old way; (2) when the suffering and want of the oppressed classes have grown more acute than usual; (3) when, as a consequence of the above causes,

---

[3] Lenin, *Selected Works*, vol. II, p. 365, in 'Marxism and Insurrection'.
[4] Lenin, *Collected Works*, vol. 26, p. 212, in 'Letter to comrades'.

there is a considerable increase in the activity of the masses, who uncomplainingly allow themselves to be robbed in 'peace-time', but, in turbulent times, are drawn both by all the circumstances of the crisis *and by the 'upper classes' themselves* into independent historical action.

Without these objective changes, which are independent of the will, not only of individual groups and parties but even of individual classes, a revolution, as a general rule, is impossible. The totality of all these objective changes is called a revolutionary situation. Such a situation existed in 1905 in Russia, and in all revolutionary periods in the West; it also existed in Germany in the sixties of the last century, and in Russia in 1859-61 and 1879-80, although no revolution occurred in these instances. Why was that? It was because it is not every revolutionary situation that gives rise to a revolution; revolution arises only out of a situation in which the above-mentioned objective changes are accompanied by a subjective change, namely, the ability of the revolutionary *class* to take revolutionary mass action *strong* enough to break (or dislocate) the old government, which never, not even in a period of crisis, 'falls', if it is not toppled over.[5]

Lenin returned to the subject on numerous subsequent occasions, stressing again and again that the social and political preconditions mentioned above were indispensable.[6] The extracts quoted – which could easily be multiplied – show what immense, indeed decisive importance he attached to the question of the political preconditions for revolution. It is these preconditions which determine the maturity of a revolutionary situation; they were therefore the invariable criterion adopted by Lenin in deciding problems of a historic order. Should the Party set about the immediate organization of insurrection? Or, on the contrary, should it continue its ordinary work of revolutionary mobilization of the masses, i.e. should it wait for a more favourable moment for the insurrection?

It goes without saying that Lenin never considered insurrection as an isolated act, unrelated to the other moments of the class struggle. Insurrection is prepared by the entire class struggle of the country in question, and is only the organic continuation of that struggle. All the activity of the revolutionary party – the struggle for peace; against imperialist intervention (in China, in the USSR, etc.); against the imperialist wars in preparation (in Europe, America, etc.); against capitalist rationalization; for higher wages; for social security in general; for the raising of the proletariat's standard of living; for nationalization

[5] Lenin, *Collected Works*, vol. 21, p. 213.
[6] See *Left-wing Communism: an infantile disorder* for Lenin's struggle against the ultra-left dogmatists at the Third World Congress of the Communist International, and especially his articles and speeches of September–October 1917.

of the land; the parliamentary struggle, etc. – all this must be directed towards the preparation and mobilization of the masses, with a view to a higher form of struggle during the paroxysm of the revolution: with a view to insurrection.

Basing itself on Lenin's doctrine, the draft programme of the Communist International outlines as follows the conditions under which the Party must lead the masses into battle for the overthrow of bourgeois power:

When the revolutionary tide is rising, when the ruling classes are disorganized, the masses are in a state of revolutionary ferment, the intermediary strata are inclining towards the proletariat and the masses are ready for action and for sacrifice, the Party of the proletariat is confronted with the task of leading the masses to a direct attack upon the bourgeois State. This it does by carrying on propaganda in favour of increasingly radical transitional slogans (for Soviets, workers' control of industry, for peasant committees, for the seizure of the big landed properties, for disarming the bourgeoisie and arming the proletariat, etc.), and by organizing mass action, upon which all branches of Party agitation and propaganda, including parliamentary activity, must be concentrated. This mass action includes: strikes; a combination of strikes and demonstrations; a combination of strikes and armed demonstrations and finally, the general strike conjointly with armed insurrection against the state power of the bourgeoisie. The latter form of struggle, which is the supreme form, must be conducted according to the rules of war; it presupposes a plan of campaign, offensive fighting operations and unbounded devotion and heroism on the part of the proletariat. An absolutely essential precedent condition for this form of action is the organization of the broad masses into militant units, which, by their very form, embrace and set into action the largest possible numbers of toilers (Councils of Workers' Deputies, Soldiers' Councils, etc.), and intensified revolutionary work in the army and the navy.

In passing over to new and more radical slogans, the Parties must be guided by the fundamental role of the political tactics of Leninism, which call for ability to lead the masses to revolutionary positions in such a manner that the masses may, by their own experience, convince themselves of the correctness of the Party Line. Failure to observe this rule must inevitably lead to isolation from the masses, to putschism, to the ideological degeneration of Communism into 'leftist' dogmatism, and to petty-bourgeois 'revolutionary' adventurism. Failure to take advantage of the culminating point in the development of the revolutionary situation, when the Party of the proletariat is called upon to conduct a bold and determined attack upon the enemy, is not less dangerous. To allow that opportunity to slip by and to fail to start rebellion at that point, means to let all the initiative pass to the enemy and to doom the revolution to defeat.[7]

---

[7] *Programme of the Communist International*, Chapter VI, 1928.

It is one thing to define theoretically the indispensable conditions which, when present, make the success of the insurrection possible. It is another, totally different and far more complicated, to *evaluate in practice* the degree of maturity of the revolutionary situation, and thus decide the question of when to launch the insurrection. This problem of timing is extraordinarily important.

Experience proves that it is not always possible to resolve the problem of timing as the circumstances would require. It frequently occurs that, under the influence of revolutionary impatience, or of the terror and provocations of the ruling classes, the degree of maturity of a revolutionary situation *is exaggerated*, and the insurrection fails. Or, on the other hand, a situation which demands decisive action by the Party of the proletariat *is underestimated*, and the propitious moment for organizing a successful insurrection is thus let slip. In illustration, we will quote a few historical examples.

On 14 August 1870, the Blanquists organized an insurrection in Paris. The masses did not support the insurgents, who were crushed. Three weeks later on 4 September, when the French troops had been beaten by the Prussians at Sedan, all Paris rose. At the moment of the Blanquist action, the ferment was already great among the masses and the ruling classes were already disorganized. But what was lacking was the shock necessary to set the masses in movement. It was Sedan that provided that shock. The Blanquists had not understood this, they had chosen the date for their insurrection badly, prematurely, and had been defeated.

Kamenev, Zinoviev and others in 1917, when the question of seizing power was discussed in the Party, considered that the circumstances were not yet ripe; that the Bolsheviks would not be able to hold onto power; that the masses would not take to the streets; that they were not sufficiently revolutionary; that 'nothing in the international situation obliges us to act immediately, and we would if anything damage the cause of socialist revolution in the West if we allowed ourselves to be massacred'; that the Party was isolated while the bourgeoisie was still fairly strong, etc. In short, they considered that the right course was to wait for the constituent assembly, which would decide the destiny of the Russian revolution.

Happily, Zinoviev and Kamenev had no support in the Party. But it is easy to imagine what would have happened if these comrades, members of the Central Committee, had had on their side even if not the majority of the Party at least a fraction, however small, oi it, and had dragged out the discussion on the seizure of power. The circumstances might have changed to the disadvantage of the revolutionary pro-letariat; for, in general, there is no situation which does not offer some way out for the ruling classes. The favourable moment might have been lost, and thereafter the seizure of power might have been postponed for a long time. It is certain that if the Party had adopted the position of Zinoviev and Kamenev, the revolutionary crisis of 1917 could have ended in an impasse, just as the revolutionary crisis in Germany did in 1918. There would have been no party considering it as its duty to assume responsibility for organizing a genuine pro-letarian government.

The position of Zinoviev and Kamenev in 1917 provides a typical example of the way in which a revolution may sometimes be missed.

In July 1917, the revolutionary part of the Petrograd proletariat was burning to intervene, and did indeed intervene, with the aim of overthrowing the provisional government. The Bolsheviks, and fore-most among them Lenin, warned the masses: 'It is still too soon.' The July Days (3–5 July) ended in a defeat. In September–October, the opposite happened. Lenin, despite major disagreement in the Central Committee of the Bolshevik Party concerning the seizure of power, ceaselessly repeated: 'Today or never! The revolution is in mortal danger!' Simultaneously, he issued all kinds of directives of a political, military and practical character, to ensure the success of the insurrection. Here is how he evaluated the situation in September 1917:

On July 3–4 it could have been argued, without violating the truth, that the correct thing to do was to take power, for our enemies would in any case have accused us of insurrection and ruthlessly treated us as rebels. However, to have decided on this account in favour of taking power at that time would have been wrong, because the objective conditions for the victory of the insurrection did not exist:

1. We still lacked the support of the class which is the vanguard of the revolution. We still did not have a majority among the workers and soldiers of Petrograd and Moscow. Now we have a majority in both Soviets. . . .

2. There was no country-wide revolutionary upsurge at that time. There is now, after the Kornilov revolt; the situation in the provinces and assumption of power by the Soviets in many localities prove this.

3. At that time there was no *vacillation* on any serious political scale among our enemies and among the irresolute petty bourgeoisie. Now the vacillation is enormous. Our main enemy, Allied and world imperialism (for world imperialism

is headed by the 'Allies'), *has begun to waver* between a war to a victorious finish and a separate peace directed against Russia. Our petty-bourgeois democrats, having clearly lost their majority among the people, have begun to vacillate enormously, and have rejected a bloc, i.e. a coalition, with the Cadets.

4. Therefore, an insurrection on July 3–4 would have been a mistake; we could not have retained power either physically or politically. We could not have retained it physically even though Petrograd was at times in our hands, because at that time our workers and soldiers would not have *fought and died* for Petrograd. There was not at the time that 'savageness', or fierce hatred *both of* the Kerensky's *and of* the Tseretelis and Chernovs. Our people had still not been tempered by the experience of the persecution of the Bolsheviks in which the Social-Revolutionaries and Mensheviks participated.

We could not have retained power politically on July 3–4 because, *before the Kornilov revolt*, the army and the provinces could and would have marched against Petrograd.

Now the picture is entirely different.

We have the following of the majority of a *class*, the vanguard of the revolution, the vanguard of the people, which is capable of carrying the masses with it.

We have the following of the *majority* of the people, because Chernov's resignation, while by no means the only symptom, is the most striking and obvious symptom that the peasants *will not receive land* from the Social-Revolutionaries' bloc (or from the Social-Revolutionaries themselves). And that is the chief reason for the popular character of the revolution. . . .

Our victory is assured, for the people are close to desperation, and we are showing the entire people a sure way out . . .[8]

This highly instructive extract from one of Lenin's works shows what enormous importance he attributed to the political conditions for insurrection, when deciding upon its timing. His evaluation of the situation in July was absolutely correct. The Party did not yet have the majority of the people on its side, the enemy was not yet sufficiently embroiled in its own contradictions, 'the oppressed were still able to live as they had done previously, and the ruling classes were still able to govern as they had previously'. In two months, the situation changed totally. Our party already had the majority of the people on its side, and Lenin now decided in favour of insurrection. Those who believed – as Zinoviev, Kamenev and others did – that he would destroy the Russian revolution, and with it the international revolution, were utterly mistaken.

In September, Lenin saw clearly that the majority of the people was behind the Bolshevik Party; judging the situation correctly, he knew

[8] Lenin, *Selected Works*, vol. II, p. 366, in 'Marxism and Insurrection'.

that the moment had come for a successful insurrection. Knowing the enormous responsibility which our party bore, not only toward the Russian but also toward the international proletariat, he was afraid that there might occur some radical modification of the situation to the advantage of the ruling classes, with the result that the seizure of power would for the time being be postponed. This is why he insisted in so imperious and categorical a fashion on an insurrection in October: Today or never! Delay means death! Victory is certain, to wait is a crime against the revolution!

This is why Lenin, seeing that the moment was ripe for a victorious insurrection, attacked Zinoviev and Kamenev so furiously, calling them strike-breakers, demanding their expulsion from the Party. He was a thousand times right. Kamenev and Zinoviev underestimated the maturity of the revolutionary situation in Russia and the West, and exaggerated the forces of counter-revolution. They held views which were basically no different from those of the social democrats.

By contrast, a negative example with respect to the timing of an insurrection was provided by the action of March 1921 in Germany – or more precisely by the tactics of the German Communist Party in connection with that March action. A certain 'theory of the offensive' was used to justify the March action theoretically.[9]

This theory was condemned by the Third Congress of the Comintern, and characterized by Lenin as putschist. The workers of the mining regions of Central Germany, in March 1921, were more revolutionary than those in other parts of the country. The government began to adopt various repressive measures against them. The Central Committee of the Communist Party responded by calling the working masses of Germany out on a general strike, which was planned to culminate in an insurrection. In Central Germany, the directive was followed; a general strike broke out, and in certain regions this escalated into an armed insurrection. But since the proletariat in the remainder

---

[9] Certain 'theoreticians' of German Communism in this period came up with the 'theory of the offensive', in other words the theory of revolutionary attack. They argued as follows: since the imperialist war of 1914–18 and the October Revolution have opened the epoch of proletarian revolutions, the only correct tactic for the Communist International must be one of revolutionary attack to overthrow the bourgeoisie. These 'theoreticians' did not take into account the Leninist principle that capitalism, in the epoch of its decomposition, is still capable of rallying temporarily, and that at such moments the tactic of revolutionary attack must be replaced by a different tactic – more appropriate, and incidentally no less revolutionary.

of the country did not actively support the workers of Central Germany, the latter were crushed by the superior forces of counter-revolution.

The Central Committee of the German Communist Party had over-estimated the revolutionary character of the situation. It had not understood that 'tens of millions of men do not make the revolution on the simple advice of a party' (Lenin); that 'victory cannot be won with a vanguard alone';[10] and that 'tens of millions of men do not make the revolution to order; they only make it when the people has been faced with an impossible situation, in which the collective pressure and the determination of tens of millions of men break all old barriers and are truly capable of creating a new life' (Lenin). The Communist Party had forgotten that the German proletariat as a whole had suffered so many heavy defeats, and had been pushed so far back onto the defensive since the days of March 1920, that it could not without prior political preparation respond sufficiently actively to the Party's directive for a general strike and an insurrection (i.e. a call for decisive mass actions to seize power). The vanguard, accompanied by a small section of the working class, rushed into the decisive battle without knowing at all whether it would be supported by the mass of workers throughout Germany, or whether its initiative would remain isolated.

In this instance, the date for the decisive action had been fixed incorrectly by the Central Committee of the German Communist Party; the call for a general offensive was premature.

Naturally, the fact that the rising was badly timed does not at all mean that we should condemn the March insurrection. The point is a quite different one – to find the reasons for the defeat. In certain regions of Central Germany, the proletarian masses did participate in the March insurrection. They fought the police and the troops. In view of this, it is not possible to condemn the insurrection – for it would not be the action of a revolutionary to condemn a mass struggle simply because its outcome was not such as one would have wished. But at the same time we must criticize the role and conduct of the leadership in this episode, and not cover up such faults as it may have committed.

While on the subject of how to choose the moment to strike, the Reval insurrection of 1 December 1924 should also be mentioned. Here, only 230–250 participants were involved. As we shall see below,

[10] Lenin, *Selected Works*, vol. III, p. 399, in *Left-wing Communism: an infantile disorder*.

in our detailed study of this insurrection, there were no large-scale mass actions on the part of the proletariat – either before, during or after the movement. The Party acted alone, with a tiny body of revolutionaries, in the hope of getting in a decisive first blow against the government forces and thereafter drawing in the proletarian masses to carry through the insurrection. But the rebels, as a result of their numerical weakness, were crushed before the masses could ever have moved into action.

The mistakes of the Communist Party of Estonia are evident here. The Reval experience once again confirms the truth of Lenin's principle that it is impossible to act with a vanguard alone, and that any intervention by such a vanguard which does not enjoy the active support of a majority of the working class is doomed to failure.

Lastly, the second Shanghai insurrection of 21 February 1927 is not devoid of interest from the point of view of how to time an uprising. It was launched at a moment when the general strike was already declining, and when half the strikers, under the impact of government terror, had already gone back to work. Two days earlier, the revolutionary movement of the Shanghai proletariat was at its peak: some 300,000 workers were on strike. Yet the Party, because its technical preparations were incomplete, postponed the insurrection. Two days were lost in preparations. During that time, the general situation changed to the disadvantage of the proletariat. The insurrection, therefore, could not succeed.

The example of the second Shanghai insurrection shows that sometimes a day or two can be of decisive importance.

After what has just been said about timing, we do not need to linger on the question: 'Can an insurrection be timed for a prearranged date?' – though in its time (in 1905, before the December insurrection), this gave rise to quite an argument between Lenin and the new *Iskra*, notably Martinov. As we know, the Petrograd insurrection of 1917 was timed for 7 November, to coincide with the opening of the Second Congress of Soviets. Many proletarian insurrections in other countries have been timed for precise dates, and executed according to a plan. It is certainly impossible to order a revolution or a workers' action for a fixed date. 'But if we have really prepared an uprising, and if a popular uprising is realizable by virtue of the revolutions in social relations *that have already taken place*, then it is quite possible to time the uprising. . . . An uprising can be (timed), if those preparing it have influence among the masses and can correctly estimate the situation.'[11]

Insurrection in the broad sense of the word is of course not a purely military operation. It is basically and above all a powerful revolutionary movement; a powerful thrust by the proletarian masses – or at least by the active fraction of those masses, even if numerically this only constitutes a minority of the proletariat – against the dominant classes. It is an active and determined struggle on the part of the active majority, at the decisive moment and on the decisive issue. The military operations of the combat organization *must coincide with the high point of proletarian action*. Only in these conditions can the insurrection succeed. The intrinsically most favourable of revolutionary situations is not sufficient to ensure the revolution's victory. *The insurrection must be organized by a party*. Power will not come of its own accord, it must be seized. 'The old government . . . never, not even in a period of crisis, "falls", if it is not toppled over' (Lenin).

It is in this sense that Lenin wrote, in his previously quoted, 'Marxism and Insurrection', after listing the political conditions necessary to guarantee the success of the insurrection:

In order to treat insurrection in a Marxist way, i.e. as an art, we must at the same time, without losing a single moment, organize a *headquarters* of the insurgent detachments, distribute our forces, move the reliable regiments to the most important points, surround the Alexandrinsky Theatre, occupy the Peter and Paul Fortress, arrest the General Staff and the government, and move against the officer cadets and the Savage Division those detachments which would rather die than allow the enemy to approach the strategic points of the city. We must mobilize the armed workers and call them to fight the last desperate fight, occupy the telegraph and the telephone exchange at once, move *our* insurrection headquarters to the central telephone exchange and connect it by telephone with all the factories, all the regiments, all the points of armed fighting, etc.[12]

Not only was Lenin the great strategist of revolution. He also knew better than anyone Marx's pregnant thesis: 'insurrection is an art'. Moreover, he knew how to apply it in masterly fashion to the practical struggle for power. It was only by correctly estimating the moment for insurrection, and by treating the latter as an art – i.e. by applying all the necessary political, technical and tactical measures, that the October Revolution was made possible.

[11] Lenin, *Collected Works*, vol. 8, p. 153, in *Two Tactics*.
[12] Lenin, *Selected Works*, vol. II, p. 369.

On the question of how the proletariat's decisive struggle for power should be prepared, let us first examine the problem purely from a general political standpoint. It is essential to know *when to orient* all the Party's *political action* towards *immediate* practical preparation (both political and technical) for insurrection; *when* to give the masses slogans such as 'workers' control of production', 'peasant committees for the occupation of big landlord and state-owned estates', 'create a red guard', 'arm the proletariat and disarm the bourgeoisie', 'organize Soviets', 'seize power by armed insurrection', etc. – i.e. *when to shift the centre of gravity of daily practical agitation towards slogans which raise the final objective of the working-class struggle, and when to concentrate all the Party's attention on mobilizing the masses around these slogans*, which must in view of the situation, become *the dominant slogans of the day*.

This moment is essentially the beginning of a new phase in the life of the Party, and in the life of the proletariat in general. Timing it accurately is as difficult as timing the insurrection itself. It must not be fixed too early – i.e. when the general situation still requires agitation and propaganda for the ordinary partial demands of the masses; when the latter are still insufficiently prepared for the slogans of the final struggle and for that struggle itself, and are not sufficiently impregnated with revolutionary spirit; when the enemy is not sufficiently embroiled in his own contradictions. For in that case, the slogans of all-out struggle will not be understood by the masses and the call on them to fight for these slogans will appear too sudden. Thus the Party's decision to reorient itself towards immediate preparation for insurrection will not prove to be viable, and will have no positive result.

Furthermore, any 'tailism' shown in this question of reorienting the Party and its mass activity, any delay in resolving it, will inevitably have grave consequences. These consequences could severely hamper the preparation of the uprising, and its entire subsequent evolution. Moreover, an excessive delay may liquidate the struggle for power during the period in question; whereas a correct policy on the part of the Communist Party and a correct solution to the question of reorienting the latter towards immediate preparation for the seizure of power, may make that struggle possible and indeed victorious.

If one examines the purely military aspect of insurrection, it is evident that, like any military operation, it cannot be improvised. On the contrary, it demands prolonged, systematic and thorough preparation, for a long time prior to the date fixed. Unless insurrection is regarded as an art; unless every aspect of it is prepared systematically, and as a military operation, it is absolutely impossible for it to succeed, even if the general political situation is favourable for a seizure of power by the proletariat. This is a principle which is valid for all countries, and especially for those in which the bourgeoisie, thanks to its long domination, has been able to constitute a flexible and powerful government apparatus. Hence (even on the basis of purely military conditions, and leaving aside the more important political factors) it is of the greatest importance that the Party should decide in good time whether to orient itself towards immediate preparation for insurrection, or whether to continue to mobilize the masses in a struggle around day-to-day working-class demands.

The Party must therefore be capable – as a result of its correct analysis of the situation in the country, its close and direct relationship with the masses, and its knowledge of the adversary's situation and the thinking behind his internal and external policies – of foreseeing in good time the approach of a revolutionary situation, and of orienting sufficiently early all its political work and its organization towards immediate preparation for insurrection.

One reason for the defeat of the German revolution in 1923 was the fact that the German Communist Party *had reoriented itself too late towards immediate preparation for insurrection.* The approach of an immediately revolutionary situation could certainly – given a Bolshevik leadership in the Party – have been foreseen from the moment of the French military occupation of the Rhineland and the Ruhr (or at least immediately after that). From that moment, a deep economic and political crisis began in Germany. From that moment, in certain regions (Saxony, Halle, Merseburg, etc.) proletarian fighting 'Hundreds' began to be formed, on the initiative of the workers themselves. And yet the Central Committee of the Communist Party only began to orient itself towards arming the workers and towards insurrection on the occasion of the three-day general strike at the beginning of August – the strike which overthrew the (nationalist) Cuno government. *A lot of time had been wasted:* the Proletarian Hundreds were being formed without suitable cadres or leadership; they had not been able to obtain enough arms; work in the army and police had been carried out in a quite inadequate fashion. All these factors, combined with the other causes,[13] could not fail to influence the outcome of the revolutionary crisis of autumn 1923.

The German Communist Party, or to be more accurate its leadership, did not realize soon enough the importance of the French occupation of the Ruhr and Rhineland. It did not evaluate as it should have the loss suffered by the German economy (eighty per cent of iron and steel production; seventy-one per cent of coal), and hence the meaning of the government's policy of 'passive' resistance. For this reason, it was unable to foresee in good time the economic crisis which subsequently created the revolutionary crisis.

On the other hand, if the Chinese Communist Party, immediately after the disastrous Shanghai insurrection of February 1927, had not understood that the moment was becoming favourable for a new revolutionary attempt, and had not prepared for this with as much energy as it in fact did, accepting every sacrifice, then the insurrection of 21 March, even if it had still succeeded (as a result of the extraordinarily propitious conditions), would certainly have cost far more than it did after such careful preparation.

One can say the same about the Russian Bolshevik Party in 1917. The firm orientation of the entire Party towards a seizure of power by the Soviets had been adopted from the moment of Lenin's arrival (April Theses). From that moment, all the political and organizational work of the Party was consciously directed to preparing the masses for the seizure of power. It is easy to imagine what would have happened if the Party had hesitated on this essential point, if it had delayed carrying out that change of orientation, or if it had adopted the position which Zinoviev, Kamenev and others subsequently took up. Naturally, in that case there would have been no question of the victory of October, for the extremely favourable situation of October 1917 did *not* derive *solely* from objective causes (prolongation of the war, economic crisis, agrarian revolution, etc.), and had not so to speak simply created itself; *it was to a great extent the result of the conscious action upon events by the Bolshevik Party* (*revolutionary education of the masses, organizational work among the people, in the army, in the fleet, etc.*).

[13] We shall say nothing here of the opportunist errors of the Central Committee of the German Communist Party on a whole series of issues – errors which played an essential role in the defeat of the 1923 revolution, and which were dealt with in detail at the Fifth World Congress of the Communist International. We are here simply concerned with certain factors of a political and military character.

By way of illustration, numerous examples could be cited. But this is unnecessary. The importance of the question under examination here, and the need for resolving it correctly, are clear. This question is no less important, as far as preparing for insurrection is concerned, than choosing the right moment to strike when a revolutionary situation has fully ripened.

It remains for us to deal with a question of principle – namely, that of partial proletarian insurrections.

The proletarian revolution does not follow a straight line. It proceeds by way of partial advances and victories, temporary declines and defeats. The definitive victory of the revolution is inconceivable without these ascents and descents on the long path of its development. The proletariat becomes hardened in this prolonged revolutionary struggle; it learns to know its own strength, and the strength and policies of the enemy. Thanks to this experience it succeeds in creating policies and tactics of its own. It stores up the lessons of history and goes into battle with new energy to realize its class aims. In this sense, the temporary defeats suffered by the proletariat should not be considered solely as defeats. Each of them contains the elements of an inevitable victory in the future. Engels said somewhere: 'Beaten armies get a good schooling.' These admirable words are even more applicable to revolutionary armies, recruited among the advanced classes (Lenin). Without the dress rehearsal of 1905, it would be impossible to imagine the victory of the Russian proletariat in October 1917. Without the succession of victories and heavy defeats costing innumerable sacrifices that the Chinese proletariat has experienced in the course of the last few years, it would be impossible to imagine the inevitable victory of the proletarian revolution in China. This is an incontrovertible fact. It is in these terms that we should examine the problem of insurrections which are not general but partial – the problem of the partial (not universal) struggle of the proletariat and oppressed peasantry against the ruling classes:

It is absolutely natural and inevitable [wrote Lenin in 1906 in his article 'Guerrilla Warfare'] that the uprising should assume the higher and more complex form of a prolonged civil war embracing the whole country, i.e. an armed struggle between two sections of the people. Such a war cannot be conceived otherwise than as a series of a few big engagements at comparatively long intervals and a large number of small encounters during these intervals. That being so – and it is undoubtedly so – the Social Democrats must absolutely make it their duty to create organizations best adapted to lead the masses in these big engagements and, as far as possible, in these small encounters as well.[14]

This conflict, extending over quite long intervals of time, cannot be seen as a continuous victory, which has no partial failures or defeats. It frequently happens that the proletariat takes up arms and intervenes against the established order without having any chance of decisive victory, and that by doing so it obliges the ruling classes to satisfy one or other of its demands. It is quite wrong to believe that armed action by the proletariat is only permissible when there is a perfect guarantee of victory. This is an illusion. Armed insurrection is an operation 'which is based on the principles of military science' and, as such (like any other operation), it cannot have an absolute guarantee of success. Setbacks, as a result of some circumstance or other – even of a purely subjective kind (since the proletariat does not and will not always have leaders in sufficient numbers, or sufficiently prepared militarily and technically) – are always possible and even inevitable.

Marx wrote to Kugelmann, when the latter had allowed himself to express certain doubts during the Paris Commune as to the Parisians' chances:

World history would indeed be very easy to make, if the struggle were taken up only on condition of infallibly favourable chances. . . . The bourgeois *canaille* of Versailles . . . presented the Parisians with the alternative of either taking up the fight or succumbing without a struggle. The demoralization of the working class in the latter case would have been a far greater misfortune than the fall of any number of 'leaders'.[15]

In our epoch too, can there not and indeed do there not occur cases in which the proletariat of a particular country or industrial centre, even though it has no chance of victory, is nevertheless obliged by certain circumstances (notably by the provocations of the ruling classes) to commit itself to armed struggle? Have we not seen examples of spontaneous insurrection (for example in Cracow in 1923, in Vienna in 1927, etc.), when the proletariat does not stop to calculate the probable outcome of the conflict, but simply takes up arms and joins battle? Could the party of the proletariat refuse to join the struggle of the masses, or refuse to lead it? Could it condemn it, or remain neutral? Such a party would cease to be the party of the

[14] Lenin, *Collected Works*, vol. 11, p. 222.
[15] Marx/Engels, *Selected Works*, vol. II, p. 464, quoted by Lenin.

proletariat, and would deserve to see the masses turn from it with contempt.

The Communist Party must be in the front rank of every mass struggle, every armed struggle, without exception. It puts itself at the head of the masses and leads them, *independently of the conditions in which the particular struggle takes place and whether it has a hundred per cent chance of victory or no chance at all.* The Party, as vanguard of the class, *is obliged to decide on the utility or otherwise of the action before the conflict begins,* and to agitate among the masses accordingly. But once armed struggle has begun, there must be no further hesitation about what the Party should do – about whether or not it should support and lead that struggle. On such occasions the Party must act as Marx did during the Paris Commune, and as Lenin did during the July Days in Petrograd. From September 1870 on, Marx was warning the Parisians against an insurrection, which he regarded as madness. But once the insurrection had broken out, he ranged himself with the insurgents. During the struggle of the Parisian proletariat, Marx wrote: 'However that may be, the present rising in Paris – even if it be crushed by the wolves, swine and vile curs of the old society – is the most glorious deed of our Party since the June insurrection in Paris.'[16]

Lenin, as we know, was against the July insurrection. 'The moment has not come,' he warned. But after the masses had taken to the streets he was with them.

There are various kinds of insurrection: victorious insurrections; mass insurrections which none the less end in failure; small-scale guerrilla warfare (minor skirmishes); putschist insurrections, i.e. those which are organized by a party or other organization on its own, without the participation of the masses.

The main criterion governing the Party's attitude towards these various kinds of insurrection is the following: do the masses take part or not? *The Party rejects putsches, as a manifestation of petty-bourgeois adventurism.* The party supports and leads every mass struggle, including minor skirmishes or guerrilla operations, if the masses really take part in them.

It would however be a crude error to draw the conclusion from this that, if such and such a detachment of the proletariat is ready to

---

[16] ibid., p. 463, also quoted by Lenin.

engage in armed struggle against its class enemy, the Party is obliged, irrespective of the general and local circumstances, to urge it to insurrection. Such a party would not deserve the name of leader of the vanguard class.

Insurrection [said Lenin in 1905] is an important word. A call to insurrection is an extremely serious call. The more complex the social system, the better the organization of state power, and the more perfected the military machine, the more impermissible is it to launch such a slogan without due thought.[17]

When it calls on the masses to rise, the Party must always take the consequences into account. It must be aware that isolated risings will not achieve any decisive success. Its duty is to call upon the masses to rise at the moment when the local and general conjuncture is most favourable to success; when the balance of forces is favourable to the revolution; when there is a chance of seizing power – if not throughout the country, at least in a number of centres which can serve as a base for developing the revolution.

Certain local organizations of the Chinese Communist Party can be cited as examples of the way not to proceed in calling for insurrection. In late 1927 and early 1928, the communist organizations in several provinces (Chihli, Hunan, etc.), aware that an immediately revolutionary situation existed, repeatedly called on the proletarian masses to rise; they did this without considering at all whether these risings had any chance of success – whether they strengthened or weakened the positions of the proletariat. These appeals to the masses and attempts to organize insurrections reflected the ultra-left mentality of a certain fraction of the Chinese Communist Party.

The Party supports every mass insurrection. However, if the insurrection does not break out spontaneously, but is organized by the Party, if the masses embark on armed struggle in response to the Party's call, then the latter bears the responsibility both for the timing and for the conduct of the struggle.

Now, insurrection is an art quite as much as war or any other art, and is subject to certain procedural rules which, when neglected, will bring about the downfall of the party neglecting them. These rules, logical deductions from the nature of the parties and the circumstances you have to deal with in such a case, are so plain and simple that the brief experience of 1848 made the Germans fairly well acquainted with them. Firstly, never play with insurrection unless you are fully prepared to

[17] Lenin, *Collected Works*, vol. 9, p. 367, in 'The Latest in *Iskra* Tactics, or Mock Elections as a New Incentive to an Uprising'.

go the whole way. Insurrection is an equation with very indefinite magnitudes, the value of which may change every day; the forces opposed to you have all the advantage of organization, discipline and habitual authority; unless you bring strong odds against them you are defeated and ruined. Secondly, once you have entered upon the insurrectionary career, act with the greatest determination, and on the offensive. The defensive is the death of every armed rising; it is lost before it measures itself with its enemies. Surprise your antagonists while their forces are scattered, prepare the way for new successes, however small, but prepare daily; keep up the moral superiority which the first successful rising has given to you; rally in this way those vacillating elements to your side which always follow the strongest impulse and which always look out for the safer side; force your enemies to retreat before they can collect their strength against you; in the words of Danton, the greatest master of revolutionary tactics yet known: *de l'audace, de l'audace, encore de l'audace.*[18]

As we study the problems of insurrection, we shall continually bear in mind this remarkable passage from Engels so rich in content and so profound; it oriented Lenin and the Bolshevik Party in their tactics of insurrection, and it *must serve as a guideline* to all communist parties as they prepare for and lead the armed struggle for power.

As we analyse the character of past insurrections in various parts of the world, we intend not only to concern ourselves with problems of principle but also, wherever possible (wherever precise information is available to us), to study in detail questions of technical organization and military tactics involved in preparing for insurrection and in the conduct of the operation itself.

A study, as complete as possible, of the various examples of insurrection offered by history will provide the necessary material for certain general conclusions concerning the organization and conduct of proletarian armed struggle.

The history of the class struggle of the international proletariat in the twentieth century is extremely rich in examples of armed struggle. Our task does not involve studying every proletarian insurrection, nor even the most important ones. We shall analyse solely the most characteristic examples. For these are the most instructive, both from the point of view of political principles – i.e. the evaluation of social and political conditions and the timing of the insurrection – and also from the point of view of the preparation and military conduct of the insurrection itself.

[18] Friedrich Engels, *Revolution and Counter-revolution in Germany*, quoted by Lenin in 'Can the Bolsheviks retain State power?', *Selected Works*, vol. II, pp. 419–20.

3

The Reval Uprising

GENERAL POLITICAL SITUATION IN ESTONIA IN 1924

The proletarian uprising which took place in Reval [Tallin] on 1 December 1924 provides us, from every point of view, with an extremely instructive example of the armed struggle of a section of the Estonian proletariat. A study of this insurrection is absolutely indispensable for the entire international revolutionary proletariat, and for all revolutionary parties seriously preparing for the seizure of political power.

In the autumn of 1924, the political situation in Estonia[1] was reckoned by the Communist Party to be favourable for organizing a successful insurrection, and for establishing the dictatorship of the proletariat. Broadly speaking, its characteristics were as follows.

[1] A. Estonia is the old Estonian province of the Russian Empire, which became independent in 1918 after the October Revolution. It covers an area of 48,100 square kilometres. Peasants make up seventy per cent of the population.

B. The Estonian trade unions, at the end of 1922, had about 27,000 members. This out of a total of some 34,000 industrial workers. At the beginning of 1924 all the unions, with the exception of a few local organizations, were under the organizational and political influence of the Communist Party.

The agricultural workers were about 60,000 strong, and of these some ten per cent were unionized. This low percentage is explained by the dispersal of the population in numerous hamlets (khutors), which made organization difficult. A further factor was government terror, which used every available means to hamper the progress of the trade unions among the rural population. In 1924 the unions were dissolved and forced underground.

C. At the beginning of 1924, the Communist Party had about 2,000 members, 500 of them in Reval. It was illegal. Ideologically, it was sound. Government terror, from the very beginning of Estonian independence, had continually decimated its ranks, taking the best militants. It nevertheless maintained close contact with the masses, and continued to lead their struggles. The proof of this was given by the number of votes which the lists of the United Workers' and Peasants' Front won in the municipal elections of autumn 1923. In Reval, this communist list won about thirty-six per cent of the vote; in Pernov [Pärnu] and other large towns about thirty per cent. In numerous rural areas, the Communist Party won absolute majorities. The most numerous arrests took place in 1921. More than 200 comrades were arrested, and of these 115 were brought before the courts. In spring 1924, 250 comrades were arrested and 149 brought to trial (the 'Trial of the 149').

Before 1924, industry and commerce had to a large extent been sustained by government subsidies, supplied by the State Bank mainly at the expense of its gold reserves. At the beginning of 1924, the opposition parties discovered that these reserves had been almost totally drained by the friends of the ruling landowner and big bourgeois party. A group of petty-bourgeois opposition parties was formed in parliament, calling itself the Democratic League (christian democrats, national democrats, labourites); with the help of the social democrats these formed a government of centre parties.

This new government was obliged to cut the credits to the shareholders and speculators of the big bourgeoisie and landowning class. There ensued a general shut-down of factories and a series of big business failures. Unemployment, in the summer of 1924, reached proportions that were without precedent in Estonia: 15,000 people were out of work. During the course of the summer, the number of workers in employment sank to 6,000.

The fall of the mark, towards autumn, had raised the cost of living by about fifty per cent while wages remained stationary.

There was a foreign trade gap. The budget showed a large deficit. The industrial and commercial crisis was further aggravated by an agricultural crisis. The 1923 harvest had been a poor one, and although the summer crop in 1924 had been a slight improvement, the winter crop looked like being down again on the previous year.

The government's attempts to obtain further loans had failed. On the contrary, England, France and the United States demanded repayment of the old loans they had granted to Estonia during the civil war and the war against the USSR. Crime reached proportions that were unheard of in Estonia, as did corruption, peculation, etc. According to official figures, 28,000 crimes were penalized in 1919; 44,000 in 1922; 64,000 in 1924. Discipline in the army had deteriorated appreciably. According to the military high command, every soldier or sailor spent on average at least one period under arrest each year.

The ruling classes showed clear signs of disintegration. After the formation of the new Centre government, the internal struggles and scandals provoked by the various ruling cliques had taken on an exceptional intensity. The Right openly accused the Centre of having usurped power, and of being incapable of extricating the country from the economic and political crisis; the Centre in turn accused the Right of speculation, theft, etc. In the parliament, these attacks regularly ended in brawls or exchanges of insults. Parliament had lost all authority over the masses.

The landowners and big bourgeois were cynically calling for a change in the Constitution in favour of the property-owning classes, and spoke of the need to suppress the 'democratic government' and to hand over power to a strong man, to a dictator.

The government had to all intents and purposes no programme, no real means of consolidating its authority or of putting the country on its feet economically. The only 'effective' achievement of that wretched government of failed speculators, gamblers and drunkards (the Minister of Defence was found drunk in a Reval street) was the savage war it waged against the revolutionary workers and peasants. In November 1924 it put on a gigantic trial of 149 communists. By murdering working-class leaders (the trade-union president Tomp was shot during the 'Trial of the 149' for contempt of court), by sentencing revolutionary militants and destroying working-class organizations, in short by sword, fire and prison, the Estonian bourgeoisie thought that it could put paid to the revolutionary movement.

Despite everything, *the revolutionary aspirations of the working class and in general of all workers escalated rapidly throughout 1924.* More and more frequently, workers were heard to demand dissolution of the government, and the establishment of worker and peasant rule. The demonstration of 1 May and the anti-war week of early August took place under the slogan of civil war. *The meetings and demonstrations were almost always joined by groups of soldiers. The workers were not alone in showing this combative attitude. Agricultural labourers, farmers and poor peasants, and even the petty bourgeoisie of the towns, sympathized with the Communist Party's agitation.*

It was clear to the Party that the only way of resolving this situation was boldly to take the path of active revolution. The Central Committee decided *in April to orient itself towards the preparation of an armed insurrection. From that moment, all the meetings or congresses called by the Party, all the Party's political and organizational work, had the aim of preparing the masses* for a revolutionary action and for Estonia's adhesion to the Soviet Union. The balance of social forces, unquestionably favourable to revolution, demanded such an attitude. The Party reckoned that in the spring of 1924, in the event of action, it would have a fifty per cent chance of success. The balance of real forces in the autumn was even more favourable. It was reckoned that if the insurrection was organized well, success would be certain.

MILITARY PREPARATION OF THE INSURRECTION

From the spring of 1924 onwards, the Party's main military objective was the formation of a proletarian force capable of smashing, at the moment of the attack, any counter-revolutionary units who might offer resistance (military academies, etc.). Combat squads – at first in the form of groups of three, termed 'defence groups' or anti-fascist groups;[2] subsequently in the form of groups of ten – began to be created in the spring. A week before the Reval uprising, the groups of ten were fused into companies, and then the latter into battalions of 120–150 men apiece. After the first successes had been achieved, these battalions were to be reinforced by such workers and soldiers as might be willing to fight. In the country as a whole, some one thousand men were organized in this way by the autumn. Of this number, about two thirds were non-party workers.

Military specialists were attached to the Central Committee and to the communist committees in the various towns, to direct the organization of the combat squads and in general the entire military preparation of the insurrection.

At the moment of the insurrection, there were three battalions in Reval, with the following strengths: 1st Battalion, 170 men; 2nd Battalion, 120 men; 3rd Battalion, 110 men; making a total of 400 men.

Most of these had had some military training (they could handle rifles or certain models of revolver, hand-grenades, knew the elementary rules of combat, etc.). There were, however, certain of them who hardly knew, or did not know at all, how to use their weapons. The insurrectionary command (i.e. the company and battalion commanders) was not adequately prepared for its role of military leadership. The need for secrecy, and the impossibility of bringing the men or even their commanders together, very often made it extremely difficult to give either of them any training.

At the moment of the insurrection, the armaments of the entire Reval military organization consisted of:

[2] These titles were made necessary by the conditions of clandestinity.

(*a*) 100 Parabellum revolvers, with fifty rounds apiece;
(*b*) about 60 carbines and rifles, with a small supply of ammunition;
(*c*) 3 Thompson sub-machine-guns, with about 100 rounds apiece;
(*d*) a few dozen hand-grenades, and 20 percussion bombs.

The counter-revolutionary forces in Reval – i.e. those who, according to the calculations of the Party and the military organization, might take up arms against the insurrection – amounted to: the *junker* academy and the officer-cadets, 400 men; the college of NCOs, 200–250 men; the garrison commander's troop, 110–120 men; the mounted police reserve, 50–60 men; a total of 760–830 men.

In addition there were about 500 fascists with arms, who however did not constitute a serious fighting force.

As for the police and the garrison units (a battalion of the 10th Infantry Regiment, a tank squadron, a telegraph battalion, the shore batteries, the artillery and an airborne squadron), the Party and its military command – on the basis of information received concerning the results of the work that had been carried out among these units to subvert them and win them over politically – reckoned that they would not take up arms against the insurgents. Indeed it was thought that, given skilful organization, once the insurrection was launched they would come over to the workers. The Party arrived at this conclusion because of its belief that the garrison had been extensively subverted by the communist cells which existed in every unit, and by the personal relations linking communists and soldiers.

It must be stressed that the Communist Party of Estonia had always paid great attention to agitation among the troops. During 1924, this work had been carried out even more intensively, with the result that the influence of communism in the army, above all in the garrison of the capital and in the units quartered in the Pechory [Petseri] district (on the border with the USSR), was very considerable. Proof of this was furnished by secret reports to the General Staff which fell into the hands of the Communist Party. Needless to say, government terror put the greatest obstacles in the way of this work in the army.

Shortly before the insurrection, the Party's influence in the army had weakened to some extent. The old soldiers, their term of service over, had been demobilized and with them the most revolutionary elements had departed. New recruits had only recently arrived. Although a great deal of agitation was carried out among these young soldiers, the Party's overall influence had none the less been reduced. Some of the new communist and youth groups had not had the time to get properly organized, and had not yet been able to establish adequate links with all the revolutionary elements who had been called to the colours. This circumstance played a considerable role in the struggle for power launched by the Reval proletariat on 1 December.

After long months of weighing up the chances of success in the event of an armed rising, the active nucleus of the Party, headed by the Central Committee, had reached the unanimous conclusion that to start the insurrection with a political strike or some similar mass movement on the part of the workers would be disastrous; it would give the adversary warning of the attack, and expose the working-class masses to the machine-guns of the bourgeoisie's henchmen – who despite everything represented a powerful force in Reval itself. *It was decided that the insurrection would be launched suddenly by the combat squads so as to take the enemy by surprise, and that only after the first successes would a general strike be organized and the working masses be brought into the fight, to complete the revolution and consolidate the insurgents' hold on power.*

Furthermore, simultaneous action in the various parts of the country was not thought to be of any advantage. The insurrection was to break out in Reval and Pernov (it did not in fact break out in the latter; the orders had been received too late, it was postponed for a day, and then naturally after the defeat of Reval it did not take place); after these places, and particularly Reval, had been occupied, the other towns would follow.

Everything was subordinated to this idea of a surprise attack. The insurrection was prepared for in the greatest secrecy. After the anti-war week, the Party organized no further actions on the part of the working-class masses, for fear of being crushed by counter-revolution. Even during the 'Trial of the 149', and on the occasion of the brutal murder of Tomp, the Communist Party did not call the masses onto the streets. It calculated that if it could succeed in striking a sudden and unexpected blow at the points selected as targets for the planned attack, then, in spite of the enormous superiority of the enemy's military strength over that of the combat organization, victory would be certain. In this respect, the organization of the insurrection had the character of a conspiracy.

At the end of November (a few days before the insurrection) the decision was taken to act before dawn on 1 December (during the night of Sunday to Monday).

According to the account given by participants, the plan was as follows: *at the very outset the insurgents would seize control of the military headquarters, the communication services, the citadel (seat of the government, national assembly, etc.); they would arrest the members of the government; they would free the prisoners; they would destroy the police-reserve building,* capture the tanks and use them against the army, police or fascist league if these dared to take up the government's defence; they would seize control of aircraft; they would sack the military academy; they would empty the arms and artillery depots (some 120,000 or 130,000 rifles, together with every kind of war *matériel,* were kept near the military academy).

In addition, they were to blow up the railway bridge between Taps [Tapa] and Iouriev [or Dorpat, now Tartu], in order to delay all transport between these two points for a few days, and prevent the despatch of troops loyal to the government from Iouriev to Reval. They were also to put the railway bridge between Reval and Taps out of action, so that the enemy would not be able to send an armoured train loaded with counter-revolutionaries from Taps to Reval. These two missions were more or less successfully carried out by small sapper units.

In the event of prolonged fighting in Reval, they were to blow up the railway bridge close to the city. After the occupation of the capital, other actions were to begin in the direction of Taps-Narva-Iouriev and Fellin [Viljandi], using the railways and also road transport.

In order to assemble the combat squads in secrecy, they had secured in advance secret apartments as near as possible to the chosen targets, and arms had been stocked in these. The squads were to move into action at set times, planned so that the attack would be simultaneous at every point. All squads were to be ready and assembled by 10 p.m. on 30 November. For security reasons, the members of the squads did not know that the operation was in fact an insurrection planned to start on 1 December. They had only been informed of an illegal meeting, which all those who possessed arms were to attend carrying those arms with them. In these same secret apartments, during the night of 30 November, the squads were taught to handle the arms which had just been distributed to them.

The commanders of the three battalions did not succeed in assembling all their men by 10 p.m. By 4 a.m. on 1 December, the numbers present at the various assembly-points were as follows: 56 men out of the 170 of the 1st Battalion; 91 men out of the 120 of the 2nd Battalion; 80 men out of the 110 of the 3rd Battalion; a total of 227 men out of 400.

The failure in mobilization is certainly attributable to the fact that 30 November was a Sunday and that it was difficult to contact everyone (they were not at home). Moreover, since they did not know that an insurrection was planned, a number of them refused to attend an ordinary meeting called for such a late hour.

In spite of the tiny number of men who had been assembled, the Central Committee confirmed its decision to begin the action on 1 December, at 5.15 a.m.

The battalions had been allotted the following targets:

1st Battalion – disarm the *junker* academy and the officer-cadet school; seize the arms depots and the narrow-gauge railway station.

2nd Battalion – disarm the police reserve and the garrison commander's troop; win over the tank and airborne squadrons; take the headquarters of the 10th Regiment and win over the men of that regiment to the insurgent cause.

3rd Battalion – capture the administrative centres, the telegraph office, the seat of government and the parliament, the war ministry, the army headquarters, the Baltic station and free all the prisoners being held in preventive detention.

THE COURSE OF THE INSURRECTION

On 1 December, at 5.15 a.m. precisely, all units set about carrying out their missions. The course of the insurrection was as follows (see map, p. 69):

Operations of the 1st Battalion. The preparation of the attack on the *junker* academy had to be effected at absolutely lightning speed. The commander of the battalion, with his immediate aides, returned from the meeting of the Party's military leadership at 4 a.m. The battalion had to leave the assembly-point by 4.45 (it was half an hour's march from the *junker* academy) in order to be able to begin the attack at

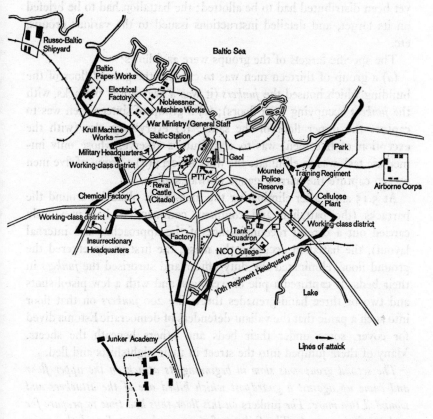

1. The Insurrection in Reval 1923

5.15 precisely. In the space of three quarters of an hour, the men had to be organized into units (in the case of some groups, only single members had turned up at the assembly-point); such arms as had not yet been distributed had to be allotted; the battalion had to be briefed on its target, and detailed instructions issued to the various groups, etc.

The specific targets of the groups were as follows:

(*a*) a group of thirteen men was to capture the ground floor of the building which housed the *junkers* (it was a two-storey barracks, with the *junkers* occupying both floors); (*b*) a group of sixteen men was to capture the upper floor of the same; (*c*) everybody else (with the exception of five men) was to constitute a reserve, whose only immediate task was to eliminate the duty officer; (*d*) a group of five men was to capture the narrow-gauge railway station.

At 5.15 a.m., after eliminating the man-made obstacles around the barracks (the battalion and company commanders had previously carried out a careful reconnaissance of the approaches and internal layout), the battalion occupied the mess; the first group entered the ground floor, eliminated the duty officer and surprised the *junkers* in their beds. It captured a pile of weapons, and with a few pistol shots and two or three hand-grenades threw the 200 *junkers* on that floor into such a panic that the valiant defenders of democratic Estonia dived for cover, some under their beds and others beneath the sheets. Many of them jumped into the street in their nightshirts and fled.

The second group was slow in beginning its attack on the upper floor and came up against a guardpost which killed one of the attackers and wounded two more. The junkers *on this floor thus had time to prepare for and repel the attack. The failure of the second group forced the entire battalion to withdraw, and the attack on the* junker *academy thus ended in defeat.* The arms depots remained totally in the hands of the enemy. The men, with five or six exceptions, dispersed.

The insurgents lost 1 killed and 2 wounded; the *junkers*, 4 killed and 9 wounded. The five men sent to capture the station carried out their mission in exemplary fashion, and without loss.

The reasons for the defeat of the 1st Battalion are obvious: in the first place its inadequate numbers (the enemy outnumbered it by eight to one); secondly, the second group's slowness; lastly the lack of determination shown in the struggle to take the academy – at the first setback the groups dispersed, although after overwhelming the

200 *junkers* on the ground floor it would have been easy to continue the fight.

Operations of the 2nd Battalion. The forces of the 2nd Battalion were deployed as follows: (*a*) attack on the mounted police reserve: 20 men; (*b*) attack on the tank squadron: 20 men; (*c*) attack on the 10th Regiment headquarters: 3 men; (*d*) attack on the 3rd Battalion of the 10th Regiment: 9 men; (*e*) attack on the airborne corps: 13 men.

The operations proceeded as follows: According to reconnaissance reports, the police reserve was barracked in a two-storey wooden building. This was the building which had to be attacked. It subsequently turned out that only a few police were housed in this building, while the main body was in a stone building attached to the former, which reconnaissance had identified wrongly as a bath-house. For this reason, and also because the group sent to attack the tank squadron had gone into action ten minutes early and by opening fire had given the alarm to the police reserve, the attack on the latter was a failure. The members of the assault group dispersed.

The attack on the tank squadron failed too. The tank hangar was occupied without the least difficulty. The combat squad included four army mechanics of whom one was a tank NCO; the latter left the hangar with his vehicle and set off towards the barracks (about a kilometre away) where the tank crews lived. But this NCO was killed by a sergeant-major. The other tanks could not get out. Then, in the plan, the sergeant-major of the telegraphists' battalion (housed across the way from the tank squadron) was supposed to bring forty of his men over to join the insurgents. This sergeant was a traitor, and the men did not arrive. Thus the attack on the tank squadron was a failure.

As a result of this failure, the attack on the officer-cadet school did not take place. For the group detailed to carry it out was supposed at the start of the insurrection to cover the attack on the tank squadron from the officer-cadet school side, and subsequently to attack the school with the help of the tanks.

The headquarters of the 10th Regiment was taken: three officers who attempted resistance were shot.

The 3rd Battalion of the 10th Regiment refused to side with the insurgents and remained neutral. The nine men sent there, in view of their numerical weakness and the absence in the battalion of an adequate nucleus of revolutionary soldiers, did not succeed in winning the men over.

The thirteen men sent to capture the airborne corps carried out their mission in exemplary fashion. On the way (the airborne corps was stationed about two kilometres from the town), they disarmed the 11th Precinct police station and captured several rifles and revolvers. Suddenly, without a shot, they entered the barracks where about eighty men of the airborne corps were housed, seized their weapons, and declared that power was in the hands of the workers and soldiers, and that the airmen had only one choice – to join the insurgents. The airmen, unanimously, at once replied that they were with the revolutionary workers. The officers surrendered their arms and declared themselves neutral (provisionally of course). After the defeat of the insurrection these officers were shot for their neutrality by order of the War Council.

But the insurgents immediately committed a major error whose consequences were fatal both to themselves and to all those taking part in the uprising. Although they now had with them fifty men, 100 rifles, ten machine-guns, plenty of ammunition, two lorries and two cars, they nevertheless did not return to the city to help their comrades. Instead they remained where they were and merely sent a motorcyclist to the insurrectionary headquarters, with a report and a request for further orders. The messenger did not return, and the unit did not move until the *junkers* arrived in armoured cars and, after a fierce engagement, dispersed them (at 11 a.m.).

Operations of the 3rd Battalion. The forces of the 3rd Battalion were divided up for their respective missions in the following way: (*a*) occupation of Reval castle (parliament, President, government offices): 12 men; (*b*) occupation of the telegraph and telephone exchanges: 12 men; (*c*) occupation of the War Ministry and of military headquarters: 12 men; (*d*) occupation of the Baltic station: 20 men; (*e*) occupation of the preventive detention gaol: 12 men.

The group sent to take the citadel carried out its mission. The eleven-men guard was disarmed, and the officer in command shot when he offered resistance. The prime minister escaped. The citadel remained in the hands of the group until the counter-revolutionary forces arrived, whereupon the group dispersed without much resistance.

The telegraph and telephone exchanges were very quickly occupied. The insurgents held out there for three hours. They took prisoner a number of police – among them the police chief of Reval who was later freed by troops loyal to the government.

The attack on the War Ministry and on the military and police headquarters was a failure. The prisoners held in preventive detention were not released, since the squad entrusted with this task was not warned in time and remained inactive throughout the entire operation.

The Baltic station was occupied without resistance. At the same time the 5th Precinct police station was disarmed, and the arms there taken. The Minister of Roads and Communications, who was found at the railway station, was shot attempting to arouse the public against the insurrection. The precinct police chief too was arrested here. The station remained in the hands of the insurgents until 8 a.m.: they beat off several attacks by the mounted police and *junkers*.

The insurrection was definitely crushed inside the city towards 9 a.m. The airborne corps was retaken at about 11 a.m. by counter-revolutionary units freed after the insurrection inside the city had been crushed.

The defeat of the insurrection was accomplished by sections of the NCO training college, groups from the *junker* academy, the mounted police reserve and the fascists. Characteristically, the bourgeoisie did not entrust this mission to the ordinary officers: the small squads which were hastily formed from the above-mentioned units were led by colonels and generals acting as squad and company commanders.

The December insurrection inflicted serious losses on the Reval proletariat. Excluding those suffered during the rising itself, some 500 proletarians were shot (among them several dozen soldiers) by decree of the War Council, and roughly the same number were imprisoned. The number killed during the insurrection came to twenty or so. There was no measure from which the Estonian bourgeoisie flinched in its savage revenge upon the Reval proletariat for this attempt to establish worker and peasant power.

REASONS FOR THE DEFEAT

What were the reasons for the defeat of the Reval insurrection? The account we have given of the preparation and course of the uprising shows that the insurgents committed a series of organizational and tactical errors with grave consequences. These can, broadly speaking, be summed up as follows:

1. *The insurrectionary leadership had over-estimated the degree of demoralization of the garrison, as they had the strength of the Party's military organization.* For them to have accomplished the objectives which they had set themselves, *their forces were clearly inadequate.* In our view this would have remained true even if the leadership had succeeded in mobilizing all those who on paper were members of its military organization. The exaggerated view that was held of the degree of demoralization of the government troops is revealed by the fact that the Party leadership thought that by sending a group of nine men to the 3rd Battalion of the 10th Regiment they could bring over the entire battalion to participate actively in the overthrow of the bourgeois government. Similarly for the tank squadron and the telegraphists' battalion. The soldiers of the 3rd Battalion, the telegraphists and the tank squadron did undoubtedly sympathize with the Communist Party, and were hostile to their officers and to the entire bourgeois régime. These units would have joined the ranks of the insurgents if there had been among them a solid nucleus of communists or of young communists, or even a group of revolutionary soldiers who had been instructed in advance by the Party and who were capable of resisting the reactionary officers. But such was not the case. The Communist Party had not directed all its activity towards securing the participation of soldiers and sailors in the insurrection, either by entire units or at least by constituted fractions. It had not organized an adequate political agitation within the army. Instead, it had in fact isolated the revolutionary soldiers from their own units, by attaching them to the workers' groups. That was a great error. It was naïve to think that the men of the 10th Regiment, without communist soldiers, would actively join the insurgents at the behest of nine unknown workers. Imagine the scene: it is 5.15 a.m., still dark, the men are asleep. They are awoken by an unimpressively small group of men whom nobody knows; these men assure them that the insurrection has broken out, and invite the battalion to take the side of the insurgents. The soldiers cannot see this insurrection, the streets are empty, there are no workers. They know nothing of any preparations for an insurrection. What could one expect them to do? The men of the battalion, as should have been expected, remained neutral until they could get more information.

The majority of soldiers did not know who was organizing the revolt: the workers, or the fascists. Perhaps there was indeed something to be hoped from the 3rd Battalion (this does seem probable, since it did not take any part in action against the workers and for that reason was partially disarmed). But these hopes could only have been realized if a larger group of workers had presented themselves to the men, or if the battalion had included in its ranks organized communists and revolutionary soldiers.

2. *The plan for the insurrection and the targets of the various groups did not correspond to the strength of the combat organization.* If one studies the way in which the revolutionary forces were deployed and the targets which were assigned to them, one is forced to conclude that the leadership of the insurrection attempted *to be equally strong everywhere, although it lacked the necessary man-power for this: the result was an extreme dispersal of its strength.* What real advantage could the insurgents have drawn, and what advantage did they in fact draw, from the immediate occupation of objectives like the narrow-gauge railway station, the Baltic station, or even the citadel with all the government buildings? How could such actions strengthen the revolutionary forces or weaken the enemy? The groups who carried out these tasks successfully by occupying the stations and the citadel in the event had a negligible influence on the outcome of the insurrection.

In our view, once the decision had been taken to launch an insurrection, a more rational plan would have concentrated all available forces – at least initially, at 5.15 a.m. – for the seizure of the four or five most important targets. Subsequently, after these had been successfully secured, the insurrectionary forces could have turned their attention to the targets next in order of importance. The first targets could have been the men of the 10th Regiment, the tank squadron and the airborne corps, the preventive detention prison and the *junker* academy (or perhaps the NCO training college). When the prisoners had been freed and the men of the 10th Regiment and the airborne corps won over, even if the attack on the *junker* academy had not been completely successful, the struggle for the next series of objectives would have been very much easier. Moreover, at least the insurgents would have had at their disposal a considerable force, which would have allowed them to operate in the light of the circumstances.

From a military point of view, the entire plan for the insurrection had not been worked out thoroughly. The principle that strength must be concentrated at the most important points had not been observed.

It is hardly necessary to stress the fact that the operations of the group which captured the airborne corps were nothing but a whole series of errors. The group's hesitation after its initial success exemplifies how not to act during an insurrection. A blunder by the leadership too was involved here, since it had not given advance instructions concerning the tasks which were to be carried out once the first objective had been achieved. A rapid appearance in the city of this group riding on cars armed with machine-guns, and an energetic offensive on its part wherever it met the enemy, would have changed the balance of forces appreciably in favour of the insurgents. Furthermore, the psychological effect of so spirited and resolute an action would have been very great. In reality, however, the commander of the group showed no initiative at all. He remained where he was with his men up to the moment when the government troops arrived to crush them.

The capture of the airborne corps, and the rapidity with which its members were won over to the insurrection, are of great interest for their bearing on one particular problem: what is the best way of bringing out on to the streets a unit which on the one hand is already subject *en masse* to the effects of revolutionary propaganda and the prevailing revolutionary mood, but which on the other hand is not yet ready to reject military discipline? If the insurgents succeed in disarming such a unit, it is then relatively easy to re-establish it for subsequent actions on the side of the insurrection – by explaining the situation to it, isolating (with the help of the communist group) elements hostile to the revolution, and then returning their arms to the revolutionary soldiers. The Reval insurgents proved incapable of acting in this way with respect to the units of the 10th Regiment. They merely harangued them, the soldiers hesitated, and the whole operation ended in a fiasco.

3. *Despite the great superiority of the enemy forces, the military groups went into action with very great enthusiasm. But this enthusiasm disappeared at once after the first defeats, at least in the case of the majority of combat squad members. With the exception of the squads which took the Baltic station and the airborne corps, no ardour whatever was displayed in the fighting. This goes a long way towards explaining the fact that when the moment came to go on to the defensive, no barricades at all were*

erected. And yet, once forced on to the defensive, the insurgents should have adopted the methods of barricade fighting and exploited its advantages. If they had wished to continue the struggle resolutely, the means were not lacking.

4. *Not all the members of the combat squads knew how to use the weapons they were carrying. The Thompson machine-guns, powerful weapons in street fighting, were hardly used at all because the men did not know how to operate them;* in addition, the supply of ammunition (one hundred bullets per machine-gun) was utterly insignificant. A number of hand-grenades as well, thrown at a moment when the outcome of the battle depended on a well-thrown grenade (directed at the police reserve), failed to explode because the thrower did not know how to handle them. This fact too influenced the outcome of the battle.

5. *The reconnaissance of certain targets had been carried out in an extremely superficial fashion. Ignorance of the precise location of the police reserve was to cause the failure of the attack at this point.* Similarly for the citadel. *The occupation of the citadel in fact missed its mark, since the insurgents failed to capture the government as a result of not knowing exactly where to look for it.*

6. *Liaison and mutual support between the various groups was also very inadequate. When a group had failed to carry out a particular task, instead of joining a neighbouring group and continuing the fight as part of a common effort, in most cases it dispersed. If there had been any real will to fight and a minimum of initiative, the necessary mutual support would have been possible, even in the absence of an overall leadership.* The most blatant examples of this lack of initiative or willingness to assist the other groups occurred in the operations at the *junker* academy (dispersal after a defeat) and the airborne corps (inaction).

7. *All the mistakes enumerated above exercized an immense influence on the outcome of the Reval insurrection.* It goes without saying that mistakes of all kinds are inevitable in the preparation and execution of something as complex as an armed insurrection. The Party and the proletariat do not possess and will perhaps never possess a sufficient number of good military leaders. Nevertheless, some of the blunders mentioned above could have been avoided, given adequate organization.

However, without in any way playing down the importance of the subjective factor, whose role was enormous, we consider that at Reval the outcome of the insurrection *did not depend on the mistakes which we have been discussing. What played the decisive role in the outcome of the insurrection was the fact that the small groups of revolutionary workers who were militarily organized remained isolated from the mass of the proletariat after they had launched the insurrection. The* working-class masses, with the exception of isolated groups of workers (above all women workers) who joined them during the fighting or provided various forms of assistance, *did not actively support the insurgents against the counter-revolution. The Reval working class, as a mass, was a disinterested spectator during the fighting. This was the decisive factor.*

Moreover, this happened in spite of the fact that the Party exerted an immense influence upon the mass of workers; in spite of the fact that the workers had lost all confidence in the policies of the bourgeoisie or in any successful economic development of 'Independent Estonia', and were demanding that Estonia should join the Union of Soviets – believing that only the slogans of the Communist Party which called for the overthrow of the bourgeoisie and the establishment of a workers' and peasants' government would provide a way out of the state of disorder, the impasse, into which they had been forced by the policies of a bankrupt bourgeoisie.

The inactivity of the mass of workers was by no means due to any lack of revolutionary spirit on the part of the Reval proletariat, but rather to the fact that the latter was not politically or materially prepared to act precisely on 1 December. After the anti-war week, the Communist Party had not tried to organize a single mass demonstration; had not once called on the workers to strike or to take to the streets. They feared that the workers would be crushed prematurely by the government's armed mercenaries. Even on the occasion of the savage murder of the communist Tomp, president of the Estonian trade unions, shot three days before the insurrection, *the Communist Party did not invite the masses to protest. The Party had exaggerated the importance of the military factor in insurrection, and underestimated that of the mass revolutionary movement.* The principle of surprise action, in a purely military sense, dominated every other consideration as the Party prepared the uprising. *The events of 1 December were not understood at all by the proletariat, for the Party's switch to direct action was too sudden. The insurrection was unexpected not only by the bourgeoisie but also by the working classes of Estonia, and of Reval in particular.* The Party hoped to use small groups of dedicated revolutionaries, the vanguard of the vanguard so to speak, to seize power from the bourgeoisie in a surprise military action. Or at least they hoped to pierce a first breach in the bourgeois State, *in such a way that they would then draw in the masses and crown the battle by a general uprising of the working people.*

We saw earlier the conditions in which the draft programme of the Communist International considers the organization of an armed insurrection possible:

When the ruling classes are disorganized, the masses are in a state of revolutionary ferment, the intermediary strata are inclining towards the proletariat and the masses are ready for action and for sacrifice, the Party of the proletariat is confronted with the task of leading the masses to a direct attack upon the bourgeois State. This it does by carrying on propaganda in favour of increasingly radical transitional slogans (for Soviets, workers' control of industry, for peasant committees, for the seizure of the big landed properties, for disarming the bourgeoisie and arming the proletariat, etc.), and by organizing mass action, upon which all branches of Party agitation and propaganda, including parliamentary activity, must be concentrated. This mass action includes: strikes; a combination of strikes and demonstrations; a combination of strikes and armed demonstrations and finally, the general strike conjointly with armed insurrection against the state power of the bourgeoisie.

At Reval, the Communist Party did exactly the opposite, and that is why the insurrection of 1 December was bound to end in defeat. Government repression of every least manifestation of revolutionary activity on the part of the workers, and fears for the premature crushing or the disorganization of mass actions, *must not become a reason for renouncing such mass actions. They must rather be reasons for preparing them in the light of the decisive battle against the bourgeoisie, i.e. of the armed uprising.* But even if it is admitted that it was extremely difficult in Reval to mobilize the masses for decisive battles or organize strikes and demonstrations immediately on the eve of the insurrection, nevertheless *it was absolutely indispensable to take measures in advance to ensure the support of specific groups of workers, in adequate numbers, after the rising itself.* This was not done.

The reason for the low level of militancy and determination in battle on the part of the combat units was, in our view, the fact that *the insurgents felt themselves isolated from the mass of workers, and did not receive adequate assistance from them. The masses displayed no more than a passive sympathy for their vanguard.*

It is not the military actions of an armed vanguard which can and must arouse the active struggle of the masses for power, it is rather the mighty revolutionary impetus of the working masses which should provoke the military actions of the vanguard detachments. The latter should move into action (according to a plan which has been properly worked out in advance in every respect) as a result of the revolutionary impetus of the masses. Whatever role the purely military factor may play in insurrection, it is still, from this point of view, a subordinate role. The mighty revolutionary impetus of the masses must constitute the social base, the social and political backdrop for the bold, audacious, decisive military actions of the advance detachments of the revolutionary proletariat determined to smash the bourgeois government machine. The armed uprising must be fixed for a moment of the rising revolution in which the preparation of the decisive strata of the proletariat and its allies (peasants and urban poor) has reached its maximum point, and in which the decomposition within the ranks of the ruling classes and in particular within their armed forces has also attained its apogee.

4

The Hamburg Uprising

THE GENERAL SITUATION IN GERMANY IN 1923

The economic and political situation in Germany in 1923 was characterized as a whole by the following features:

The occupation in January 1923 of the Ruhr and Rhineland deprived Germany of the great, essential bases of its economy: eighty per cent of iron and steel production, seventy-one per cent of coalmining. The result was a severe economic crisis for industry and for the entire national economy. This reached its peak at the end of the 'passive resistance' with which the German government opposed the Allies in the occupied territories (October/November).

The catastrophic state of the German economy was characterized by three factors: industrial stagnation and growing unemployment; the disorganized state of the country's finances; the depreciation of the mark.

The proportion of unemployed in relation to the number of unionized workers in the whole of Germany in 1923, according to official figures, was as follows:

	Unemployed	Semi-employed	Total
January	4·2%	12·6%	16·8%
April	7%	28·5%	35·5%
September	9·9%	39·7%	49·6%
October	19·1%	47·3%	66·4%
November	23·4%	47·3%	70·3%
December	28·9%	39·9%	62·2%

The monthly average of unemployment in previous years had been:

1913	2·9%	1919	3·7%	1921	2·8%
1918	1·2%	1920	3·8%	1922	1·5%

The total number of unemployed and semi-employed (i.e. working a few days per week or a few hours per day), in the last three months of 1923, reached *eight million: more than half the entire German working class.*

The enormous expenditure involved in the policy of inaction pursued in the Ruhr and on the Rhine (there are no exact figures, but on average this expenditure reached 2–300 million gold marks a month), together with the complete exoneration of the possessing classes from taxation (in consequence of the collapse of the monetary system), brought about a rapid and continuous increase in the budgetary deficit. Thus, the proportion of incomings relative to outgoings was 1·8 per cent in August 1923. At the end of the same month, the total of the floating debt was 1,666,667 thousand million marks. The State's revenue in November barely reached 12.3 million gold marks.

Almost all government expenses were covered by issues of paper money, i.e. by inflation, *a form of tax whose entire weight falls on the working class and middle strata.*

The depreciation of the mark proceeded at an unbelievable pace. Thus, the dollar was quoted in Berlin, Hamburg and Frankfurt on 18 October at 4–6 thousand million marks (four in the morning, six by the evening); on 20 October 15–19 thousand million; on 22 October 46 thousand million; on 23 October 75 thousand million.

It is obvious what the social consequences of this collapse of the German economy were: *extreme pauperization of the working class and the middle strata* (petty bourgeoisie, white-collar workers, pensioners, etc.).[1]

Simultaneously, a process ensued whereby the national wealth fell under the control of the banks, the *Konzerne* and the foreign exchange speculators. This was the moment when the notorious Hugo Stinnes was making his crazed attempts to amass ever-increasing riches at the price of the nation's starvation. The landowners liquidated their debts, paying them off with valueless paper marks. The internal debt thus evaporated, at the expense of broad strata of the population. After passive resistance in the Ruhr had been brought to an end, the govern-

---

[1] The weekly dole to an unemployed worker barely permitted him to buy a litre of milk or a pound of bread. The monthly stipend of a civil servant or a pensioner was just enough to buy a newspaper or a box of matches. The situation of those workers who still had jobs was no better. The concession which they had won, i.e. that their wages would be paid twice weekly, was not much help, since the speed with which the mark fell and food-prices rose wiped out their wages at once and subjected them to the most appalling exploitation.

ment ceased all subsidies to the unemployed in the occupied territories, while continuing to distribute them to the Ruhr industrialists as compensation for the losses which they had suffered as a result of the occupation.

The economic crisis brought about *a political crisis*. At the beginning of August a general strike broke out. This was organized by the factory committees which were under the influence of the Communist Party. It overthrew the Cuno (nationalist) government. Stresemann, whom the social democrat president of the republic, Ebert, called on to form the new cabinet, declared that he was heading 'the last bourgeois government'. He was convinced that the government would be overthrown and that the dictatorship of the proletariat would be established in Germany.

Indeed, under the weight of their impoverishment, the German working class rapidly became revolutionary. The petty bourgeoisie no longer hoped for salvation except by proletarian action, and turned towards revolution. The influence of the Communist Party among the workers grew rapidly, while that of social democracy was steadily on the wane. 'Food riots' took place throughout the country; the workers broke into food shops and shared out the contents. The working class spontaneously formed combat 'Hundreds', and prepared for the decisive conflict. By October there were 250,000 men, some of them armed, in the Proletarian Hundreds.

In September, workers' governments of communists and left social democrats were formed in Saxony and Thuringia, subsequently disbanded by the troops of the *Reichswehr*. Power passed into the hands of the *Reichswehr* commander (General Seeckt), and the country was declared to be in a state of siege. While in the rest of Germany the military command was busy re-establishing order, in Bavaria the counter-revolution was organizing fascist bands to march on Berlin and install a strong central power, a dictatorship. In the West, separatists supported by the occupation authorities became a force. On 20 October they succeeded in taking power in Aachen, Trier, Koblenz and other towns, and proclaimed the 'Independent Republic of the Rhine'.

The various political and economic factors mentioned above clearly show that in the second half of 1923 Germany was in an acute revolutionary situation. Given a strong and ideologically coherent Bolshevik Party; given skilful and resolute action aimed at revolutionary mobilization of the masses and at directing their struggle; given intensive work by the Party to prepare the masses and the Party itself for insurrection; given these conditions, the success of the revolution was certain.

However, in fact this subjective factor – essential for victory – was missing.

The decision to prepare for insurrection was only taken after the three-day general strike in August. However, the Central Committee of the Communist Party did not have any clear idea of the preparations to be made for an insurrection, nor did they have any firm determination to carry it through. The Communist ministers of Saxony and Thuringia, instead of utilizing the apparatus of government to organize, mobilize and arm the masses for a revolutionary action aimed at seizing power, in fact followed a line of conduct which hardly differed in essence from that of the left social democrats. On this question of the Saxony government, as on many others for that matter, the Central Committee of the Communist Party, led by Brandler and supported by Radek, followed an extremely indecisive and opportunist policy, which was categorically condemned by the Eighth Congress of the German Communist Party and the Fifth World Congress of the Comintern.

The Party paid too little attention to organizing the unemployed, who constituted the most revolutionary element of the German working class; they were excessively preoccupied with bringing the petty-bourgeois elements of the towns into the revolutionary front; they hardly bothered at all about the peasants, and they did *absolutely nothing* to subvert the army or police. The united front tactic, when it was applied at all, was applied in an opportunist spirit (Saxony and Thuringia) which had nothing in common with the Comintern's directives. Revolutionary action inside the trade unions, the decisive sector of the struggle, was greatly weakened by a communist exodus from those unions.

All these opportunist errors on the part of the Party leadership had as their consequence – indeed could not fail to have as their consequence – the defeat of the German revolution, in spite of extremely favourable conditions and in spite of the will to fight shown by the decisive elements of the proletariat.

Such was the social and political background against which the events of 23–25 October 1923 took place in Hamburg.

THE POLITICAL SITUATION IN HAMBURG

On the initiative of the Communist Party, a congress of factory committees had been called to take place on 21 October in Chemnitz. According to the Central Committee's plan, this congress was to proclaim a general strike which would subsequently turn into an armed struggle for power. The Hamburg Party organization was convinced that the situation in Central Germany was such that very shortly (on the occasion of the Chemnitz congress) the signal would be given for the insurrection that would set all Germany ablaze. This opinion was further strengthened by the fact that immediately before the Hamburg action, troops had been sent from the north-west to crush the revolutionary movements in Central Germany. The departure of these troops greatly emboldened the Hamburg proletariat.

All the conditions were clearly present for a revolutionary intervention by the masses. With a week still to go before the Chemnitz congress, the shipyards, the transport system, and factories of every kind were already on strike. If a general strike did not break out, it was for the sole reason that the Communist Party, waiting for the decisive battles which were due to be engaged throughout Germany when the Central Committee gave the word, did not call upon the masses to down tools. On 21 October, the conference of North German shipyard workers sitting in Hamburg sent a delegation to Chemnitz to obtain the order to move. Another delegation, headed by Urbahns, was sent by the Portworkers' action committee. *The masses wanted an offensive, and were only waiting for a call from the Communist Party.* On 20 October, the streets of Hamburg saw innumerable clashes between the workers and the police. Despite the declaration of a state of emergency and a ban on public meetings and demonstrations, the masses fought for the right to remain on the streets. In this extremely tense situation, the petty bourgeoisie clearly showed its sympathy for the demonstrating workers. The police themselves frequently did not hide their sympathy for the starving people. Certain police stations, on orders from the city council, surrounded their entrances with barbed wire, doubled their sentries, and sent out patrols armed with repeating rifles. The entire police force was put on a war footing.

Simultaneously, the active sections of Hamburg social democracy redoubled their agitation against the communists and tried to discredit the communist programme as leading directly to civil war and a blood-bath. They tried to dissuade the workers from any idea of fighting against the police or the state military apparatus, and advised them to refrain from preparing for a general strike. Moreover, they refused to form action committees with the communists.

On Sunday 21 October, the streets were animated, but the city remained relatively calm throughout the holiday.

On Monday 22 October the strike spread. In some quarters there were new skirmishes between the workers and the police.

Here is how the situation, particularly in the Barmbek district, was described by a Hamburg worker, in an article published by a clandestine newspaper just after the insurrection:

22 October was a day of great excitement. The streets in the working-class district of Barmbek did not, however, reveal any outward animation. The women walked along in twos and threes with empty baskets – some of them silent, others talking loudly and gesticulating. What were they to buy? What were they to eat? Prices were rising by the hour.

On the Saturday a number of shops had been looted, particularly bakeries. The Barmbek police had used their guns. Nobody had had enough because of that.

Monday afternoon was calmer. But the blood of all the workers was racing. The men clenched their fists. The women crossed their arms under their aprons. The children stopped playing. Everybody seemed to be waiting for something. What?

A comrade whom I met told me: 'Well, tomorrow we won't be walking around so peacefully', before going off to search for a bit of bread. Another comrade, who was standing in front of a butcher's shop looking at the meat, caught me by the hand and said: 'If the communists don't do something and do it at once, their party will fall apart.' That evening there was a women's meeting in the district. On the agenda: hunger. The hall was packed. Some of those present were extremely wrought up, having spent the day vainly looking for something to eat. The orator spoke calmly, but the interruptions from the audience exploded like whip-cracks. After the speech, the applause sounded like a call for vengeance. There was only one slogan: to battle! On the streets, the men formed small, dark groups. New additions arrived continually. Night had fallen.

The main streets of Hamburg were crowded. The police used their guns again. Cries went up from women who had been wounded. Curses from men running from the police bullets. Everywhere, in the back streets, the scattered groups reformed. The excitement was greater than it had been when the masses demanded the resignation of Cuno.

People were whispering to each other: 'Is it beginning? When? Tonight? To-morrow?' Nobody knew anything for certain.

Thus there was a more revolutionary mood in Hamburg than anywhere else in Germany. For that reason, and also because there were no

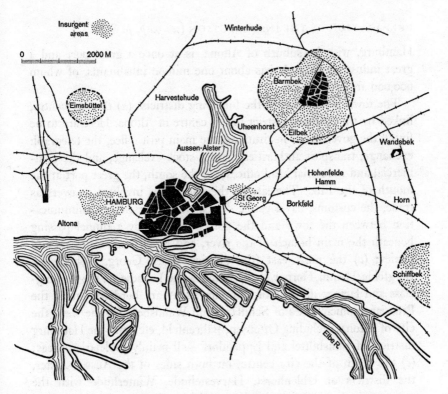

2. The Insurrection in Hamburg, 1923

troops in the area, the Central Committee of the Party, counting on a favourable outcome to the Chemnitz Congress, gave the Hamburg Party organization the word to launch an insurrection. This was also to be the signal for a general uprising throughout Germany.

PREPARATION OF THE INSURRECTION (*see map, p. 87*)

Hamburg, with its suburb of Altona, is at once a great port and a great industrial town. It has about one million inhabitants, of whom 600,000 are proletarians.

The town is made up of the following districts: (*a*) the city centre, linked by the St Pauli district to the centre of Altona. Here are to be found the government institutions, the main post office, the telegraph exchange, transport authorities, banks, stock-exchange, and the commercial and industrial head offices; (*b*) the south, the great port at the mouth of the Elbe. The site of the companies involved in overseas trade, the customs, naval yards, docks, warehouses, etc. Communication between the town and the port is assured by a tunnel passing beneath the main branch of the river, and by all kinds of boats and ferries; (*c*) the north-east (the districts of St Georg, Hohenfelde, Borgfelde, Hamm, Horn, Eilbek, Barmbek, etc.) – these are the working-class and factory districts of Hamburg; they are bordered on by the Prussian municipalities of Schiffbek and Wandsbek; (*d*) the west, the city of Altona, including Ottensen, Bährenfeld, etc., and the Hamburg districts of Eimsbüttel and Eppendorf – all mainly proletarian areas; (*e*) the north of the city centre, on both sides of the Aussen-Alster, the districts of Uhlenhorst, Harvestehude, Winterhude with the mansions and villas of the big bourgeoisie.

There were no *Reichswehr* units in Hamburg. The units stationed to the north and south were already on their way to Central Germany. Hamburg had some 5,000 police, armed with pistols and repeating rifles. They also had machine-guns, carbines, and six armoured cars. Large stocks of arms were maintained, mainly in some fifty police stations and in various other depots, with which to arm the fascists so that they could be mobilized in the event of any armed action by the proletariat. Armoured cars were stationed at the police barracks and at Wandsbek.

No systematic organizational work or political agitation had been carried out by the Party in the ranks of the police. In general, the latter were prepared to carry out the orders of its reactionary commanders.

Although the influence of social democracy upon the mass of the Hamburg proletariat was insignificant, the social democrat organization in the city nevertheless totalled some 40,000 members, of whom a part (the full-time officials) were certainly hostile to any revolutionary action and ready to oppose it by every means.

The Communist Party had about 18,000 members. Its combat organization had about 1,300; this was the active nucleus, the *Ordnerdienst* as it was called or OD for short. It was organized on a territorial basis, in groups of five or ten, under the command of military organizers responsible to the district committees; these in their turn, via the intermediary of the city military organization, were responsible to the Hamburg committee. Shortly before the insurrection, the structure of the OD had been given the following form: at the base, groups of eight men with a commander; four such groups formed a squad, and four squads formed a section commanded by a section head. Each section had attached to it a number of cyclists and motorcyclists, several nurses (from the Workers' Aid Association) and some scouts, mainly women.

The OD was originally designed to act as a guard for the Party's private and public meetings, and demonstrations. Its functions also included sentry-duty at district committee headquarters and communist presses, and sticking up posters and proclamations. The OD in Hamburg had about eighty firearms of various calibres, mostly revolvers.

In the month of August, when in accordance with the Central Committee's directives the Proletarian Hundreds began to be formed, the OD provided them with cadres. At the moment of the October action, there were fifteen Hundreds in Hamburg, militarily organized but with no arms. Each had between forty and sixty men. These Hundreds were meant to constitute the great combat force of the proletariat, the red guard which, once armed, would have to bear the brunt of the struggle against the forces of counter-revolution at the moment of the general uprising. However, the purpose of the Hundreds was not clear to the Party organization as a whole. No concrete directive was given, no effort was made by the Central Committee to clarify it. The Party, or at least a certain fraction of it and in particular the OD, saw the Hundreds as a fighting body, an auxiliary to the OD. The OD was the base of the red guard. The Party devoted all its attention to the military training of the OD members, to a search for arms, etc. It must be said that the military training of the OD was of a high standard. Generally speaking, the OD had learnt to use its weapons, knew the essentials of street fighting, was reconnoitring the deployment of the enemy's troops and especially of the police, and had obtained a quantity of useful information on how the enemy might be disarmed and the plan for the insurrection drawn up. In short, the OD was actively preparing to launch the decisive struggle against the police and fascists as soon as the Party gave the word.

On the evening of Sunday 21 October a meeting of the city's active militants decided on action. They reckoned that the situation was favourable for a mass action, and that Hamburg should give the signal for the general proletarian uprising. The example of Hamburg would draw in the other cities. Moreover, it was useless to wait for a general strike to be declared: the aim should be to draw ever wider categories of workers into the strike which had already begun in Hamburg, and thus make it general. The situation in the city encouraged expectations of a spontaneous and non-organized move by the workers, if the Communist Party did not place itself at the head of the movement and direct it. Such an occurrence would of course be a terrible blow to the Party's authority among the proletarian masses.

The decision was taken to begin by declaring a strike on the railways, to prevent the troops being sent to Saxony.

Once this decision had been taken the meeting broke up; it reconvened on Monday the 22nd at 8 p.m. to reach a final decision on the question of insurrection.

According to the account of one of those present, the plan adopted was as follows:

(a) a surprise attack by the armed units in the working-class quarters, with immediate occupation of the arms depots; (b) disarming of the police and fascists in the suburbs; (c) simultaneous concentration of the worker detachments, equipped with arms, in the central area of Hamburg at the head of a mass demonstration; the enemy (police and fascists) to be driven back from the city centre towards the south (towards the river, where the crossings are to have been occupied by the insurgents), and there disarmed definitively; (d) occupation of the post and telegraph offices, the main stations (both those of the urban transport system and those serving other parts of the country), the aerodrome, etc., by communist forces within these establishments –

this to take place before the units from the suburbs arrive in the centre of the city; (e) to prevent enemy reinforcements being sent from outside, barricades to be erected on the main entry roads along which enemy forces might be expected to arrive. These barricades to be erected by the local working-class organizations, who were also to destroy roads and railway lines in a 25-kilometre radius around the city. The Party organizations of Hamburg, Wilhelmsburg, Outersen and Stade to render impassable the channel of the Elbe.

This plan was approved at the 8 p.m. meeting on 22 October. During the same session, the military leaders of the districts received their detailed instructions – the addresses of the liaison centres, the overall command, etc. It was fixed that the OD would go into action at 5 a.m. on 23 October. The attack had to take the enemy by surprise, and the first successes were to be the signal for the mass of workers to move into action with the aim of seizing power.

Lack of information prevents us from analysing the other measures which were decided once the general decision had been taken to launch an insurrection. Therefore, since we have at our disposal a fairly lengthy report by the Barmbek military commander (under whose command this meeting also placed the leaders of Uhlenhorst and Winterhude), we will now describe the course of the insurrection in the working-class neighbourhoods of the north-east. It was here in any case that the main events of the insurrection took place.

Since his orders were to attack at 5 a.m. on 23 October, the Barmbek military commander took various preparatory measures in the area for which he had been made responsible. As he had himself only been appointed at the Monday meeting, he found himself in quite a difficult situation, not knowing the men, lacking information about the combat organization or the enemy's forces, etc. (He had in fact once before been military commander of the district, but had been dismissed several months earlier.)

His fundamental objective was to assemble his subordinates, obtain information from them about their forces and those of the police, and assign them their specific missions. In addition, the plan of attack had to be coordinated with the mobilizing activity of the district committees, so that the mass of workers would enter the fray as soon as the armed units began to move into action. There was very little time left for all of this.

At the women's meeting already mentioned, the Barmbek commander had instructed those comrades whom he knew to assemble the commanders of the combat organization at 11 p.m. in a clandestine apartment. There he met the secretaries of the district organizations of Barmbek and Greater Hamburg.[2] It turned out that they knew nothing of the decision to attack on the morning of the 23rd. Everything had to be explained to them in haste. By agreement with the secretary of the Barmbek committee, it was decided to meet once again during the night in order to fix a definitive plan of action.

By 11 p.m. the military commanders had been assembled, but those of Uhlenhorst and Winterhude did not arrive. A further meeting had therefore to be called for 1 a.m.

At the 11 o'clock meeting, the Barmbek commander started by explaining the Party's decision, and gave the order to mobilize the combat squads at certain prearranged addresses where they would be assigned their missions. Each squad member was to bring, in addition to his arms, a hunk of bread and a roll of bandage.

The Barmbek combat organization, including those of Uhlenhorst and Winterhude, had nineteen rifles and twenty-seven revolvers. The enemy had twenty police stations in the area, of which eight had been specially reinforced; in addition the Wandsbek barracks contained some 600 police, with six armoured cars each armed with two machine-guns. Thus the enemy had an overwhelming superiority.

When they discussed the plan of attack, the leaders of the combat organization came to the conclusion that the best course would be to concentrate their forces for a surprise attack on the Wandsbek police barracks; they would seize all arms to be found there and the six armoured cars, and then turn part of their forces against the eight reinforced police stations and capture these or at least besiege them. They decided that this plan was preferable to a simultaneous attack on all twenty police stations, as the military command of the Hamburg committee had prescribed. But the latter did not approve their arguments, and the Barmbek commander had the order confirmed that he must base his plan on a simultaneous attack on all twenty police stations, leaving the Wandsbek barracks untouched in the first instance.

To characterize the preparations which were made during the night of 22/23 October, the following feature must be mentioned: the secretary of the Barmbek Party organization, who had already received

[2] The name 'Greater Hamburg' was used to designate the north-eastern periphery of the city.

some information in the Hamburg committee about the insurrection that was being prepared, instructed the Barmbek military commander that in accordance with higher orders he should wake all Party members and bring them onto the streets at 4 a.m. on 23 October, to join the insurrection and mobilize the workers for the conflict. When the Barmbek military leadership asked the overall command of the insurrection how this order could be reconciled with a surprise action by the combat-squad members (such as formed the basis of the entire plan for the rising), it met with the answer that this order should not be viewed in such a tragic light, since it had no importance at all!

As planned, all the military leaders met again at 1 a.m., including this time those of Uhlenhorst and Winterhude. The Barmbek commander once again briefly described the situation in Germany as a whole and in Hamburg itself, and then explained the plan of action and briefed everyone on their specific missions. The deployment of forces was as follows:

Each police station was to be attacked by one or two combat squads. Twice this number were to be involved in the attack on the 46th Precinct station (Essenstrasse) and the one at the Mundsberg Gate, since these had been specially fortified. Each group was to have two revolvers, or one rifle and one revolver. The Wandsbek barracks were to be attacked after the police stations had been disarmed. Each group was to be at its battle station at 4.55 a.m., and was to attack its appointed target at 5 a.m. precisely. To ensure precision, all watches had been checked and synchronized.

As soon as the commanders returned from the meeting, the squad members assembled to a man and at the appointed hour in the various clandestine apartments to which they had been told to go. Morale was excellent.

As we have seen, the armament of the combat organization of Barmbek and its affiliated districts was minimal. Not a single machine-gun! In order to obtain one, the military commander sent men during the night to Bergedorf (twenty kilometres south-east of Hamburg) to beg one from an OD member who had one hidden. The plan was to use this machine-gun for the attack on the Wandsbek barracks. Although the messengers were personally known to the owner and carried unquestionable authorization (in the form of a prearranged password), they came away empty-handed since the Bergedorf comrade knew nothing about the insurrection and did not trust them. None the less, the communist leadership in Bergedorf sent a group of cyclists armed with revolvers to Barmbek and mobilized its combat-squad members locally so that it would be able to move into action simultaneously with Hamburg if the insurrection really was launched.

On their way back, the messengers stopped at Schiffbeck (a working-class suburb) and informed the local Party committee of the insurrection planned for the morning of the 23rd. There too, nobody knew anything about it. Nevertheless, they took measures immediately to act simultaneously with the other districts.

The orders of the military commander were to disarm the police in the stations to be attacked and to remove all arms and distribute them to the squad members and to any workers in the area who were ready to take part in the fighting. The police were to be shut up under close guard, and all squad members remaining available were to assemble immediately at a prearranged rendezvous so that they could be given new missions.

THE COMBAT ORGANIZATION'S ATTACK
AND THE COURSE OF THE INSURRECTION

The insurrectionary leadership, even while the men were assembling, still feared that the squad members – when they learnt that they were to move into battle almost unarmed, and that the promise previously made to them that they would be given arms in adequate quantities when the moment came had been broken – would become so disillusioned that they would lose much of their high morale. This is precisely what happened. On the way from the assembly points to the police stations, about one third of the men disappeared. Two squads even melted away entirely before reaching their objective.

By about 5.30 a.m., the insurgents had *captured and disarmed seventeen police stations* (Barmbek, Wandsbek, a number of stations in Winterhude, Uhlenhorst and other districts). The fortified 46th Precinct station at Essenstrasse was not disarmed through the clumsiness of a squad leader who opened fire from the street when the other squads were already inside the building and on the point of disarming the police. The squad members inside thus had the impression that they were under attack from outside. For this reason – and also because one of the policemen had skilfully thrown a hand-grenade among the squad members and had thus allowed his colleagues to prepare for resistance – the attack failed.

By 6 a.m., about 130 men armed with machine-guns and revolvers were at the assembly point. Three sub-machine-guns had also been captured. The police prisoners were used as instructors to teach the squad members to use these. It turned out that the police stations did not contain any large quantity of hand-grenades or ammunition. No doubt the squad members had in fact failed to discover where they were kept. For instance, forty rifles were discovered in one police station at about 10 a.m., although they had passed unnoticed earlier.

There were two reasons for the great success of the squads in occupying the police stations: (1) long before the attack, the commander of the combat squads had carefully reconnoitred the surroundings of the police stations and their internal layout. The organization of the attack had been studied exhaustively, and every smallest detail foreseen. The attackers showed infinite daring and determination; (2) the police had been in a state of 'third degree combat readiness'[3] for several days as a result of 'unrest in the city', and this had been reduced to first degree readiness on the evening of the 22nd. The reason for this was that the men were extremely weary after the previous few days. Hamburg Police Headquarters, which had given the order in question, naturally did not know about the insurrection. On the night of 22/23 October the police were asleep. The attack caught them unawares.

These two reasons explain the extraordinary success of squads which were almost unarmed against seventeen heavily armed police stations.

Police-colonel Hartenstein, one of the men in command of the struggle against the insurrection, very correctly remarked of the attack on the police stations: 'If the plan for insurrection had been known by the police on the eve of the action, one may presume that the enemy action would have been crushed by appropriate counter measures before it was able to develop.'

At the beginning of the uprising, the insurrectionary command sent comrades (those who had no arms) to the railway stations, the factory gates and other points where workers gathered, to proclaim a general strike and draw the workers into the fighting. Their success was total.

[3] The German police had three degrees of combat readiness: the third meant that the entire force was on constant alert.

All transport stopped functioning, the factories ceased work, and the workers congregated at the various theatres of combat.

Reinforcements for the police, in the form of a number of armoured cars, soon began to arrive at those police stations which had not been disarmed; it therefore became impossible for the insurgents to take them. The failure of the attacks mounted thereafter to disarm the remaining police stations was also due to certain tactical errors committed by the insurgents or rather by their leaders (lack of coordination between the attacks of the respective squads).

Given these circumstances and the arrival of police reinforcements,[4] any question of an attack on the Wandsbek barracks was automatically ruled out. Guerrilla fighting broke out. Small groups of armed workers were formed. The overall direction of operations decreased notably. The insurgents, in short, had been thrown on to the defensive. Towards 7 a.m., the order was given to erect barricades.

Although the masses had not known that the insurrection would begin precisely on 23 October, when they learnt on the morning of that day of the fighting already in progress, they at once joined the fray in one way or another. The general cry went up: *Give us arms!* But the supply of arms was totally inadequate. As soon as the slogan: *Build barricades!* had been launched, these could immediately be seen springing up in almost every district of the city. *This was only made possible thanks to* the participation of the working-class masses, in particular the women.

The insurrectionary command in the districts which we have been discussing knew nothing of the course of events in other areas. It thought that the workers of Barmbek and its neighbouring districts had only suffered a temporary setback, not of decisive importance, which could not influence the outcome of the insurrection as a whole. It imagined that the insurgents in other areas had perhaps won great successes, and that therefore Barmbek should hold what it had won at all costs and defend itself doggedly until reinforcements arrived. The Barmbek comrades had had no contact with the Hamburg political or military leadership since the beginning of the battle. A number of reports had been sent to the Hamburg committee and to the overall

---

[4] Colonel Hartenstein recounts in his book that all the police of the port of Hamburg were replaced by fascist volunteers, and the forces thus freed sent against the insurgents. He adds that during the day of 24 October some 800 fascists were thus employed in carrying out police duties.

military commander, but none of these had arrived at its destination. It was only during the second half of the day that the insurgents learnt that there was no longer any insurrection going on in the centre, or in Altona, and that on the contrary everything was calm there. How was this to be explained? The workers of the insurgent districts had no idea.

The rest of our account will show why the struggle of the north-eastern districts remained an isolated one.

The Altona OD had not carried out its mission of disarming the police. According to the account of one of the leaders of the Hamburg rising, this was for the following reasons:

1. As was later recognized, the insurrectionary headquarters was mistaken in supposing that Altona had been able to procure, several days before the action, arms for 240 men. *Nothing of the sort was the case*.

2. The commander of Altona OD had been named at the last moment. It is clear that he did not have time to get his bearings in his new situation. Furthermore, he discarded the previously adopted plan of action.

3. It had been planned to attack the police stations with one, and sometimes two, OD groups apiece. While the groups were assembling, many of the members were alarmed by rumours claiming that traitors had already warned the police of the attack being prepared. Thus, out of the five groups which were to attack the main police stations, only one succeeded, at 6 a.m., in getting inside the Ottenzen police station and disarming six policemen. There then took place a quarter-hour-long gun battle between the attackers and those of the police who had not been disarmed; but when scouts announced the approach of three police trucks, the attackers dispersed with the arms they had captured.

On 23 October in the morning there were a few more attempts at insurrection in other districts (St Georg, etc.). but, with bad military and political leadership and lack of arms, they had no success. Only Schiffbek was an exception: the insurgents there disarmed the police and held power for two days.

In Eilsbek, Barmbek, Hammbek and other districts a bitter struggle between the police and the insurgents lasted until 5 p.m. The police concentrated a large force in the southern part of Barmbek and launched two vigorous attacks against the barricades. Both were repulsed, and the attackers suffered heavy losses. The insurgents, hidden on rooftops, at windows, on balconies and behind the barricades had an admirable field of fire and made every bullet count. The losses on their side were negligible. Before each attack, the police blazed away with rifles and machine-guns at the barricades in the belief that the main enemy force was behind them. In reality, the insurgents had left only a small number of defenders there, while their main force was on the roofs, at the windows and on the balconies of the neighbouring houses.

A third large-scale attack by the police on the Eilsbek barricades once again failed. The police detachment assembled for this attack sent ahead an armoured car to machine-gun the barricade, so that they could then storm it with impunity. But an insurgent appeared unexpectedly and killed the driver, and the rest of the crew abandoned the vehicle and took to their heels. The police did not proceed with their attack.

Subsequently, that particular barricade was not attacked again until after the insurgents, without the knowledge of the police, had themselves abandoned it to withdraw to new positions. The withering fire that was bestowed on it by considerable police forces was therefore wasted as there was not a single insurgent behind it.

Throughout the insurrection, the insurgents did not limit themselves to defensive action: wherever the situation was favourable, they at once went over to the offensive, mounted sharp counter-attacks, carried out flanking movements, etc., and thereby tired and demoralized the enemy.

In this way, by energetic and skilful operations, the insurgents kept up a determined struggle against the armoured vehicles of the police. On one occasion, two armoured cars advanced along a street and came up against barricades: at once new barricades went up behind them, and the vehicles found themselves surrounded and put out of action for several hours. Similar occurrences, proving the daring, the determination and the initiative of the insurgents, were extremely numerous.

Before recounting the remainder of the insurrection, one question must be considered: why did the struggle remain isolated in the north-eastern districts? Why did the plan for mobilizing the masses throughout the entire city for a concerted attack on the centre not even begin to be carried out? Why did the struggle in several districts where it had started in the morning subsequently come to a halt?

The reason for this was that on 23 October, at the moment when the Hamburg proletariat more than ever needed a firm leadership, *it did not have that leadership*. News arrived from various districts that they had received orders to stop fighting, that the insurrection had been called off, and that consequently the workers were hiding their arms until they received new orders from the Party leadership.

Certain comrades on the Regional committee[5] thought that since some districts had begun the attack, the others should follow suit; but it was already too late, since, as a result of the order that had unfortunately been given to stop the insurrection, the struggle had already been called off in all districts except Barmbek and the neighbouring areas. At about 10 p.m., it was learnt that the order to stop the insurrection had been given by Urbahns, secretary of the Hamburg committee, who had just arrived back from the Chemnitz Congress.[6] Urbahns was searched for in vain everywhere in order to find out the reasons for the counter-order.

Urbahns, as was subsequently ascertained, had given his counter-order on the basis of the results of the Chemnitz conference. This conference was supposed to decide on the launching of a general strike, which in the Central Committee's plan was to turn into an armed insurrection aimed at seizing power; the Hamburg insurrection was to play the role of signal for this general uprising. But the conference had been badly organized, and when the question of a general strike was put to the vote, a majority (though a small one) was won against it by the social democrats. Since the conference had thus refused to declare a general strike, the Party leadership decided to abstain for the moment from any insurrection.

The Chemnitz conference had taken place on 21 October. Why its results had not been communicated to Hamburg during the 22nd, together with the Central Committee decisions which followed from it, is impossible to understand.

The new order only arrived at the Barmbek insurrectionary headquarters which was encircled by police, at 5 p.m. on the 23rd.

In spite of the Party's countermanding order, the proletarian masses of Hamburg on their own initiative organized a series of demonstrations and public meetings in the streets, stopped work, and waited for directives which would tell them how to act. A great crowd of workers

[5] In Hamburg, in addition to the City committee, there was also a 'Seaboard' committee.
[6] Urbahns has now been expelled from the Communist Party.

formed in front of the Trade Union Building, broke the police cordon which the reformists had called for, forced its way inside, and began to thrash those of the reformist leaders who had not fled. It was not until fire had been opened on it that this crowd dispersed.

In the southern part of Barmbek, the fighting lasted until nightfall (5 p.m.). The police suffered heavy losses, but thanks to constant reinforcements succeeded in pushing the insurgents gradually back towards the north. At 6.30 p.m. Colonel Denner, commander of the police forces, decided that it was useless to continue the battle and gave the order to cease fire for that day.

The night of 23/24 October was calm. The Barmbek insurgents, who held good positions with plenty of cover, opened fire from time to time at such groups of police as showed themselves, and dispersed them. Spies were everywhere in the streets. Although by now they knew that there was no rising in progress in the other districts, and that the counter-order had been given by the Party, the insurgents nevertheless decided to continue the struggle. The population of Barmbek gave them every kind of assistance: they helped construct barricades, brought bread and cigarettes, gave the enemy false information, etc.

The women played a particularly important part in the insurrection. Apart from the information about the end of the insurrection, various rumours circulated among the insurgents – e.g. that a general strike had broken out in Central Germany; that Russia was sending aid (a shipload of arms, etc.). .... It was only during the night of 23/24 October, when one of the principal members of the Hamburg committee arrived in Barmbek with the order to stop fighting, that the insurgents began to go home.

On the morning of the second day a cruiser from Kiel, the *Hamburg*, and two torpedo-boats carrying 500 police from Lübeck, arrived in the port of Hamburg. The forces of counter-revolution had been further strengthened by the fact that the fascist organizations of the city had been provided with arms from secret stocks and were now on a war footing.

At dawn, the police began a concerted advance on Barmbek. All available forces, both police and fascists, took part in the operation. Reconnaissance was carried out by aeroplanes which flew over the area. The detachment of marines from the cruiser *Hamburg* refused to march. The attack was unnecessary, since the insurgents had already abandoned their positions. Only a few snipers scattered on the rooftops continued to pick off the police.

At 11 a.m. Colonel Denner sent his superiors a report on the 'fall' of Barmbek.

After the occupation of Barmbek, the main force of police turned towards Schiffbek to overthrow the soviets in that area, and also towards the other south-eastern districts to put down the 'troubles' there. A fierce struggle lasting several hours was needed to dislodge the insurgents from the barricades.

On 25 and again on 26 October, in Barmbek, isolated groups of insurgents attacked small police detachments searching houses or pursuing those who had participated in the action.

The police lost about sixty dead and a large number of wounded during the course of the entire operation. On the insurgents' side, there were 4–6 dead (the number of wounded is not known). There were a large number of dead and wounded among the civilian population (i.e. those who did not actually carry arms and fight), since the police frequently opened fire upon them. Among the dead and wounded there were even a number of children.

The low casualties of the insurgents were due to their skilful use of barricades, to their positions on rooftops, balconies and in their general use of good cover.

The Hamburg insurrection was accompanied by minor attacks by workers on the police and the authorities, and by the looting of food shops etc., in several surrounding towns and villages (Bergedorf, Itzehoe, Kiel, etc.).

CONCLUSIONS

In the first place, the Hamburg insurrection lasted two days and, despite the overwhelming superiority of the enemy forces, *it was not crushed by counter-revolution*. It was halted at the Party's orders, and the armed forces of the proletariat *stopped fighting voluntarily*. The Hamburg Prefect of Police, in a special report, admitted to his Berlin superiors that, despite his efforts, he had not succeded in breaking the insurgents' resistance, and that the latter had not been crushed but had voluntarily left the battlefield and gone into hiding bearing their arms. He stressed at the same time the courage and daring displayed by the insurgents from start to finish. He acknowledged the powerlessness of the police to counter an insurrection which employed the most modern methods of active defence, made large-scale use of barricades, rooftops, balconies and windows, and enjoyed the support of the population.

We are fully in agreement with this judgement by an enemy.

Secondly, the Hamburg insurrection was without any doubt *an insurrection of the proletarian masses*. The number of combat-squad members who took an active part in the fighting and bore arms was, it is true, relatively small – about 250–300 men. But the mass of the proletariat showed by its attitude that it was on the side of the insurgents. The rapid erection of a whole network of barricades was only possible thanks to the participation of the working-class masses. They further showed their active sympathy by stopping work in almost all factories, docks and shipyards. There was a near-complete halt to all working-class activity in the city.

The Hamburg insurrection was supported by working-class actions in several other neighbouring towns. It was not conceived as an isolated operation, having no connection with the proletariat of the other regions of Germany. The Communist Party's idea was that it should serve as a signal for a general uprising in the main industrial centres. It broke out at a moment in which the revolutionary ferment was everywhere at its peak, and in which the political and economic crisis was at its most acute.

However, and this is the third point, political preparation for the insurrection had been *extremely weak*. The political secretaries of the various districts only learnt of the order for a rising at the last minute, and some of them only did so at all by accident; this made it impossible for them to carry out the necessary work of political and material preparation.

With respect to the leadership, the Hamburg insurrection was a classic example *of the way an insurrection should not be organized, and of the attitude which should not be adopted towards an insurrection*. If the leadership was to remain faithful to Marxism, it was not permissible for it, once the insurrection had broken out and had achieved a number of significant successes, to sound the retreat. This was all the more impermissible in that the insurrection had been launched on orders from the Party. 'One does not play with insurrection' (wrote Marx). Certain leaders of the Hamburg organization (Urbahns, for instance) did play with insurrection. Despite the outcome of the

Chemnitz conference, since the insurrection had already begun, the correct policy would have been to mobilize all the forces of the revolutionary proletariat of Hamburg and the other regions, with the aim of extending the movement in Hamburg itself and supporting it by energetic action wherever this was possible. In Hamburg, *the slogan of soviets should have been launched, and vigorous agitation begun for their creation.* However, in Hamburg the Communist Party, vanguard of the proletariat, whose duty was to organize and lead the mass uprising, did not simply remain inactive, it even hampered the development of the insurrection. The Party, or to be more precise its leaders, in practice betrayed the insurrection in the same way Plekhanov said in 1905: 'They should not have taken to arms.'

Without organization, without the leadership of a revolutionary party, no successful insurrection is possible. In Hamburg, leadership from the Party was lacking, and the insurrection could not have finished otherwise than it did.

Fourthly, despite everything, despite the lack of leadership and the poor preparation, and although the combat organization was numerically very weak and almost without arms, the insurgents nevertheless succeeded – through their limitless dedication to the cause of revolution, through their courage, through their decisive and skilful actions, and thanks to the help of the working-class masses – in waging a successful struggle against the numerically superior and highly armed forces of the police. This fact testifies to the courage of the active nucleus of the proletariat of Hamburg, and especially of Barmbek, and shows that given good military and political leadership, even though they have very few arms at their disposal, combat units can hope to triumph over counter-revolution. It is easy to imagine what the outcome of the Hamburg insurrection would have been if the errors of leadership which we have pointed out had not been committed – and they were avoidable.

Fifthly, it is inconceivable that the insurrection, if it had been victorious, i.e. if it had seized power, could have held it supposing that red Hamburg had remained isolated and had not been supported by similar insurrections in the main centres of the country. Insurrections in the other towns, or at least in those of the Baltic region, were the precondition of a revolutionary victory in Hamburg itself. In our view Hamburg, given the state of the country in 1923, could have been the signal for a general uprising in a good number of centres and regions. The Hamburg proletariat was capable of taking power, despite the treachery of social democracy. But for that to happen there would have had to be a Bolshevik leadership at the head of the German Communist Party. There was no such leadership.

5

The Canton Insurrection

GENERAL REMARKS

The universal historical significance of the Canton insurrection is unquestionable, and so widely recognized that it is not something which needs to be proved. The Sixth World Congress of the Communist International spoke of the insurrection in the following terms:

> The Canton uprising was a heroic rearguard action of the Chinese proletariat in the preceding period of the revolution, and notwithstanding the grave errors committed by the leaders in the course of the rising, it marks the beginning of the new Soviet phase of revolution.[1]

> The Canton insurrection has been conceived by the workers as a sample of the great heroism of the Chinese workers.[2]

Previously, during the Shanghai insurrections and in general during the entire revolutionary struggle prior to the Canton uprising, the Chinese proletariat had been closely allied to the radical national bourgeoisie. Its vanguard, the Communist Party, during that whole period had formed a bloc with the Kuomintang – which at that time was the political expression of the bloc of four forces: proletariat, bourgeoisie, peasants and urban poor. In the Canton insurrection, however, the Chinese proletariat *for the first time presented itself as a genuinely independent class*, struggling against the bourgeoisie, the warlord or feudal cliques and against foreign imperialism; struggling for the revolutionary democratic dictatorship of the proletariat and peasants, i.e. *for Soviet power*. The Canton proletariat, under the leadership of the Chinese Communist Party, succeeded in seizing power in a town of one million inhabitants and in holding it for fifty-eight hours. By doing so it demonstrated to the whole world that the Chinese proletariat has definitively become conscious of itself as a class, has constituted itself politically, has become an independent class capable of acting as the directing and guiding force of the Chinese

[1] *Theses and Resolutions of the Sixth World Congress of the Communist International*, 'The International Situation and the Tasks of the Communist International', Section 54.
[2] 'Manifesto on the Chinese Revolution', voted at the opening session of the Sixth World Congress of the Communist International.

revolution. Finally, it demonstrated that the subsequent course of the great Chinese revolution will unfold under proletarian hegemony.

The revolutionary events which followed the Canton insurrection in China serve to confirm the truth of this assertion. The Chinese bourgeoisie, even before the insurrection, had ceased to be a revolutionary force, and had passed definitively over into the camp of counter-revolution. Side by side with the feudal and warlord cliques and with foreign imperialism, it was waging a savage war against the proletariat and its allies, the peasants and the urban poor. After the Canton insurrection, this onslaught by the reactionary forces against the revolution only increased. The sole force capable of leading the revolutionary struggle of the labouring classes of China is the proletariat.

We propose here to reconstruct the situation in China (particularly in Kwangtung province) which formed the background to the struggle, and to analyse the reasons for the defeat. It is not the Chinese proletariat alone who should profit by the lessons of the Canton insurrection. Its positive sides, like its mistakes, must be appreciated by the international proletariat; for the experience of Canton is one of the most precious lessons of the international revolutionary struggle in recent years.

THE SITUATION IN CHINA

In the autumn of 1927 the overall situation in China,[3] particularly in the Centre and the South, was characterized by the following features:

(*a*) the national bourgeoisie was continuing progressively to turn away from the national democratic revolution and to pass into the camp of militaristic and imperialist counter-revolution. All the counter-revolutionary forces were engaged in a bitter struggle against the revolutionary fraction of the proletariat and against the mass of the peasant population: dissolution of peasant organizations and trade unions, savage repression of all revolutionary movements, physical extermination of the revolutionary cadres of the working class, etc.;

(*b*) a deep crisis was becoming apparent in every domain of economic life: there was a steady deterioration in the financial situation, in commerce, in industry, in transportation. The crisis was assuming catastrophic dimensions;

[3] Excluding Manchuria. The political and economic situation of that province, a semi-colony of Japanese imperialism, has always been very different from that of the rest of China.

(*c*) the counter-revolutionary forces were proving manifestly incapable of creating a stable situation, or of achieving unity in their own camp; the division of China among multiple hostile political groupings, in a state of war among themselves, had reached an unprecedented level;[4]

(*d*) a powerful revolutionary movement was growing up, and this expressed itself in strike actions in the industrial centres (Shanghai, Canton, Hankow, etc.); in the growing revolutionary movement of the peasantry, which in the provinces of Hunan, Hupeh, Kiangsi, Honan and Kwangtung took on the form of a veritable civil war in the countryside against the big landowners and kulaks (gentry) etc.; in the insurrection of the armies of Yeh T'ing and Ho Lung on 30 July [1927] at Nanchang; in the establishment of Soviet power at Haifeng and Lufeng, etc.

At the same time the period which preceded the Canton insurrection was characterized by a low level of activity on the part of the Communist Party. The Party as a whole did not prove capable of organizing the revolutionary movement of the masses or giving it political leadership. It had not yet freed itself definitively from illusions about the 'Left' Kuomintang, and was guilty of serious errors of opportunism, above all in rural and military policy, etc. In addition, the activity of the counter-revolutionary forces; the savage terror which they practised against the Communist Party; the lack of any close contact (in space or time) between the main revolutionary fronts: the working-class struggle, the peasant insurrections and the mutinies among the soldiers;[5] all these factors could not fail to have a negative effect on the development of the revolution.

[4] The following were the main rival political groupings: Chang Tso-lin in Manchuria, Inner Mongolia and Chihli; Chang Tsung-ch'ang in Shantung; Yen Hsi-shan in Shansi; Yang Sen in Szechuan and Hupeh; the Kwangtung group (Chiang Kai-shek) in the provinces of Kiangsu, Chekiang and Fukien and in a part of Kiangsi; the Kwangsi group, headed by Pai Ch'ung-hsi the Kwangsi warlord and hero of the 12 April shootings in Shanghai and his clique, in the provinces of Kwangsi, Kweichow, Hunan and a part of Kwangtung; the Hunan group of generals, headed by T'an Yen-kai, in the province of Hunan; the group of Chang Fa-k'uei and Wang Ching-wei in Kwangtung. In addition to these main groupings, which represented a serious military and political force, there existed throughout the various provinces small cliques controlling minor forces, e.g. the generals of Yunnan, Anhwei, etc.

[5] These three revolutionary fronts emerged in isolation, without coordination in time or space. There was no unity of action between them. The insurgent armies of Nanchang did not prove capable of winning over the peasant movement in the regions in which they operated. The peasant uprisings were not coordinated with the revolutionary struggle of the workers in the towns.

In its plenary session of October 1927, the Central Committee of the Chinese Communist Party took stock of the concrete situation in the country. Its view was that, in spite of a series of defeats (Shanghai – crushing of the workers' movement in April; Wuhan – disarming of the workers, etc.; Swatow – defeat of the army of Yeh T'ing and Ho Lung, etc.), the situation in China *remained immediately revolutionary*, and that the slogan of insurrection was still appropriate.

THE SITUATION IN KWANGTUNG

The essential factors characterizing the situation in Canton and the province of Kwangtung immediately prior to the insurrection were as follows:

(*a*) on 17 November, General Chang Fa-k'uei – whose inspirer was Wang Ching-wei, the 'Left' Kuomintang leader, and who based himself on a section of the Kwangtung bourgeoisie – carried out a *coup d'état* in Canton and drove out Li Chi-shen, the ideologue of the comprador bourgeoisie who had seized power in a counter-revolutionary coup on 15 April 1927.

Chang Fa-k'uei and Wang Ching-wei, although they sought to win general sympathy by lying words, in reality waged a ruthless war against the revolutionary workers, against the peasant movement and above all against the Communist Party, which had been driven underground. In this respect, the members of the Kuomintang 'Left' yielded nothing to the pure reactionary Li Chi-shen. The government of Wang Ching-wei and Chang Fa-k'uei, as soon as it was installed, cancelled the gains which had been made by the Hong Kong strikers (it expelled them from the flats which the employers had been forced to provide; closed the people's restaurants; drove the strikers out of Canton, etc.). It carried out mass arrests of workers, dissolved the revolutionary trade unions and occupied their premises, put up posters calling for extermination of the communists, and even defended the bourgeois organizations which were demanding a boycott of English and Japanese goods;

(*b*) immediately after the *coup d'état* of 17 November, hostilities broke out in the province of Kwangtung between the two military groupings – that of Chang Fa-k'uei and that of Li Chi-shen, allied to General Li Fu-lin. Since Li Chi-shen made every effort to avoid decisive engagements, the war did not take the form of large-scale battles. Li Chi-shen led his troops in various directions, and Chang Fa-k'uei's forces followed in his wake. Nevertheless, the change of government and this 'bloodless' war did greatly weaken the ruling classes; it accelerated their disorganization, discredited both the political leaders of the Kuomintang and the Kuomintang itself, and hastened the economic disintegration of the province and city of Canton;

(*c*) after the departure of Li Chi-shen's forces with Chang Fa-k'uei at their heels, Canton gradually freed itself of government troops. The latter were progressively despatched to the front, with the aim of concentrating a sizeable force there which could strike a decisive blow at Li Chi-shen's rear as he retreated.

At the moment of the insurrection, the following units of Chang Fa-k'uei's army were actually in Canton: the training regiment, one infantry regiment, an artillery regiment, a regiment carrying out guard duties, and a few other minor units. These troops did not represent a serious military force, since they had to a considerable extent been subverted by the agitation and propaganda of the Communist Party. For example, there was a 200-strong illegal cell of communists and young communists in the training regiment.[6] In the other units the cells were numerically weak, but despite this the revolutionary ferment had affected a great many of the soldiers.

Apart from these troops of Chang Fa-k'uei's in Canton, who had been extensively subverted by the Communist Party, there were two of Li Fu-lin's regiments on the island of Honam. The Party had done nothing to subvert these or win them over politically, so they represented a reliable force in the hands of the reactionary command.

Around Canton, in the province of Kwangtung, there were some 50,000 reactionary soldiers in the armies of Li Chi-shen and Chang Fa-k'uei. The soldiers of these regiments followed the slogans of the Kuomintang. The slogans of the Communist Party were largely unknown to them, and even if they did have some idea of them they did not make any distinction between them and those of the Kuomintang. These soldiers were at the disposal of the reactionary command and carried out its orders without argument. The Party had done no work among them, for lack of men and resources;

[6] The presence of so large a cell in this training regiment was due to the fact that it contained a large number of students from Whampoa, and also to the fact that for a long time it had had a communist as its commander (though he was in fact dismissed before the insurrection).

(*d*) the revolutionary ferment among the oppressed classes was still growing, thanks to a constantly worsening economic situation and to the terror of the Kuomintang generals. The grouping of the working-class masses of Canton around the illegal red trade-union federation and around the communist organization of the city proceeded at a brisk pace. Clandestine meetings of trade-union delegates and clandestine conferences of Communist Party delegates were held regularly and amid growing interest. Already in September the situation was such that when the army of Yeh T'ing and Ho Lung approached Swatow, the Kwangtung provincial committee decided to embark on immediate preparations for insurrection in Canton. The defeat of the Nanchang troops outside Swatow at first, it is true, had an unfavourable impact on revolutionary activity in Canton, but the enthusiasm of the working class was not dampened by it, and the Communist Party, in spite of the defeat and the savage terror which followed it, continued to prepare the masses actively for the decisive conflict. At the same time, it took all kinds of technical and organizational measures to ensure the success of the insurrection.

On 14 October, in connection with the sailors' strike, the movement took on the form of a genuinely spontaneous uprising. On that day great mass demonstrations took place throughout the city. Several thousand demonstrators stormed the premises previously occupied by the red unions, drove out the police and put several government agents to death. After this, the terror redoubled. A section of the members of the Kwangtung provincial committee then considered that the situation was ripe for the immediate launching of an insurrection. However, the majority decided to wait longer; they called on the members of the Party to continue mobilizing the masses, stressing the connection between economic and political demands, and propaganda in favour of insurrection.

The revolutionary fraction of the Canton proletariat marked the date of 7 November by a huge demonstration, which was dispersed by the police. It should be noted that some members of the Kwangtung communist committee once again called for an insurrection during the course of that day. But the balance of forces, in the opinion of the other leading comrades in the committee was not yet favourable enough, and the insurrection was postponed.

During the first days of December, the revolutionary movement in Canton continued to grow. Once again the sailors went on strike; the bus drivers joined them, and so did a number of factories and the postal workers. The relatively strong upsurge of proletarian class struggle after Chang Fa-k'uei's *coup d'état* expressed itself in new demonstrations, in the mass circulation of clandestine communist publications, in the freeing of imprisoned communists by the mob, etc.;

(*e*) but in addition to the red unions, there existed numerous trade unions in Canton whose administration was in the hands of reactionary Kuomintang supporters. These unions, containing tens of thousands of workers, were grouped round the reactionary engineering union. The latter had backed the government's counter-revolutionary measures throughout the period of reaction, and had given active assistance to the government's troops in repressing the insurrection. This circumstance, i.e. the presence of this large number of members of reactionary unions (exceeding the number of active supporters of the red unions), constituted the main difficulty of the insurrection; it paralysed the preparations for it to a considerable degree, and exercised a negative influence upon its outcome. In these trade unions, the Communist Party's influence was negligible.

The petty bourgeoisie, as a mass, had not yet freed itself from its illusions about the 'Left' Kuomintang, and awaited some improvement in its wretched situation from Chang Fa-k'uei;

(*f*) in Kwangtung province, the revolutionary peasant movement expressed itself by establishing Soviet power and putting into practice the slogans of agrarian revolution in six districts around Haifeng and Lufeng (250 kilometres east of Canton). At Haifeng, a congress of worker, soldier and peasant delegates, which opened on 7 November in the presence of 300 delegates and a public of some 10,000 people, set up a Soviet government of all the insurgent areas in Kwangtung. At the beginning of December, the power of the Soviets extended over territory containing half a million inhabitants. The government was headed by a member of the Central Committee of the Communist Party. On Hainan island too, there was a powerful peasant movement.

Unfortunately, at the moment of the Canton insurrection, the revolutionary movement in the regions immediately surrounding the city was extremely weak.

The Party was not capable of carrying out the necessary agitational work in the peasant areas immediately surrounding Canton. The old mistakes of the Party in the agrarian field were now making themselves strongly felt.

THE IMMEDIATE PREPARATION OF THE INSURRECTION

At its 26 November session, the Kwangtung provincial committee of the Communist Party decided to orient itself decisively towards immediate preparation for insurrection. It was deeply convinced that all the conditions for victory were present, and that success was certain given good technical and political preparation.

In the period between 30 November and the start of the insurrection, the communist organization worked away intensively at mobilizing the masses for the insurrection. It also worked out a general political programme, drew up military plans, gave thought to the future organization of the Canton Soviet, etc.

The Party carried on its agitation among the masses with the following slogans: 'Down with Chang Fa-k'uei and Wang Ching-wei!', 'Down with the Kuomintang!', 'Full democratic freedom of the press, of speech, of assembly, of association and the right to strike', 'Extermination of the Chang Fa-k'uei provocateurs', 'Arms for the workers and peasants', 'Immediate liberation of all political prisoners', 'Restoration of the government subsidy to the Hong Kong strikers', 'Unemployment allowances to equal full pay', 'Higher wages and workers' control of production', 'Expropriation of the big bourgeoisie', 'Improvement of the material and juridical condition of the peasants', 'Creation of revolutionary soldiers' committees', 'Liquidation of all individuals who participated in or directed the Kuomintang terror', 'All land to the peasants, the rice to the workers', 'Down with militarist wars!' 'All power to the Soviets!', etc.

As for the organizational measures taken in preparation for the insurrection, after 26 November the Party at once proceeded to set up a revolutionary military committee which would provide the overall leadership, and also a red guard command which would provide the technical leadership for the insurrection itself. It worked out in detail the plan for the rising. It prepared the military mobilization of the communists (there were about 1,000 Party members in Canton, including the youth; 200 of these, as we have already stated, were in the training regiment) and the organization of the red guard. It set about forming special groups of actively revolutionary workers to carry out special missions (liquidation of the counter-revolutionary leaders); grouping and training drivers and truck-crews; adding to the number of instructors in enemy units, etc.

The Canton revolutionary committee was made up of five comrades, of whom one (Yeh T'ing) was appointed leader of the military side of the insurrection (commander-in-chief). Comrade Yeh T'ing only arrived in Canton six hours before the operation was launched, and therefore took no part in its preparation. This circumstance, as we shall see later, had a very unfortunate effect on the course of events.

The Soviet, elected on the eve of the insurrection, was composed of sixteen members. Of these, ten were appointed from a meeting of the Red Federation of Chinese Trade Unions, three represented the Canton garrison and three the Kwangtung peasant organizations (only one of these latter comrades was in Canton for the start of the uprising).

The Party's work in the army was mainly limited to the units of the Canton garrison. Because the necessary resources and men were lacking, no work was done among the troops outside.

The same can be said with respect to work among the peasants. A clandestine Party school for peasant militants had been organized in Canton. The comrades attending it acted as a link between Canton and the peasant organizations, transmitted the Kwangtung committee's instructions, distributed literature among the peasants, etc. But given the limited number of militants involved, this could not achieve any serious results and did not in fact do so.

The balance of armed forces in Canton, on the eve of the insurrection, was as follows:

Forces of Reaction

2 of Li Fu-lin's regiments on Honam island	3,000 men
1 artillery regiment in the outskirts of Canton to the north, with thirty cannon	500 men
1 infantry regiment, stationed next to the foregoing	600 men
1 infantry battalion, stationed at the same spot	250 men
1 battalion guarding the arsenal, near the San-shui station	300 men
the cadets of Whampoa academy, on Whampoa island	1,000 men
1 newly-recruited regiment of the 2nd Division at Hsi-kuan	800 men
1 newly-formed regiment of the 3rd Division	approx. 600 men
the municipal police	2,000 men
the battalions guarding Li Chi-shen's house	(numbers unknown)

In addition, the headquarters of the 2nd Division, the 12th Division and the 4th Army Corps and Chang Fa-k'uei's headquarters were all situated in Canton. Each of these headquarters was guarded by a Mauser company of between fifty and one hundred men (we do not have exact figures); these were made up of picked and well-paid professional soldiers.

All these units, with the exception of Li Fu-lin's two regiments and the Mauser companies, had been extensively subverted by the Communist Party. For this reason, they did not constitute a very serious force in the hands of the reactionary command. Li Fu-lin's two regiments and the Mauser companies, however, had not been affected by the revolutionary agitational propaganda. The insurgents could only hope to demoralize these by force of arms.

Insurgent Forces

The training regiment, in the Cha-hei barracks	1,000 men
1 squadron of the town gendarmerie	50 men
1 section of the arsenal guards	50 men
2 sections of the Whampoa cadets	100 men
the Canton red guard	2,000 men

In addition, the insurgents were counting on the support of the peasants who, once the insurrection broke out, were to send an armed detachment of 1,500 men to Canton (in fact, only about 500 of them arrived).

At the moment of the insurrection the training regiment was under the command of a reactionary officer, and some of the officers sided with him; but the regiment as a whole, with its 200-strong communist cell, and even including some of its officers, was firmly for the insurrection and only waiting for the Party's orders.

As we have seen, the balance of organized military strength hardly appeared favourable to revolution. But if one takes into consideration the fact that the forces of the bourgeoisie were hemmed in on every side by the generally revolutionary ferment, and that they were politically extremely unreliable from the reactionary command's point of view, then it can be reckoned that the respective military strengths in Canton were equally balanced. Given good organization (at the start of the insurrection), this balance could even quite easily be modified in favour of the insurgents, and that is what happened.

As for the organization and armament of the red guard, things stood as follows:

After the provincial committee had gone over to preparation for insurrection (August 1927), Canton was divided into ten districts, with a military commission in charge of each.

These military commissions had the job of organizing the work of subverting the government troops stationed in Canton, and winning them over politically; of forming detachments of red guards and giving them some military training; of accumulating arms and ammunition; of setting up a network of informers inside Chang Fa-k'uei's units and headquarters and in government institutions; in short, of preparing the insurrection in general from a technical point of view.

The district military commissions operated under the direction of the military commission of the Kwangtung provincial committee, composed of five comrades. The district commissions were ordinarily made up of three comrades, except in certain cases where there was only one 'representative of the commission'.

The military commissions operated secretly. In view of the need for absolute secrecy, the red guard created in the various districts took the form, during this first period, of isolated and carefully camouflaged ten-man groups, without any larger units. These groups of ten were subordinated to the military commission of the area (or more precisely to the comrade appointed from this commission to organize the red guard detachments). Subsequently, when the number of these groups of ten increased and the decisive moment was drawing near, the question arose of combining the groups into larger units so that they could be utilized more rationally during the insurrection. Immediately prior to the insurrection (i.e. some two weeks before it), the task of forming and commanding the red guard detachments was taken away from the district military commissions and entrusted to military leaders specially appointed from the trade unions under Party influence.

At the start of the insurrection, there was a total of about 2,000 workers organized in the Canton red guard, of whom 300 were strikers from Hong Kong.

The arms' situation was fairly bad. The red guard had hardly any weapons at all. In the whole of Canton, it only had 29 Mausers and some 200 grenades; not a single rifle.

Similarly, the men had not been given adequate military training. Many of the red guards did not know how to use their weapons. Most

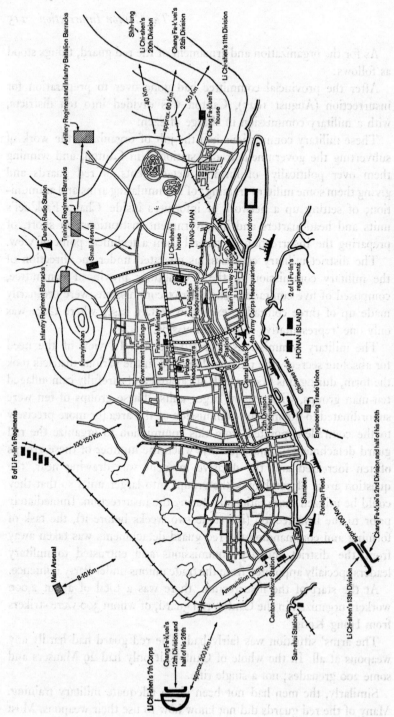

3. The counter-revolutionary forces in Canton, 11 December 1927

Shih-lung

Li Chi-shen's 20th Division

Chang Fa-k'uei's 25th Division

40 Km

Li Chi-shen's 11th Division

approx. 60 Km

Chang Fa-k'uei's house

50 Km

Artillery Regiment and Infantry Battalion Barracks

Danish Radio Station

Training Regiment Barracks

Small Arsenal

Infantry Regiment Barracks

Kuanyinshan

Li Chi-shen's house

TUNG-SHAN

Aerodrome

Government Buildings

France Ministry

Park

Police Headquarters

Radio Station

Central Bank

Main Railway Station

2nd Division Headquarters

4th Army Corps Headquarters

2 of Li Fu-lin's regiments

HONAN ISLAND

Chinese Fleet

12th Division Headquarters

Engineering Trade Union

5 of Li Fu-lin's Regiments

100-150 Km

Main Arsenal

8-10 Km

Shameen

Foreign Fleet

Ammunition Dump

Canton-Hankow Station

Chang Fa-k'uei's 2nd Division and half of his 26th

Li Chi-shen's 13th Division

San-shui Station

approx. 100 Km

Chang Fa-k'uei's 12th Division and half of his 26th

approx 200 Km

Li Chi-shen's 7th Corps

group-commanders were ignorant of the most elementary principles of military science or street-fighting tactics.

The meagre military training of the Canton red guard was due to the special conditions in China. In China there is no compulsory military service; all Chinese armies are mercenary armies. The Chinese people has a genuine hatred of soldiers, and only those who have no other way of keeping themselves alive (ruined peasants, urban *lumpen*) go into the army. The workers do not go into the army. For this reason, the Chinese working class hardly has any chance to learn the art of war by legal means. This circumstance had the most disastrous results on the fighting quality of the Canton red guard.

THE PLAN AND COURSE OF THE INSURRECTION (*see map opposite*)

In its 7 December sitting, the provincial committee of the Communist Party unanimously decided to organize the rising for the night of 10/11 December, at 3.30 a.m. It considered that all the social and political conditions required to ensure the victory of the insurrection were now present. The decisive shock had been given by the news that Chang Fa-k'uei, on orders from Wang Ching-wei, was recalling one of his divisions from the front and posting it to Canton to disarm the training regiment and re-establish 'order'. It was clear that, once the training regiment had been disarmed, reactionary terror would be redoubled, and that Chang Fa-k'uei would stop at nothing until he had eliminated all revolutionary possibilities in Canton by fire and sword. The issue was thus posed as follows: to accept defeat without a fight, or to act with a reasonable chance of taking power? The Party chose the second alternative.

After several plans had been considered,[7] the following was decided on: on 11 December, at 3.30 a.m., the insurrection would break out in the training regiment. The soldiers would disarm the infantry and artillery regiments, and also an infantry battalion quartered in the same area. Meanwhile, in the city, the red guard would disarm the

---

[7] One of these rejected plans was as follows: at noon on 11 December, the Party organizes a demonstration in which the training regiment participates. During this demonstration a general strike is declared, and at the same time the soldiers of the training regiment, together with the red guard units, seize the government buildings, disarm the police, etc. This plan was abandoned because it seemed to the revolutionary committee that the chances of success would be far more slender if they did not take the enemy by surprise in a sudden night attack.

police and the guard regiment; attack the headquarters of the 2nd and 12th Divisions and the 4th Corps, and also Li Chi-shen's house; open the prisons in which some 3,000 political prisoners were held; capture police headquarters, the government buildings, the arms depot near the San-shui station (which contained about 4,000 rifles with ammunition, and 5,000 hand-grenades), and the main arsenal, situated some eight kilometres outside Canton, together with all its arms.

The arms taken in the first stages of the insurrection would at once be distributed to the workers, allowing new armed units to be formed.

The Party would proclaim a general strike. All its forces would then have to be deployed for the task of drawing the mass of workers into the struggle to overthrow the old order. Their support would have to be secured for the clandestinely-formed Canton Soviet of worker, peasant and soldier deputies, so that a proclamation could be made during the insurrection conferring supreme power upon it. Immediately the insurrection had begun, the Soviet would publish a series of decrees: on the dismissal of the old government, nationalization of the land, confiscation of the city's major private fortunes, nationalization of the banks, railways, etc.

This, broadly speaking, would complete the first stage of the insurrection.

In the second stage, all insurgent forces would have to be deployed for the task of ridding the city definitively of every last remnant of counter-revolution, and liquidating Li Fu-lin's reactionary forces on Honam island.

The third stage would involve confronting the remaining militarist troops in Kwangtung, and drawing the peasantry into the revolutionary struggle. This last stage of the plan was only sketched out in broad outline. Nothing was planned in the event of failure.

The execution of the plan went through the following stages:

At 3.30 a.m., precisely, the president of the Canton revolutionary committee Chang T'ai-lei arrived at the training regiment's barracks with a group of workers riding on trucks taken by revolutionary drivers from their employers. This regiment, when its communist organization gave the signal, assembled in full strength in the courtyard; after Chang T'ai-lei had addressed the soldiers for ten minutes, they declared that they were entirely at the disposal of the Soviet of worker, peasant and soldier deputies, and intended to participate actively in establishing the new order. The commander of the regiment and fifteen reactionary officers who attempted to take up the defence of the Kuomintang were shot on the spot.

Each of the three battalions of the training regiment was assigned its specific mission: one would go to disarm the infantry regiment, another would disarm the artillery regiment and the infantry battalion, and the third would make its way into the city and join forces with the red guard.

At precisely the same moment (3.30 a.m.), the red guard went into action inside the city.

The disarming of the infantry and artillery regiments and the infantry battalion was carried out rapidly by the detachments of the training regiment. After this operation, the latter found itself in possession of thirty cannon and a large quantity of rifles (about 1,500) and machine-guns. The captured arms were at once transported in trucks to the city and distributed to the workers. The battalions of the training regiment then left the disarmed troops under guard and proceeded into the city to carry out further revolutionary tasks.

The red guard operations designed to disarm the police in their precinct stations and occupy the government buildings succeeded no less brilliantly. On the other hand, the attacks on the 2nd and 12th Division and 4th Corps headquarters, on Li Chi-shen's house where several hundred Mauser personnel were quartered, and on the police headquarters all failed. This last objective was only taken after a combined and bloody assault by the red guard and a battalion of the training regiment. After the capture of the police headquarters, the high command of the revolutionary committee installed itself on its premises.

By 3 p.m. the insurgents held all local police stations and all government buildings in the city, with the exception of the districts of Tung-shan and Shameen; the latter, as a foreign concession, was not to be attacked. Only the headquarters of the two divisions and the 4th Corps, and Li Chi-shen's house, remained in enemy hands. Considerable forces had to be expended and great determination shown by the insurgents before these positions could be occupied. It was only towards the end of the first day that it was possible to storm the 2nd and 12th Division headquarters. That of the 4th Corps, containing some 200 Mauser personnel who put up a stubborn resistance, could only be taken at about 10 a.m. on the second day, after the insurgents had set fire to the building. About half the Mauser gunners (i.e. one hundred men) were able to escape by water to Honam island. The fire in the army corps headquarters spread to the central bank which adjoined it and burnt it to the ground.

In connection with the capture of the 4th Corps headquarters, there is one interesting circumstance which must be mentioned. One of the staff officers of this corps was a communist. Despite this, the revolutionary committee had not thought it necessary to inform him of the planned insurrection, and for that reason this particular communist, who occupied an important position, played no part in the operation.

Li Chi-shen's house – a pretty imposing fortress, surrounded by a moat and a stone wall – could not be taken throughout the time that Soviet power lasted in Canton. Li Chi-shen was not inside in any case; but it held a large number of soldiers who were devoted to him and who succeeded in fighting off every attack.

From the very first day of the rising, the insurgents lacked arms. The weapons captured from the infantry and artillery regiments or after the disarming of the police were far from sufficient to arm all the workers who were willing to fight (by 7 a.m. on 11 December, 20,000 workers were already taking an active part in the rising). Despite this, the arms depot at the San-shui station and the main arsenal were not occupied throughout the uprising. The reason for this is unknown to us. What is certain is that the capture of these key objectives would have made it possible to arm some 10,000 workers, and would thus have created a balance of armed forces extremely favourable to the insurgents.

According to certain reports, a 500-strong peasant detachment from outside the city captured the San-shui station and attempted to seize the arms depot. However, when it met resistance from the guard, it began negotiations, and in the end the depot was not occupied.

The militarist forces began their campaign to retake Canton from the very first day of the uprising. The offensive was carried out by Li Fu-lin's units from Honam island. Given cover by the guns of the foreign and Chinese fleets, Li Fu-lin's regiments managed to cross over and attack a little to the east of what had been the 4th Corps headquarters. Their four attacks were successfully beaten off. Some of the cannon captured from the artillery regiment were utilized by the insurgents at this juncture. On the second day, Li Fu-lin's troops came down from the north by the Canton-Hankow railroad, and launched several attacks without success. One of these took place only 150 metres from the headquarters of the revolutionary committee, since the enemy had got through without being spotted by the insurgents. This episode shows that reconnaissance was very inadequately organized.

From the outset, the yellow engineering union took the side of reaction. It formed fifteen armed detachments of fifty men apiece, and these took an active part in the struggle against the insurgents.

During the night of 12/13 December, the revolutionary committee weighed up the situation and concluded that red Canton was in an absolutely critical position. On the one hand, they had failed to rid the city completely of counter-revolutionary forces (Honam, Tung-shan). On the other, the proletariat and petty bourgeoisie had not afforded the new régime enough active support. They had not been able to achieve a general strike: only the drivers, printers, rickshaw-men, the sailors of the Hong Kong-Tientsin line, and a few others had come out; the railway workers, municipal employees, Hong Kong seamen, etc., had not stopped work. The petty bourgeoisie, for the most part, had adopted a waiting policy. The engineering union, and a section of the workers grouped round it, were openly hostile to the insurrection. The counter-revolutionary leaders (Chang Fa-k'uei and others) had not been successfully isolated. From their Honam and Hong Kong sanctuaries, they continued to direct the struggle against the revolutionaries. The imperialist fleet gave effective aid to counter-revolution: a haven for the fleeing bourgeoisie; transport for Li Fu-lin's troops on their way to attack the centre of Canton from Tung-shan; bombardment of the town by the guns of Chinese and foreign ships, etc.

On the other hand, the red city was already surrounded by a counter-revolutionary cordon, formed by Generals Chang Fa-kuei, Li Chi-shen and Li Fu-lin, who had come to an agreement most touchingly when faced with the common enemy. Urged on by the imperialists, they had provisionally forgotten their disagreements in order to fall on Canton together and from all sides. The San-shui railway station was already occupied by a detachment of Chang Fa-k'uei's 26th Division. Li Fu-lin's troops, transported from the other side of the river by the foreign fleet, was preparing a new attack from Tung-shan. The 25th Division was advancing from the east. Li Fu-lin's troops continued to attack from the north. The engineering union was actively aiding the counter-revolution. At the same time, the revolutionary committee was informed of the imminent arrival of other army units stationed in Kwangtung province.

Lacking weapons (rifles), the insurgent forces *could not grow*. On the contrary, the inevitable losses during the fighting caused them *progressively to diminish*. It had proved impossible for them to win superiority in armed strength. Now, on the contrary, the balance of forces was shifting gradually in favour of counter-revolution.

The situation was such that the revolutionary committee wondered whether it was right to continue to defend Canton, or whether they should not rather withdraw. The decision was made to send all available armed forces out of the city, and to attempt a breakthrough towards the peasant insurrection in Hailufeng. In the morning and during the day of 13 December, the red city was evacuated by the armed forces of the insurgents; about 1,500 strong, they were what was left of the training regiment and a part of the red guard. The red guard units who remained in Canton fought to the last.

The withdrawal of this force of 1,500 men was an extremely hasty one, and the cannon, most of the machine-guns, and most of the ammunition were left behind in the city.

The bloody repression exacted by the counter-revolution cost the lives of some 4,000 workers.

LESSONS TO BE DRAWN FROM THE CANTON INSURRECTION

We must now consider in somewhat greater detail the central question posed by the Canton insurrection: what were the reasons for its defeat, and what are the lessons to be drawn by the revolutionary party when it organizes and prepares for the seizure of power in the future.

As we have seen from our description of the way in which the Canton insurrection was prepared and carried out, the Communist Party was guilty of serious errors in the military organization and conduct of the operation; these errors could not fail to have a disastrous effect on the outcome of the conflict. Briefly, they can be resumed as follows.

The plan for the insurrection had not been studied with sufficient care; the leadership proved to be extremely weak. This was to some extent due to the fact that the member of the revolutionary committee responsible for the entire military side of operations had only arrived in Canton six hours before the uprising; he had consequently not been able to study the situation adequately or draw the necessary conclusions regarding the operations to be carried out. Furthermore, this comrade, although a soldier by profession (Yeh T'ing was a general), did not have an adequate military training; nor above all did he have any experience of proletarian insurrection inside a town. The lack of any serious plan or good leadership during the insurrection explains the fact that the San-shui arms depot and the main arsenal were not occupied, that reconnaissance and liaison were not properly organized during the fighting, etc. It also explains why no use was made of the disarmed soldiers of the infantry and artillery regiments and the infantry battalion.

There is no doubt that the soldiers of these disarmed units, after a certain amount of political work had been rapidly carried out and a careful selection made, could have been used as active combatants on the side of the insurgents. Instead the military commander, when his attention was drawn to this possibility, asked for a roster of the disarmed soldiers with their political opinions marked on it. Naturally, such a bureaucratic way of resolving a revolutionary problem in time of insurrection could not and did not produce any good result. Time was short, it was wasted in useless paper-work, and in the end the soldiers of these units remained unutilized. Subsequently, they simply dispersed throughout the city. Yet the majority of these soldiers hardly differed politically from those of the training regiment. If this had not been true, they would not have let themselves be disarmed so easily by a few insignificant detachments from the latter. The revolutionary ferment among the soldiers of the two regiments of infantry and artillery was an undeniable fact, as it was also with respect to the other units of the Canton garrison. It is this which made it possible to neutralize them so swiftly.

As a result of poor leadership, tasks were not properly distributed among the various red units. A number of these units remained entirely unused, as Yeh T'ing indicates in his report: a section of gendarmes; a section of the arsenal guards; two sections of Whampoa cadets. These units, which were considered to be devoted to the revolutionary cause, nevertheless were not assigned any active mission; they received no communication from the leadership of the insurrection and remained inactive throughout. Yet the shortage of manpower was acute.

A further serious error on the part of the leadership was its failure to make use of the communist staff officer who at the start of the insurrection was stationed at 4th Corps headquarters. This comrade, as we indicated earlier, was not informed of the plans of the Kwangtung communist committee. By virtue of his position, he might have been able seriously to influence the entire course of events in favour of the proletariat. But in order to have done so, he would have had to be kept informed and to be assigned specific tasks by the revolutionary committee.

When working out its plan for the insurrection, the leadership *attached too little importance to liquidating the counter-revolutionary leaders*. The revolutionaries did not succeed throughout the insurrection in neutralizing the active leaders of reaction. The entire counter-revolutionary command (Chang Fa-k'uei and other Kuomintang leaders) was in Tung-shan. The occupation of Tung-shan was not planned to take place at the beginning of the insurrection, but was left for the second stage. The result was that the counter-revolutionary leaders, as we have shown, at once fled and took refuge on Honam island and in Hong Kong; from there they were able to direct the struggle against the insurgents in complete safety.

The non-occupation of Tung-shan, and the fact that the counter-revolutionary high command was allowed to escape, were among the biggest blunders made by the leaders of the Canton rising.

In general, it should be noted that the insurgents did not devote enough energy to combating the main figures of counter-revolution. Thus Chu Jui writes in his article 'The Canton Insurrection':

Insufficient importance was attached to neutralizing the counter-revolutionaries. During the entire time that Canton was in the hands of the insurgents, only a hundred individuals were executed. Prisoners could only be executed after a regular trial by the commission for struggle against reaction. In the middle of a battle, in the middle of an insurrection, such a procedure is too slow. Thus, after the withdrawal, there were seventy or eighty reactionaries in the prisons who later emerged and took part in the repression. No attempt was made to confiscate government property or the wealth of the reactionaries. Power was in our hands for two or three days; yet the principal organs of the insurrectionary leadership hardly had the wherewithal to buy provisions, while the central bank contained several millions in hard cash which remained untouched. Neither were the other banks touched, nor the shops.[8]

Yet another serious error by the leadership was that, although by noon on the first day the centre of Canton was in the hands of the insurgents,

[8] *The Canton Commune*, a collection of articles and documents, Moscow, 1929, p. 96.

it failed to isolate the 4th Corps headquarters from the units under the latter's command. The headquarters was still in communication that evening with its forces outside the city. Telegraphic communication between Canton and Hong Kong never stopped functioning.

One fact which had a disastrous influence on the course of the conflict was that the working-class masses did not know how to use firearms. Of the thirty cannon captured from the artillery regiment, only five could be used; all the others remained inactive because the insurgents had nobody to operate them. The same was true of the machine-guns: the insurgents made no use of most of those they possessed. Not knowing how to handle their weapons, and ignorant of the elementary principles of combat, the working-class forces suffered heavy casualties while inflicting relatively minor losses on the enemy.

Barricade-fighting methods were not properly applied. Yet by the beginning of the second day the insurgents had already been thrown back on to the defensive, and the situation demanded the use of barricades, which could have presented serious advantages. The insurgents devoted far too much of their strength and attention to capturing the divisional and 4th Corps headquarters and Li Chi-shen's house. At a time when the situation required rapid and energetic action to occupy the entire city and above all the counter-revolutionary positions in Tung-shan, the correct tactic would have been to surround and isolate the headquarters in question with the minimum of forces (cutting off all communications, light, water, etc.); most of the available resources could then have been devoted to attacking the targets which were most important at that particular juncture, if the balance was to be tipped in favour of the insurrection (Tung-shan, the arms depots, etc.).

All the above-mentioned tactical and organizational mistakes, together with the poor leadership and the inability of the workers to handle firearms, had an immense negative influence on the entire course of the uprising. *The fundamental problem in every conflict, and especially during an insurrection, is the problem of how the insurgents are to achieve superiority of forces over counter-revolution; if this problem did not receive a favourable solution, it was mainly as a result of those mistakes.*

After their bold and energetic initial assault on the old order, the insurgents were quickly obliged to fall back onto the defensive as a result of the unfavourable relation of forces in the field. The initiative in the fighting from then on passed to the enemy.

Furthermore, it should be noted that the death of Chang T'ai-lei, one of the most energetic and talented leaders, killed on the second day on the way back from a meeting, further weakened the already defective leadership.

However, despite the considerable negative effects of the tactical errors we have mentioned, *the essential causes of the defeat in our view lie elsewhere.* The principal and decisive causes are to be sought in another domain: the general situation in China and the balance of forces in the province of Kwangtung did not favour an insurrection.

In Canton it was possible to seize power (though the whole town was not occupied, since Tung-shan and Honam island remained in enemy hands) thanks to the negligible size of the counter-revolutionary forces present. But this was only true for Canton. In Kwangtung province as a whole, the balance of forces was decisively unfavourable to the insurgents. At a distance of two or three days' march from Canton, in various directions, there were about 50,000 troops under the command of the militarists Chang Fa-k'uei, Li Chi-shen and other lower-ranking generals, who had no serious disagreement with each other. The Party's work among these troops to subvert them and win them over politically to the revolution had been practically non-existent (for lack of men), and most of the soldiers were totally ignorant of the communist slogans. It was this fact which permitted Chang Fa-k'uei, after the proletarian insurrection had broken out, to turn his army round and send it to repress the uprising. Li Fu-lin and Li Chi-shen did the same. All this was only possible because there was no real, bloody war going on between these militarists; they were thus able without the least hesitation to call back their troops from the front and send them against Canton. These regiments were not demoralized, they were loyal to the reactionary command, and they were supported materially and politically by the imperialists. Once their offensive had been launched against the city from all sides, it was clear that Canton could not be defended; *for superiority of forces was, by an immense margin, on the side of counter-revolution.*

At the moment of the insurrection, there were no serious revolutionary movements among the peasantry in the regions surrounding Canton. The region of Hailufeng, where Soviet power had been proclaimed in six districts, is 250 kilometres away from Canton, and for that reason the peasants in revolt were not able to give Canton any active support when it was needed. The same was true with respect to Hainan island; here too there was a powerful peasant movement, but it was completely isolated so that no assistance could be hoped for from it.

The Canton insurrection was not supported by any action on the part of the proletarian masses or the revolutionary peasantry in the other provinces of China. The Central Committee of the Communist Party had not learnt in time of the decision of the Kwangtung provincial committee to launch the movement in Canton on 11 December.

Such was the general political situation and the balance of forces between revolution and counter-revolution in Kwangtung. As far as the city of Canton itself was concerned, *there was without the slightest doubt a revolutionary mass movement there: the masses genuinely took part, in one form or another, in the uprising and sympathized with the insurrection.* (All the Menshevik arguments claiming that the Canton masses did not take part in the rising, and that the latter was merely a putsch, are to be rejected with contempt.) But it is also true that there were sections of the proletariat, like the engineering union (and many other unions, representing tens of thousands of members, which were under the latter's influence) with its membership of over 5,000 workers, which not only did not support the movement but, on the contrary, were hostile to it or at least remained passive and neutral spectators of the bloody conflict.

The insurgents *were not able to prepare or carry out a general strike: the railway-workers and seamen continued working and were used by the counter-revolution for transporting troops, refugees from Canton, etc.* This was particularly true of the river-transport workers. *The petty bourgeoisie was still attached to its illusions about the Kuomintang 'Left', and understood nothing of the communist slogans nor of what was going on in the city.*

As an illustration, here is how a member of the Canton revolutionary committee, comrade Yeh T'ing, judged the attitude of the working masses towards the insurrection:

The great masses did not take part in the insurrection at all: two big meetings produced a not very satisfactory result. All the shops were closed, and the shop-workers showed no desire to support us. We were not able to make use of all our comrades, and consequently there is nothing astonishing if the workers were very badly organized. Most of the soldiers who had been disarmed simply dispersed around the city. The insurrection was not related to the troubles that had arisen among the workers of the three railway lines. The reactionaries were still able to use the Canton-Hankow line. We did not pay sufficient attention to the fleet, which remained in enemy hands. Our party did not do what was necessary to support the base organizations of the workers. The armed detachments of the engineering union, wearing white armbands, chased their red brothers and shot them. The power-station workers put out the street lamps, and we had to work in the dark. The workers of Canton and Hong Kong, like the seamen, under pressure from the British imperialists did not dare to join those who were fighting. The sailors on the Hong Kong-Tientsin line, in a similar situation, went on strike notwithstanding and triumphed. As for the river-transport workers, they shamefully put themselves in the service of the Whites, who they helped to cross the river while we for our part were unable to find even a small number of boats. The railway-workers of Hong Kong and Hankow transmitted the enemy's cables and transported his soldiers. The peasants did not help us to destroy the railway, and did not try to prevent the enemy from attacking Canton. The Hong Kong workers did not show the least sympathy for the insurrection.[9]

Although in our view Yeh T'ing underestimates mass participation in the uprising, we are nevertheless in general agreement with him. It is clear that this inadequate participation by the proletarian masses was due to the lack of good leadership; the leaders proved incapable of taking the measures necessary to secure the collaboration of the workers in the active struggle. But something else is equally clear: the indispensable social conditions, without which the victory of armed insurrection is impossible, were not present to a sufficient degree in Canton.

The Canton insurrection, a heroic attempt by the proletariat to organize a Soviet government in China, played an enormous role in the development of the workers' and peasants' revolution. It nevertheless revealed a whole series of blunders made by the leaders: insufficient preliminary work among the workers and peasants, and among the enemy forces; a wrong appraisal of the working-class members of the yellow unions; inadequate preparation of the Party organization and the Young Communist League for the insurrection; complete failure to inform the national Party centre about events in Canton; weakness in the political mobilization of the masses (absence of broad political strikes, absence of an *elected* Soviet in Canton as an organ of insurrection), for which the leaders directly responsible politically to the Communist International (Comrade N[eumann] and others) are partly to blame. Despite all these blunders, the Canton insurrection must be considered as a model of heroism on the part of the Chinese workers, who have now the right to claim their historical role as leaders of the great Chinese revolution.[10]

The Sixth Congress of the Chinese Communist Party and the Sixth World Congress of the Communist International declared their entire agreement with this evaluation.

The new fact which these two congresses added was that the Canton

[9] Yeh T'ing's report on the Canton insurrection.
[10] *Resolution on the Chinese Question*, adopted at the Ninth Plenum of the Executive Committee of the Communist International in 1928.

uprising should be viewed as a 'rearguard action of the Chinese proletariat in the preceding period of the revolution'. The Canton insurrection broke out at a moment when the revolutionary wave was already subsiding in China.

The revolutionary wave, however, was already beginning to ebb. In the course of a number of uprisings (the rising led by Ho Lung and Yeh T'ing, the peasant uprisings in Hunan, Hupeh, Kwangtung and Kiangsu) the working class and peasantry still strove to wrest the power from the hands of the imperialists, bourgeoisie and landlords, and in this way to avert the defeat of the revolution. But in this they were not successful. The last powerful onslaught of this revolutionary wave was the insurrection of the heroic Canton proletariat, which under the slogan of Soviets attempted to link up the agrarian revolution with the overthrow of the Kuomintang, and the establishment of the dictatorship of the workers and peasants.[11]

This evaluation of the Canton insurrection as a rearguard action by the Chinese proletariat has a very considerable importance, and one of principle. By it, the Communist International indicates the fundamental reason for the defeat.

If we judge the military and political errors committed during the preparation and execution of the insurrection in the light of the overall political situation in the country, and particularly in Kwangtung and Canton, we will come to realize that these errors did not in fact have a decisive influence on the outcome of the conflict.

The Canton insurrection was crushed by the superior, combined forces of reaction: militarists, bourgeoisie, imperialists, etc. The Canton workers showed matchless heroism. The Canton proletariat and the working classes of all China will draw the appropriate lessons from the errors and the achievements of the Canton Commune. The decrees of the young Canton government will have immense significance for all Chinese workers: nationalization of the land; expropriation of large firms, the means of transport, the banks; eight-hour day; physical extermination of counter-revolution; recognition of trade unions as authorized organs of the working class; suppression of mercenary armies; all-out war against the imperialists; a campaign against militarist wars, etc. These decrees showed the workers of China that it was not merely a question of handing over power to a particular group or transferring it from one ruling class to another, but of

[11] *Theses and Resolutions of the Sixth World Congress of the Communist International*, in 'Theses on the Revolutionary Movement in the Colonies and Semi-colonies'.

transforming radically the entire social order by handing over all power to the working classes. This is where the universal significance of the Canton uprising lies.

But the importance of the rising would have been even greater if its leaders had not committed the huge blunders mentioned above. These errors could have been avoided.

In fact, if the leaders of the insurrection had had a well-thought-out plan and had put it into practice in every detail, the struggle would have taken on a markedly different character. Occupying the arms depot and the main arsenal would have allowed the insurgents to increase their armed forces to some 10,000 men. They would have been able to increase their numbers even further if they had made good use of the captured soldiers of the disarmed garrison units, and of those revolutionary units who were never called on to take part in the struggle. If they had done all this, and the workers and soldiers had really been provided with arms, they would have had a revolutionary army over 20,000 strong. Even though this army would doubtless still have been inferior in numbers, military training and armaments to the 50,000 men commanded by the militarists, it would none the less have been possible to combat the counter-revolution more success- fully with it than was possible with the negligible forces which the revolutionary committee had at its disposal in the actual event.

By this we do not mean, of course, that these 20–25,000 men of the revolutionary army, under the conditions in which the Canton insur- rection took place, would have been able to carry on a prolonged struggle against the forces of reaction. The enemy's superiority was after all overwhelming. A final victory of those 20–25,000 revolu- tionaries was impossible unless, 1) the decisive elements of the Canton proletariat gave them active armed support (in other words, if the Party had been able to get them to participate in the active struggle); 2) the peasant population along the route of the militarist troops marching to Canton from all over Kwangtung province had been able – whether by mass uprisings or by guerrilla actions – to distract the attention of at least a part of these troops. It would finally have been necessary for there to have been at least some symptoms of disaffection inside the militarist armies. If these conditions had been fulfilled, then the Canton insurrection, as a rearguard action of the Chinese revolution in 1927, could have served as a point of departure for a new revolution- ary upsurge.

The Canton insurrection showed the Chinese workers that *armed insurrection can only triumph if it is carefully prepared, if no significant* military or political mistakes are made, and if the proletarian masses as a whole are drawn into the action, together with the soldiers of the militarists' armies.

The lesson of Canton will not be lost upon the Chinese workers.

The Canton insurrection has been conceived by the workers as a sample of the great heroism of the Chinese workers. Let the next uprising of the broad masses of the workers and peasants, organized on the basis of the consistent and correctly applied principles of Leninism, supported by the international proletariat, be the victorious October of China.[12]

[12] op. cit., 'Manifesto on the Chinese Revolution.'

6

The Shanghai Insurrections

(see map p. 134)

The three Shanghai insurrections described briefly in this chapter took place in *different* conditions from those which obtained in the cases considered hitherto.

In the first place, in accordance with the absolutely correct decisions of the Communist International, the Communist Party of China *was still forming a bloc with the Kuomintang* with whom it was fighting against the feudalists, the semi-feudal militarists and foreign imperialism. The national bourgeoisie was still revolutionary, and was struggling for the national emancipation and unification of China under the hegemony of the bourgeoisie.

By the time of the third insurrection, the national bourgeoisie had without a doubt already effectively passed over into the camp of reaction. But this change of attitude had not been adequately understood by the leadership of the Communist Party and, as we shall see, its entire tactic continued to be based on a close bloc with the Kuomintang.

In the second place, these three insurrections *were prepared and executed under the following slogan: Help the troops of the national revolution* – i.e. in their war (the Northern campaign of the revolutionary army) against the Northern feudalists (Chang Tso-lin, Sun Ch'uan-fang, Chang Tsung-ch'ang). The principal tactical factor in the three insurrections was the desire to combine revolutionary actions in the enemy's rear with the direct offensive of the national army.

These two features characterized the preparation and organization of the Shanghai insurrections.

The first (24 October 1926) cannot really be called an insurrection in the true sense of the word, for it was limited to minor skirmishes between the detachments of the combat organization and the police. But the situation at the time, and the decisions of the Communist Party in favour of preparing for a genuine armed insurrection, make it worth some consideration.

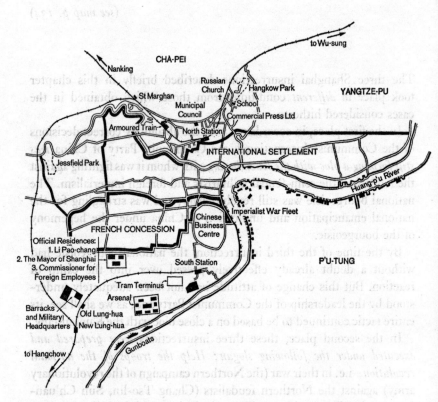

4. Shanghai at the time of the insurrections, 1926–27

THE INSURRECTION OF 24 OCTOBER 1926

In October 1926 the situation in Shanghai and on the Chekiang front was as follows. After the defeat of Wu P'ei-fu outside Wuchang on 10 October, the commander of the Northern expedition (Chiang Kai-shek) had turned his main forces against Sun Ch'uan-fang's army in Kiangsi province. It seemed unlikely that the latter would be able to resist the Southern national army. General Hsia Ch'ao, governor of Chekiang province, wished to show himself in a good light to his new master, the commander of the national army, and so assure himself a suitable position under the new government once the latter had defeated Sun Ch'uan-fang; he therefore decided to rise against Sun Ch'uan-fang. For this purpose, he came to an agreement with General Niu Yung-ch'ien, a right-wing Kuomintang member who was then in Shanghai representing the national government. Niu Yung-ch'ien had recently arrived to represent the political bureau of the Kuomintang, which had only lately become organized in the region. His task was to mobilize the forces of Shanghai, to disorganize Sun Ch'uan-fang's rear, and lastly to organize a rising in Shanghai if the Southern troops came sufficiently close to warrant it. This mission coincided with the line adopted by the Communist Party. Even before Hsia Ch'ao made his decision, the communist leaders had already come to the conclusion that the Shanghai proletariat, in the event of Sun Ch'uan-fang being defeated and Hsia Ch'ao recognizing the national government, should rise in support of the latter and assist him to seize the city. The Communist Party at the same time recognized that, in addition to the working class, it would be necessary as far as possible to draw the petty bourgeoisie and students into the uprising.

The combative attitude of the Shanghai proletariat, encouraged by the national army's victories and Sun Ch'uan-fang's difficulties, became increasingly evident. The Communist Party's influence was considerable. There was every reason to hope that if it gave the order for a general strike and an insurrection, the majority of the proletariat would follow it.

Niu Yung-ch'ien had grouped around him not only the petty bourgeoisie, but even a part of the middle bourgeoisie (Yü Ho-teh, ex-president of the Chamber of Commerce, etc.). He further succeeded in gaining the support of a part of the *lumpenproletariat.*

The Communist Party had managed to create an armed force of

130 workers; they had also organized a further 2,000 men in combat squads for which there were no arms. Niu Yung-ch'ien had a force of about 600 men, mainly recruited from the *lumpenproletariat*. He had not dared enlist workers or give them arms. Yü Ho-teh appeared to have about 500 men of the merchant militia at his disposal (subsequent events showed that in reality he had many fewer than this). All these units together made up the armed strength of the expected insurrection.

There was no overall plan, nor was there any overall commander, since none of the participants in the coalition (Communist Party, Niu Yung-ch'ien, and Yü Ho-teh representing the merchants) was willing to subordinate its forces to either of the other two partners. Each group decided to operate independently, but the date on which they were to move into action was by common accord to be fixed by Niu Yung-ch'ien, representing the national government (it is strange that the Communist Party should have accepted such a compromise).

According to the Communist Party's plan (the merchants and Niu Yung-ch'ien had no plan at all), the insurrection was to begin with a strike by the seamen, the metalworkers, the municipal water and electricity workers, and subsequently the textile workers. It was reckoned that more than 100,000 men would take part in the strike.

Sun Ch'uan-fang's forces in Shanghai comprised: one infantry battalion (about 1,000 men); more than 2,000 police; two river gunboats (one of which in fact supported Niu Yung-ch'ien); and the 76th Brigade (very unreliable), with its general Li Pao-chang quartered two days march away from Shanghai on the north bank of the Yangtze.

Such was the balance of organized armed forces.

On 16 October, General Hsia Ch'ao, who commanded some 10,000 men, declared that he had gone over to the national government. On 17 October he sent a regiment to occupy Shanghai, and towards the evening of the same day this regiment arrived within fifteen kilometres of the city. (It is incomprehensible why Hsia Ch'ao did not send all his forces against Shanghai as the situation dictated, instead of sending only one regiment.)

At the same moment the vanguard of the 76th Brigade entered Shanghai; these troops had been dispatched by Sun Ch'uan-fang to reinforce the garrison even before Hsia Ch'ao's regiment had set off. On the same day, Sun Ch'uan-fang's forces joined battle with those of Hsia Ch'ao and delayed the arrival of the latter in Shanghai.

This was the most favourable moment for the proletariat to attack. But its leaders considered that they were still inadequately prepared. On 20 October, the communist squads and Niu Yung-ch'ien's units were both more or less ready to act, but Hsia Ch'ao's situation at the front was bad. No reliable news about the front was available in Shanghai. The date for the insurrection was postponed from one day to the next. On the morning of 23 October, Niu Yung-ch'ien received an unverified report that Sun Ch'uan-fang had been defeated by Hsia Ch'ao. On the strength of this report, he gave the order to begin the insurrection during the night of 23/24 October at 3 a.m.

In fact, Hsia Ch'ao's troops had been defeated by Sun Ch'uan-fang.

Since it lacked any plan or leadership (the signal for the start of the action was supposed to be a salvo from one of the gunboats; this in turn was supposed to follow a rocket fired from Niu Yung-ch'ien's house: the rocket was fired at the correct time, but the gunboat did not notice it and thus did not fire its salvo), *the insurrection never took place*, apart from minor skirmishes with the police. At 5 a.m. the Communist Party ordered its squads to postpone the action. The entire operation cost the Party almost no casualties.

The *main* cause of the failure – leaving aside various organizational errors such as the lack of any plan or leadership, the poor intelligence about the situation at the front, and subsequently the lack of coordination between the operations of the troops and those of the proletariat – consisted in the fact that *the Communist Party relied too much at the time on Niu Yung-ch'ien. It had in effect left the direction of the insurrection to him (he had fixed the date); it had voluntarily renounced any independent policy during the preparation and execution of the operation; in short, it was tailing the Kuomintang.* For this reason, the Party *had made almost no* serious preparation for insurrection among the proletariat. It could not do so, since it had placed itself in a position of dependence on Niu Yung-ch'ien, whereas it had every reason to assume the leadership and to utilize Niu Yung-ch'ien and the merchants as auxiliary forces.

The really propitious moment for insurrection (on 17 October, when Hsia Ch'ao was only fifteen kilometres from Shanghai) had not been seized. The Party had accepted Niu Yung-ch'ien's claims that he was not ready to move. Yet the balance of forces in Shanghai was such that if the Communist Party had called the proletariat out on a general strike, the latter would certainly have responded overwhelmingly –

for the slogan of aiding the national armies meant something to the entire population. An intervention by the proletariat could have decided the struggle in favour of the insurgents and Hsia Ch'ao, even given the defective material organization. The Party *evidently under-estimated the importance of the strike and over-estimated the purely military factor* (forming the squads). It did not anticipate that Hsia Ch'ao's troops might suffer a defeat while the armed forces were being assembled inside Shanghai, and that as a result the situation would be radically modified to the detriment of the revolution. It did not understand that in such cases (combined operations by the proletariat in the enemy's rear and by an army advancing at the front), *the dominant factor is always the army*, and that the proletariat must time its own actions by it. It was therefore inadmissible to delay the insurrection for internal technical and material reasons. On the contrary, it was necessary to take up arms if there was even the slightest possibility of doing so, in order to ensure success at the front.

Our explanation of the reasons for the defeat would not be complete, indeed would be superficial, if a further factor were not discussed: the tactics of the Communist Party towards the Kuomintang, and its conception of the role of the proletariat in the Chinese revolution. Only in the light of this question will it be understood why the Party leadership in Shanghai tailed the Kuomintang, agreed that the date of the insurrection should be fixed by a member of the Kuomintang Right like Niu Yung-ch'ien, in short, renounced any policy of its own in the entire uprising.

The leadership of the Communist Party *underestimated the role of the Chinese proletariat in the revolution*. It believed that the proletariat was not yet strong enough politically to win hegemony in the national democratic revolution. Even if certain leaders of the Party verbally admitted the need for the proletariat to fight for the leading role in the revolution, this remained nothing but an empty phrase: no effort was made in that direction.

Once this kind of conception of the proletariat's role held sway in the leading circles of the Party, the conclusion was inevitable. The leading role in the democratic revolution must belong to the Kuomintang. The proletariat and its vanguard should synchronize their tactics with that of the Kuomintang, raise only demands which did not contradict Kuomintang policy, and follow the Kuomintang's lead. This is how the Party leadership understood the Comintern's directives on the temporary bloc between Communist Party and Kuomintang in the democratic revolution.

The Party leadership did not consider the possibility that the Chinese bourgeoisie might betray the democratic revolution; it overestimated the revolutionary spirit of that bourgeoisie.

These assertions can be confirmed by a study of the Party's policy on any issue whatsoever at the time of the first insurrection. 'Tailism – that is what characterized the Party leadership at that time,' writes Yang Hsiao-shen, a participant in the events of Shanghai.[1]

This tailism, this subordination of the Communist Party to the policy of the Kuomintang, characterizes not merely the period of the first insurrection but to a large extent the following period too, up to the August 1927 extraordinary conference which replaced the old opportunist leadership.

The causes indicated above for the first insurrection's failure were only possible because the leadership of the Chinese Communist Party took up an incorrect position on the following question: who should play the leading role in the revolution, the Kuomintang or the Communist Party? It was right to maintain the bloc with the Kuomintang and to fight side by side with it for the slogans of national revolution. But the Party should not for an instant have lost sight of the fact that the Kuomintang might, and indeed was inevitably bound to betray the revolution. It should ceaselessly have claimed the right to have its own policy in the national democratic revolution. It was essential for it to be aware always that the objectives of the national democratic revolution, in China as everywhere else, can only be completely achieved by proletarian revolution.

THE SECOND SHANGHAI INSURRECTION (22 FEBRUARY 1927)

After a certain pause in operations at the front (after Sun Ch'uan-fang's defeat in Kiangsi province), the offensive of the national army was relaunched in February; its aim was to crush Sun Ch'uan-fang definitively. On 17 February, the national troops (General Pai Ch'ung-hsi) occupied Hangchow and, on the 18th, the Chia-hsing station sixty kilometres south of Shanghai.

After long discussion, the Central Committee of the Communist

[1] Yang Hsiao-shen: 'The events in Shanghai in the spring of 1927', in *Documents on the Chinese Question*, no. 13, published by the Chinese Workers' University.

Party, in view of the favourable situation at the front, decided to declare a general strike in Shanghai, and to organize an armed rising as soon as the southern troops came within about thirty kilometres of the city (towards the Sung-ching station). Unlike the first insurrection, *this time* the Party leaders recognized the need to show more initiative and independence in the preparation and execution of the uprising.

Nevertheless, as early as the evening of 18 February, a meeting of the active trade-union militants of Shanghai – estimating, under the impact of the Southern army's victories on the Shanghai front, that Sun Ch'uan-fang had been definitively crushed – unanimously decided to declare an immediate general strike and call the workers to insurrection. The Central Committee representative attending the meeting was obliged to support this decision. The strike was declared, and started on 19 February. It reached its peak on the 20th, with more than 200,000 organized workers on strike.

The balance of armed forces in the city was as follows: the Communist Party had 130 squad members armed with Mauser revolvers, and about 3,000 without arms. In addition, thanks to the work which had been done in the fleet, it enjoyed an immense influence among the sailors. Of the four gunboats on the Huang-p'u river, the Party could count absolutely on one, and possessed cells on the others – so that it was legitimate to suppose that, given favourable circumstances during the insurrection, these three too would come over to the revolutionary side. The Party had no other armed forces. Niu Yung-ch'ien's men had dispersed after the first insurrection, taking the arms which had been distributed to them. Yü Ho-teh had lost all his forces too.

With respect to trained military leaders, the situation was pretty bad. There were very few of them, and those who were available to the Party had only been appointed immediately prior to the rising, so that they had not been able to get to know their men or study the city and the various tactical objectives. This circumstance was to have unfortunate consequences during the course of operations.

On 19 February, Sun Ch'uan-fang's authorities had 500 soldiers and 2,000 police at their disposal in Shanghai. The rest of their forces were at the front. Thus the balance of forces in the city was more favourable on this occasion than at the time of the first attempt, in October 1926.

Events moved very fast. The general strike had been called by others, and the Central Committee was confronted with a *fait accompli*. With the exception of one member, it had only learnt of the trade-union militants' decision at about noon on 19 February, after the strike had already begun. Hurriedly, it had to resolve a whole series of questions relating to the coming insurrection (how the new government was to be formed, etc.), and take a whole series of preparatory measures. The whole of 19 February was spent in preparations of this kind, and in discussion. The Party as a whole, especially the leadership, was in no sense prepared for insurrection.

On 20 February, it became clear that the attack on Shanghai from the south had been suspended and that the army was waiting for reinforcements. Sun Ch'uan-fang's representatives, aware of this development, began to employ terror against the strikers. Some were executed. Sun Ch'uan-fang put out a manifesto declaring every striker a traitor punishable by death.

The suspension of the offensive from the South and the terror against the strikers faced the Party leaders with a new question: whether to call off the strike, or whether to continue it with the aim of transforming it into an armed insurrection? Three opinions were voiced: one favoured calling off the strike, a second was for continuing the strike and organizing an insurrection to seize power in Shanghai, and the third wanted a continuation of the strike without any insurrection being organized.

In the end, after long discussions, it was decided to continue the strike and to fix the insurrection for 21 February, at 6 p.m. However the insurrection did not take place then, because the signal for it to begin was never given. The action was supposed to start after a gunboat salvo had been fired. The salvo was not fired, for some material reason or other. The squad members dispersed. Later, the Party leadership gave its sanction to the *de facto* situation. All this lowered the squad members' morale, and had a disastrous influence on subsequent events.

The insurrection was fixed a second time, for 6 p.m. on 22 February. However, circumstances had changed appreciably in the interim in favour of Sun Ch'uan-fang. Secure in his relatively stable position on the front (since the Southern troops had halted their offensive), he set about repressing the strike movement with increasing severity, and stepped up the executions of workers. Since the communists proved unable to draw the railway-workers into the strike, he quickly transported an infantry battalion to Shanghai to reinforce the garrison,

By 21 February, only 100,000 workers were still out on strike; the rest had been driven back to work by the wave of terror.

The plan for the rising involved a gunboat opening fire at exactly 6 p.m. on the arsenal, the barracks, the garrison commander's head-quarters (General Li Pao-chang), and a group of houses belonging to government officials.

Simultaneously, in the various districts of the city, the squad members would disarm the police and seize the administrative build-ings. The captured arms would be given to those who had none and to the workers. In addition, once the shelling had started, a detachment of 100 workers was to proceed to the gunboat to receive seventy rifles promised by the sailors.

The insurrection began at the appointed hour, and the four gun-boats opened fire. Their first target was the arsenal, which soon hoisted the white flag as a sign of surrender; they then turned their attention to the barracks, the railway station, and the garrison com-mander's headquarters, firing for two and a half hours without stopping.

The squad members who were to receive the seventy rifles failed in their mission because the craft which was supposed to take them out to the gunboat did not arrive in time. Thus the objectives which had been conquered by the artillery fire could not effectively be occupied.

In the southern part of Shanghai, the insurgents were strikingly successful. However, in P'u-tung (one of the working-class districts), after a short battle with superior numbers of police, the squad members dispersed. And Cha-pei (the biggest working-class centre, in the northern part of the city) did not take part in the rising at all because its squad members had not heard the cannonfire (the north and south of Shanghai were separated by the French concession and the international quarter, approximately ten kilometres). After waiting for the signal for some time, they dispersed.

In view of this situation (the south receiving no support from the north; the strike declining; the failure in P'u-tung), the insurrectionary leadership decided during the night of 22/23 February to give the order to halt operations.

The reasons for the defeat were clear. On the one hand, the move-ment had been adversely affected by the technical factors mentioned above: the lateness of the boat which was to enable the seventy rifles to be handed over, making it impossible to consolidate the success achieved by the gunboats; the timing of the insurrection not by a fixed hour but by an unreliable signal, with the result that Cha-pei remained inactive; the absence of any proper leadership or any liaison between the insurrectionary headquarters and the districts. Even given the fact that Cha-pei had failed to hear the signal and had not joined the battle, it was still the clear duty of the leadership, once the other districts had moved, to transmit the order to move to Cha-pei too, even at that late hour. There was inadequate intelligence on the situation at the front. Liaison between the districts and the insurrectionary command was poor.

On the other hand, one of the key reasons for the failure of the insurrection was certainly *that it had been organized at a moment when the revolutionary movement of the masses was no longer mounting but declining. The favourable moment had passed. That moment was 20 February.* This fact could not fail to have a decisive influence on the outcome of the insurrection. In view of the situation in Shanghai, it would have been infinitely more correct for the Party to have invited the masses to rise on 20 February. The proletariat's morale was at its peak then, and the Party should have responded to Sun Ch'uan-fang's executions of strikers with acts of a more radical nature than a simple strike, i.e. with an insurrection. The real balance of forces also appeared to demand such a solution.

There is another question which must be posed here: since the Sun Ch'uan-fang authorities had succeeded in disorganizing the mass movement and obliging half the strikers to return to work immediately, should we not conclude that the fighting temper of the Shanghai proletariat was insufficient for a decisive action? It is difficult to give a categorical answer, but the question cannot be avoided. The conclusion is a very plausible one. *The Party, as was shown above, was utterly unprepared; it had not carried out enough agitation among the masses in favour of insurrection; it was not capable of drawing the railwaymen and other categories of the working class into the strike.*

Furthermore, the fact that the national army halted its advance towards Shanghai precisely on 19 and 20 February and the days which followed could not fail to affect the proletariat's morale.

THE THIRD SHANGHAI INSURRECTION (21 MARCH 1927)

The insurrection of 21 March 1927 – involving combined action by the army and by the revolutionary proletariat in the enemy's rear, and a bloc between the Communist Party and the Kuomintang – was a model both of organization and timing, and also of leadership and technical execution. Exemplary use was made of the experience of October 1926 and February 1927. In this insurrection, the Shanghai proletariat acted as the real leader of the four coalition forces (proletariat, bourgeoisie, peasants, urban poor). *The insurrection was mainly prepared and executed by the proletariat*; the bourgeoisie, which had played a considerable role in the two earlier insurrections, and even a dominant one in the first, was this time used simply as an auxiliary force. In the prevailing conditions, this represented an immense step forward.

Immediately after the defeat of 22 February, the Central Committee ordered the various Party organizations to study the reasons for the failure of the two previous actions, to draw the appropriate lessons and to prepare actively for a new insurrection. The situation at the front was such that the latter might very shortly become a practical necessity.

In spite of the proletariat's defeat on 22 February, Sun Ch'uan-fang had not dared to continue the terror which he had unleashed at the moment of the strike. The Communist Party took full advantage of this to prepare itself for new and decisive battles. The military preparations carried out between the second and third insurrections can be resumed as follows: (*a*) the Central Committee of the Communist Party decided to increase the number of combat-squad members from 2,000 to 5,000. The military leadership accomplished this task successfully within a very short space of time; (*b*) the command structure of the combat squads was reviewed, and new leaders appointed. By shortly before the 21 March insurrection all the squads had been given their definitive form, with a commander for every twenty or thirty men; (*c*) huge efforts were made to give the squad members, and above all their commanders, a military formation. Training exercises for both took place regularly; (*d*) a flexible and energetic high command was set up, to direct operations during the insurrection. This high command was provided with a special liaison detachment, and another detachment of scouts; (*e*) great attention was paid to studying the city from a tactical point of view. Each commander had to know his district perfectly, and the entire city at least in broad outline. He had to make a tactical estimate of every building to be occupied during the insurrection, of every street, etc. To this end, the commanders and squad members carried out a personal reconnaissance of the targets which were to be occupied; they studied the approaches to them, planned how barricades would be positioned in the event of their being obliged to fall back on the defensive, even studied the roofs of the main buildings with a view to selecting good firing positions, etc.; (*f*) some 100 new Mausers were purchased, to add to the fifty which remained from the second insurrection.

Up to the middle of March, the Party continued to be very poorly informed about the situation at the front. In fact, on 12 March the national army had resumed its general advance on Shanghai: the Party only learnt of this, and then in only the vaguest terms, on 16 March. At the same moment, it received information that the Southern army might be expected to arrive in Shanghai on the 20th or 22nd. In the light of this information, the Central Committee made all its preparations in such a way that the insurrection could be launched on the 20th or 22nd.

Concretely, it was decided that when the Southern troops reached the Sung-ching station in the direction of Hangchow, and the Ch'ang-chou station in the direction of Nanking, both some thirty kilometres from Shanghai, the Party would call the workers and petty bourgeoisie out on a general strike and organize an armed rising.

In connection with its preparations for the rising and its collaboration with the national army, the Party and in particular its military personnel carried out a great deal of work among the railwaymen of the Shanghai-Nanking line. At this time, troops were being sent by rail from Shantung province (governor Chang Tsung-ch'ang) to assist Sun Ch'uan-fang. On 8 March, the railwaymen of the Shanghai-Nanking line went on strike. A great part of the Shantung troops, it is true, had already been conveyed to their destinations; nevertheless, this strike on a line serving the front created huge difficulties for the enemy. Trains could only circulate when drivers and other crew-members could be found and compelled to work under armed guard. Between the second and third insurrections, and above all during the strike, the railwaymen, under orders from the Party's military organization, organized the derailing of military trains and disrupted traffic by every kind of diversion. In order to keep their transport-system working, the Shantung troops had to employ a huge quantity of men to protect the railroad.

The agitational work which the Communist Party carried out

among the railwaymen was exemplary and shows the correct way of operating in such cases, in the rear of 'one's' own army.

As for the political preparation of the proletariat and middle classes of Shanghai, the Party accomplished a great deal here too. Apart from its normal work of revolutionary mobilization of the proletarian and semi-proletarian masses, it achieved considerable results by preparing and calling a delegate assembly. This assembly was to elect an executive committee which, during the insurrection, would proclaim itself the supreme authority. A great deal of preparatory work for this assembly was carried out in all parts of the city. The first session took place on 12 March and elected a committee of twenty-six members, fifteen of whom were communists. During the insurrection, this executive committee, which included representatives from the various classes of the population, appointed from among its members the new revolutionary government of Shanghai, with communist participation.

On the morning of 21 March, it was learnt that the Southern troops might arrive that evening. The Sung-ching and Ch'ang-chou stations had been occupied. At once the Central Committee decided to proclaim a general strike starting at noon, and to launch the insurrection an hour later.

The balance of forces in the city at the start of the general strike was as follows. Apart from 6,000 unarmed squad members (the Party had already succeeded in recruiting 6,000 instead of the planned 5,000) and 150 armed men, the Party had nothing. The fleet, which had taken part in the second insurrection, had left its Shanghai moorings and was now lying off the fortress of P'u-tung. It was not possible to count on its help in time. The enemy had about a brigade of infantry in Shanghai, and an armed train manned by Russian white guards. In addition, it had the entire police force at its disposal, i.e. some 2,000 men.

According to the plan, the insurrection was to begin simultaneously in all districts (except for the foreign concessions) with the disarming of the police. Once this was done, the squad members were to proceed to prearranged rendezvous to be assigned new missions, mainly concerned with disarming the troops.

The strike began at noon. For about half an hour the whole city appeared dead. The entire proletariat was on strike, together with the major part of the petty bourgeoisie (shopkeepers, artisans, etc.). At

1 p.m. precisely, the disarming of the police began throughout Shanghai. *In well under an hour, the entire police force had been disarmed.* By 2 p.m. the insurgents already had some 1,500 rifles. Immediately after this, the insurgent forces attacked the main government installations and set about disarming the troops.

Serious fighting broke out in Cha-pei (near the North station, the Russian church and the Commercial Press publishing house). Finally, by 4 p.m. on the second day of the insurrection, the enemy (some 3,000 soldiers and an armoured train with white Russian instructors) was definitively crushed. After this last bastion had fallen, all Shanghai (with the exception of the foreign concessions and the international quarter) was in the hands of the insurgents.

On 22 March in the evening the troops of General Pai Ch'ung-hsi – subsequently the sorry hero of 12 April (when troops opened fire on a workers' demonstration) – entered Shanghai.

The leaders of the third insurrection had *timed the general strike and armed insurrection well.* This was an example of *good coordination between the army's operations outside Shanghai and revolutionary action within the city. The high point in what was an unprecedented upsurge of the Shanghai workers coincided with the approach of Chiang Kai-shek's troops and a state of chaos in the enemy's ranks.* Moreover, the operation was characterized by boldness and skill on the part of the combat squads in disarming the police and troops.

In the insurrection and struggle for power of 21 March Marx's thesis that 'insurrection is an art' was put into practice in the most exemplary fashion.

This victory of the Shanghai proletariat was purchased at the cost of two previous defeats. The masses learn by experience. The experience of the previous conflicts had shown the necessity, long before the insurrection, of preparing carefully and systematically for the decisive battle; the necessity of ensuring that this battle will be directed solely by the party of the proletariat. In the third Shanghai insurrection, the Chinese Communist Party made excellent use of this experience.

One is struck by *the astonishing discipline and aptitude for combat of the Shanghai working class.* A general strike is called for a specific hour, and at that precise instant all working-class Shanghai goes on strike. At one o'clock sharp the disarming of the police begins in every working-class district. What is more, this operation is carried out by workers who are for the most part unarmed (only possessing 150 Mausers all told).

It was only possible to carry out the general strike and insurrection with such precision *because of the enormous influence which the Communists wielded at the time in Shanghai over the working class and a fraction of the petty bourgeosie.*

Readers knowing anything about Chinese events in this period may, and indeed almost certainly will, pose the following question: if the morale of the Shanghai proletariat reached so high a degree of enthusiasm at the moment of the third insurrection, and if the Chinese Communist Party exerted so immense an influence on the working classes of the city, then it is incomprehensible why Soviet power was not proclaimed; why Chiang Kai-shek's reactionary generals were able to dissolve the government set up during the insurrection; and, finally, why the proletariat allowed itself to be disarmed. For, just one week after the insurrection, Chiang Kai-shek carried out a counter-revolutionary *coup d'état*, and the working class, which had seized power before the arrival of the Southern troops, was unable to profit by its victory.

In order to answer this question, which is a quite legitimate one, it is necessary to go back to the problems of overall political strategy which we mentioned earlier, when we examined the reasons for the first insurrection's failure.

Although it followed a basically correct line with respect to the organization, preparation and execution of the uprising, the Chinese Communist Party (or rather its leadership) followed *an incorrect line* vis-à-vis *the Kuomintang: it underestimated the revolutionary role of the proletariat, and continued to see the Kuomintang as an undifferentiated whole and the entire national bourgeoisie as a revolutionary force – whereas in fact a fraction of that bourgeoisie and hence of the Kuomintang (its right wing) had already openly entered the camp of counter-revolution and was willing to ally itself both with the indigenous forces of reaction and with foreign imperialism.*

This was the basic reason for the defeat of the Shanghai proletariat after Chiang Kai-shek's troops entered the city.

The Communist Party leadership did not see or did not want to see that Chiang Kai-shek's march on Shanghai had only been undertaken in order to win control of the city – seen by the militarists as the richest of prizes in terms of its material wealth. The idea was that in this way they would be able to free themselves from the influence of the left-wing government in Wuhan, countering Wuhan with Shanghai. The Central Committee knew very well that the campaign against Shanghai had been undertaken by Chiang Kai-shek without the authorization of the Wuhan government.

In spite of this, and although Chiang Kai-shek's policy, intentions and prolonged disagreements with Wuhan were known to the Central Committee, the latter prepared the insurrection purely and simply under the slogan of aid for the Southern troops. *The Party did not warn the working class of the danger which threatened it as a result of Chiang Kai-shek's offensive.* It hoped that it would succeed somehow in influencing Chiang Kai-shek and his henchmen, so that they would not dare carry out a reactionary policy in Shanghai or the area surrounding it. It continued to see the proletariat as an auxiliary force and not as the leader of the democratic revolution. For this reason, *it did not prepare the working-class masses to resist the attempts at counter-revolution which were only to be expected from Chiang Kai-shek.*

This is the explanation for the fact that the new government formed during the insurrection – in which several communists took part, side by side with Niu Yung-ch'ien and other members of the Kuomintang right wing – remained almost inactive, waiting until it was dissolved by Chiang Kai-shek. The communists did not try to influence the other members of the government, nor did they utilize their official positions to continue the revolutionary mobilization of the masses.

The Party did nothing to prevent the appointment of a right-wing Kuomintang member to command the police, and thereby in practice handed over all executive power in Shanghai to its class enemy. There was even worse to come; a part of the Central Committee wanted to allow the workers' guard to be disarmed and were ready to surrender the weapons to the military command. It should be noted that a part of these arms had already been given to the troops as a gift. If in the event all the arms were not given up, this was only at the insistence of the military leaders.

The Party leadership, in spite of the categorical orders received from the Communist International, in spite of the categorical demands of certain leading comrades, did nothing to spread a revolutionary spirit among the garrison. Proposals were made to enrol the mass of workers in the army, and to carry out intensive political agitation within the military units; but the leading fraction of the Party's central apparatus stuck obstinately to its positions.

The following episode, recounted by Yang Hsiao-shen in the article quoted earlier, characterizes the Communist leadership of the period perfectly. Among the garrison units, the most revolutionary was the 1st Division. Chiang Kai-shek, who had begun to apply his own policy immediately after occupying the city (he arrested the 'Left' Kuomintang secretary in Cha-pei; shot all the members of the political body appointed by the Wuhan government; dismissed such commanders as he considered unreliable; demanded that the workers' battalions should surrender their arms, etc.), ordered the 1st Division to leave Shanghai and set off for the front.

Thereupon the commander of the 1st Division, Hsüeh Yüeh, presented himself to the Party and asked the following question: I have received orders from Chiang Kai-shek to leave Shanghai. What should I do? If I do not obey, I shall have no alternative but to arrest Chiang Kai-Shek. In spite of the time that had been lost, the left still had a predominant influence in Nanking, Soochow and Shanghai itself. But no clear reply was made to this proposal for a decisive attack upon Chiang Kai-shek. Hsüeh Yüeh was advised to sabotage his orders, to pretend that he was ill. However, the moment came when it was impossible to procrastinate further. Hsüeh Yüeh received an ultimatum, and when he turned to the Party there was no third choice: either he could take up arms against Chiang Kai-shek, with the support and under the orders of the Communist Party; or he could obey Chiang Kai-shek's order and remove from Shanghai a strong force of great revolutionary worth.

After the departure of the 1st Division, Chiang Kai-shek dissolved the government and disarmed the workers' battalions.

These are the essential facts which characterized the opportunist policy of the Communist leaders in the period of the bloc with the Kuomintang. This policy caused the defeat of the proletariat in March 1927. As the Comintern indicated, the Communist Party should – even while maintaining the bloc with the Kuomintang – have fought simultaneously for an autonomous policy of the proletariat in the democratic revolution.

Moreover, the situation in Shanghai and the balance of forces were such that the proletariat had every right to expect some decisive action from the Party.

7

Communist Activity
to Subvert the Armed Forces
of the Ruling Classes

The Communist International has made frequent pronouncements in its official resolutions on the attitude which the proletariat should adopt towards the bourgeois army. But with the theses on the struggle against imperialist war and on the tasks of the communists which were adopted by the Sixth World Congress after comrade Bell's report, the international revolutionary proletariat now possesses a detailed programme, in accordance with the doctrine of Marx, Engels and Lenin, on the problems of war and on the proletariat's stance with respect to the various types of war and types of army in the various phases of the proletarian revolution. These theses provide a clear orientation for the tactics of the Party, and of the entire revolutionary proletariat, in relation to the various types of army – according to their character (armies based on compulsory military service; militias or mercenary armies; imperialist armies; bourgeois volunteer organizations; national-democratic armies), and according to the class aims which they serve. The enormous importance of these theses resides in the fact that problems of war and military questions are not dealt with abstractly or academically, but in close relation with the entire policy and tactics of the revolutionary party in preparing and organizing the proletarian revolution.

It is enormously important, both in principle and also in practice, to pose correctly the question of relations between the proletariat and the army, and the line to be followed in this domain. *The army is the key element in the organization of the State. Upon its stability and its general condition depends the stability of the State as a whole. Upon the degree of disaffection within a bourgeois army depends in great measure the proletariat's chance of overthrowing the bourgeoisie and smashing the bourgeois State in the event of an immediately revolutionary situation* – when the question of overthrowing the bourgeois class in practice has to be placed on the immediate agenda.

The history of all revolutions shows that if an army and police force with good military training, provided with every modern technique of attack and defence (machine-guns, armoured vehicles, chemical weapons, air power, etc.) and with good commanders, and supported by the armed fascist detachments which exist in every country today, *fight effectively against the revolution, they are capable of rendering the latter's victory singularly difficult even if all the other conditions are favourable.*

Lenin said: 'Of course, unless the revolution assumes a mass character and affects the troops, there can be no question of serious struggle.'[1]

It is certainly beyond doubt that in periods of crisis, when there is an acute revolutionary situation, the army and police cannot escape the influence of the prevailing revolutionary mood. By virtue of their class composition, the revolutionary ferment will make itself felt among them in some degree or other. Nevertheless, it would be naïve to suppose it possible for the army, or even parts of the army, to go over openly to the camp of revolution without some prior work by the revolutionary party. It would be naïve to suppose that the revolutionary process will on its own take root and develop in the army and police. The revolutionary party must carry out political and organizational work in the army and police, both before the immediately revolutionary situation and above all during it. The more intensive this work is, the stronger the revolutionary ferment among the troops and their hesitation between revolution and counter-revolution will be, and the more numerous will be the individual units going over to the proletariat. Throughout the insurrection, this political and organizational activity within the army must be combined with methods of physical struggle against the latter.

In Germany, if a proper revolutionary agitation had in fact been carried out in the Reichswehr and police units (which was perfectly possible despite the Reichswehr's isolation), the chiefs of staff would certainly not have been able to send their troops to occupy revolutionary Saxony and Thuringia so easily as was in fact the case in September–October 1923. In Estonia during the autumn of 1924, if the *proper organization* (communist cells, groups of revolutionary soldiers, etc.) had existed in the army, the very considerable influence which the Communist Party already enjoyed among the troops would have made

[1] *Collected Works*, vol. 11, p. 174, in 'Lessons of the Moscow Uprising'.

it impossible for the forces of reaction to repress the Reval insurrection of 1 December so swiftly. Finally, if the Chinese Communist Party in Kwangtung province had been able to carry out, even to a small degree, activity of this kind to subvert and win over politically the troops of Chiang Fa-kuei, Li Chi-shen and Li Fu-lin *sent to crush red Canton* (we are not speaking here of the training regiment, or of many other units in which the Party organization had worked brilliantly), then the outcome of the battle would certainly have been different. Furthermore, the Canton insurrection began precisely with the revolt of a military unit, the training regiment, without which a general uprising would have been impossible in the conditions prevailing in Canton in early December 1927.

In all past insurrections without exception (Shanghai, Petrograd, Moscow, Cracow, the various German risings, etc.), the decisive role has always been played by the army. The actual outcome of the revolution very often depends on the degree of sympathy for the revolution in the army, and on the extent to which its commanding officers can use it against the revolutionary proletariat. For the passage of power from one class into the hands of another class is ultimately decided by material strength. And the army is the key element of that strength.

It is not solely *in the aftermath of a war* (*when it is inevitable*) that the situation in a given country may and doubtless will become revolutionary; *it may and doubtless will do so equally well in a period of 'peace', in spite of the temporary stabilization of capitalism.*

The civil wars in Germany in 1920 and 1923, in Bulgaria in 1923, in Estonia in 1924 and in Vienna in July 1927, prove that proletarian civil war may not only break out in times of bourgeois imperialist wars, but also in the present 'normal conditions' of capitalism; for present-day capitalism intensifies the class struggle to an acute degree and at any moment may create an immediate revolutionary situation.[2]

But this in no way leads to the conclusion arrived at by the rightist elements in the Comintern who claim that revolution is only possible in the aftermath of a war. The conclusion which flows from it is simply that preparation for insurrection must be carried on simultaneously by means of agitation in the army on the one hand, and on the other by the formation of actual proletarian armed forces, capable of

[2] *Theses and Resolutions of the Sixth World Congress of the Communist International*, 'The Struggle against Imperialist War and the Tasks of the Communists', section 24.

fighting with arms in their hands against that fraction of the regular army which has not yet been subverted. For it must not be forgotten that when the insurrection is launched, the struggle for the army will have to be waged with arms too. But the more the subversion of the bourgeois army is advanced, the stronger will the armed forces of the proletariat be, and the easier will be the struggle during the insurrection itself. The reverse is also true.

In time of war this principle retains all its importance. It is necessary to be aware that the slogan of transforming the imperialist war into a civil war *will remain nothing but an empty phrase unless the revolutionary party carries out regular work in the army in as serious a fashion as possible.*

Referring to the decision of the International Metalworkers' Federation, meeting in Hanover, on the need to respond to war by declaring a strike, Lenin wrote in a memo addressed to the members of the Political Bureau:

Pose the question of the anti-war struggle at the next Plenary session of the Comintern Executive Committee, and adopt detailed resolutions explaining that only a revolutionary party which has been tested and prepared in advance, with a good illegal apparatus, can successfully wage the anti-war campaign; that the correct means of struggle is not an anti-war strike, but *the organization of revolutionary cells in the belligerent armies and their preparation for making the revolution.*[3]

But this work of organization and political agitation among the troops in wartime will be made very much easier if the Party has already embarked upon it systematically in advance, when it is still peacetime.

One of the most serious mistakes the Communist Parties have committed hitherto, is that they regarded the war question from the abstract, purely propagandist and agitational point of view, and that they did not devote sufficient attention to the army, which is the decisive factor in all wars. *Unless the significance of the revolutionary policy in the war question is explained to the broad masses, and unless work is carried on in the army, the struggle against imperialist war and attempts to prepare for revolutionary wars will never reach beyond the stage of theory.*[4]

The Communist International has frequently stressed the importance of work in the army and navy. Yet numerous sections – and even a Party like that of China, which has frequently been confronted with the problem of armed struggle against militarist armies; a party which the

[3] Quoted in *Pravda,* 20 January 1929.
[4] *Theses and Resolutions of the Sixth World Congress of the Communist International,* 'The Struggle against Imperialist War and the Tasks of the Communists', section 41. Neuberg's emphasis.

new upsurge of the revolutionary wave would inevitably oblige to organize and carry out a general proletarian uprising – have until recently (i.e. until the beginning of 1928) underrated the importance of the Comintern's decisions, and have carried on almost no work in this field, except in a few isolated areas.

The essential principle for every revolutionary party is that it should carry out revolutionary work wherever the masses are concentrated. The bourgeois armies and navies always contain tens or even hundreds of thousands of young proletarians or peasants who are no less susceptible to revolutionary slogans and ideas than the factory workers or certain categories of peasants. In view of the fact that the army, the police and the navy are the main instruments of constraint, the principle means by which the bourgeois State (and every other non-socialist State) combats the revolutionary proletariat, the need for revolutionary work within their ranks *cannot be exaggerated*. A party which directly or indirectly renounces this crucial field of revolutionary activity exposes itself to consequences which are extremely deleterious to the revolution. *Such activity must be pursued tirelessly by the entire Communist Party, both in periods when the revolutionary forces are being built up, and even more during periods of revolutionary upsurge. We consider that such agitation, in the light of the considerations outlined above, is as essential as the Party's work in a whole series of other domains (winning the middle classes, etc., etc.).*

Agitation in the army is frequently non-existent or insufficient because it is extremely difficult and involves many risks. This is especially true of mercenary armies like those of China, and of certain European armies: Bulgaria, Germany, etc. Obviously, the structure of an army, military discipline, the isolation of soldiers from the population, etc., create enormous difficulties. The bourgeoisie resorts to terror against any parties which carry out revolutionary work in the army. *But that only means that every communist party must carry out such work with all the more energy, resolution and persistence.*

The main objective of work in the army, navy and police (or gendarmerie) *is to bring the mass of soldiers, sailors and police, into the common front of the proletarian class struggle ; it is to ensure that the soldiers know and adopt the Communist Party's slogans and objectives.*

The activity of the Party and Young Communist League to subvert the bourgeois army and navy must be carried out on two main levels: (*a*) inside the army and the fleet; (*b*) through the general activity of the

Party as a whole outside the army: e.g. the parliamentary group's activity on military questions; agitation by word of mouth or via the press to popularize some particular slogan within the army, etc., etc.

These two modes of action, inside the army and outside it, *must be intimately linked, under the direction of a single centre*, the Central Committee of the Party.

The methods and forms of propaganda and agitation in the army vary from country to country. Every Communist Party, orienting itself in the light of local conditions in its own country and army, must work out the appropriate forms and modes. The essential thing here is that the subversion of the bourgeois army must be pursued as energetically as possible; that the work of the Party's military organization inside the army (such an organization must be created) and the work of the Party as a whole to subvert the army, should *be closely related to everyday political activity and to the slogans which the Party issues regularly to guide practical, day-to-day struggles.*

Revolutionary work within bourgeois armies and navies almost everywhere is bound to be strictly illegal and clandestine. The bourgeoisie is prepared to devote all its efforts and all its resources to protect its armed forces against any revolutionary influence liable to subvert them; it enforces draconian measures against any revolutionary elements discovered within them. Nevertheless, with the sharpening of the class struggle, and in particular with the approach of an immediately revolutionary situation (whether this is in a 'peaceful' period or in wartime), in other words *when an open struggle for the army begins between the proletariat and the ruling classes,* then the scope of the Party's secret work increases progressively, and ever greater numbers of soldiers, inspired by the communist slogans, are drawn into the revolutionary struggle. At such moments, the revolutionary Party has to achieve the correct combination of secret methods inside the army with revolutionary mass action to win the latter over.

An excellent illustration of this is provided by Bolshevik activity inside the army during the various phases of the Russian revolution. From 1902 onwards, the Bolshevik Party carried out a tireless clandestine revolutionary agitation in the Tsarist army. During the 1905 revolution, in a number of garrisons this activity had reached a scale which permitted it genuinely to affect the masses. The Bolsheviks knew how to combine organized secret activity with mass agitation among the troops. After the defeat of the 1905 revolution, when the

Party was obliged by the Tsarist terror to resort to clandestine methods as it prepared the masses for new revolutionary battles, its work in the army took on a yet more secret character. This situation lasted right up to the revolution of February 1917. Nevertheless, immediately after the overthrow of the Tsarist government, the Bolshevik Party began mass activity among the troops on a vast scale. Clandestine methods gave way to legal methods of subversion: communist cells, soldiers' committees, conferences of soldiers' delegates, soldiers' newspapers, etc., etc.

The real Leninist policy of the revolutionary proletariat with respect to imperialist war is to transform the latter into a civil war. With respect to the army – the main factor in imperialist war – the strategy of the Party and the revolutionary proletariat as a whole must aim at the total disintegration of the imperialist army, and at the passage of its soldiers into the proletarian camp. This is the final aim of all agitation inside the army. It can only be achieved completely with the victory of the proletarian revolution. As long as power remains in the hands of the bourgeois State, the bourgeois army will subsist as one of the key elements of that State. *The aim of the proletariat – independently of the political situation of the country – is to subvert the bourgeois army as much as possible and infuse it with revolutionary ideas.*

In order to win the bourgeois army over to revolution, and in order to weaken it generally, it is necessary to rely to a considerable extent on agitation for partial demands, and on the revolutionary struggle to reform various aspects of military life under the bourgeois State. In every country – depending on the nature of the regular armed forces, the method of recruitment, the length and character of service in the conscript units, the material and juridical situation of both officers and soldiers, etc. – the partial demands of the proletariat on military matters will vary. The revolutionary party, at every given moment, must present partial demands whose realization will on the one hand interest the mass of soldiers and on the other be comprehensible, in the given concrete situation, to the greatest possible number of workers.

Here is how the Sixth Comintern Congress defines the aims of the communists with respect to partial demands on military matters:

In conducting the struggle for revolution and for Socialism, we do not refuse to bear arms. The aim of our struggle is to expose the militarization the imperialists introduce for the benefit of the bourgeoisie.

As against this sort of militarization we advance the slogan: Arm the proletariat. Simultaneously, the Communists must advance and give support to the partial demands of the soldiers which, in a concrete situation, stimulate the class struggle in the armies and strengthen the alliance between the proletarian and peasant soldiers and the workers outside the ranks of the army.

The partial demands are approximately as follows:

1. *Demands in Connection with the System of Defence*: Dissolution of mercenary forces; dissolution of standing and principal military units; disarming and dissolution of the gendarmerie, police and other special armed forces for civil war; disarming and dissolution of Fascist Leagues; concrete demands for the reduction of period of military service; introduction of the territorial system of military service; abolition of compulsory residence in barracks; soldiers' committees; the right of labour organizations to train their members in the use of arms, with the right to the free selection of instructors. . . .

In the case of volunteer, mercenary armies, the demand should not be for the reduction of the period of military service, but for the right to leave the service whenever the soldier desires.

2. *Demands in Connection with the Legal Rights and Economic Position of the Soldiers*: Increased pay for soldiers; improved maintenance; the establishment of stores committees composed of soldiers' representatives; abolition of disciplinary punishments; abolition of compulsory saluting; severe penalties for officers and non-commissioned officers inflicting corporal punishment on private soldiers; the right to wear mufti when off duty; the right to be absent from barracks every day; furlough, and extra pay while on furlough; the right to marry; maintenance for soldiers' families; the right to subscribe to newspapers; the right to organize in trade unions; the right to vote; the right to attend political meetings.

The fact that in numerous imperialist countries a considerable percentage of the armies are recruited from among oppressed national minorities, whereas the officers either entirely or for the greater part belong to the oppressing nation, provides very favourable ground for revolutionary work in the army. Consequently, among the partial demands we advance in the interests of the masses of the soldiers should be included demands corresponding to the needs of these oppressed nationalities (for example: military service in their home district; the use of the native language in drilling and instruction, etc.).[5]

This list of partial demands could easily be extended. Only the most important have been mentioned here – those which can be presented on behalf of the soldiers of most capitalist States.

The theses continue:

The demands of both of the above-mentioned categories (only a few of which have been enumerated) must not only be put forward in the army but also outside it – in parliament, at mass meetings, etc. Propaganda in support of these demands

[5] ibid., section 45–6.

will be successful only if they bear a concrete character. In order that they may do so it is necessary:

1. To have a close acquaintance with the army, with the conditions of service, with the needs and demands of the soldiers, etc., which can only be acquired by maintaining close personal contact with the army.

2. To give consideration to the system of defence in the given States and to the situation in regard to the military question at the given moment.

3. To take into consideration the morale of the army and the political situation in the country at the given moment. For example, the demand for the election of officers, as a rule, can be advanced only when the army has reached an advanced stage of disintegration.

4. To link up closely partial demands with the principal slogans of the Communist Party – arming the proletariat, proletarian militia, etc.

These demands will have revolutionary significance only if they are linked up with a distinct political programme for revolutionizing the bourgeois army.

Special attention must be paid to organizing the soldiers for the protection of their interests, in alliance with the revolutionary proletariat, prior to their being called up for service (recruits' leagues, mutual aid clubs), during the period of military service (soldiers' councils) and also after the conclusion of military service (revolutionary ex-servicemen's leagues). It must be the special task of the trade unions to maintain contact with their members in the army and to help them to form the above-mentioned organizations.

The conditions for revolutionary work in volunteer armies differ from the conditions for such work in conscript armies. In volunteer armies it is usually much more difficult to carry on agitation in support of partial demands like those mentioned above. Nevertheless, the work must be undertaken. The fact that in a majority of cases volunteer armies are recruited from among the proletariat (the unemployed) and from among the poor peasants, provides a social base for mass work among the soldiers. The forms of this work must be carefully adapted to the social composition and the special features of the troops. Strenuous agitation must be carried on among the masses against the special forces the bourgeoisie organize for class struggle against the proletariat (gendarmes and police) and especially against their volunteer forces (the Fascists). The reformists who talk loudly about the 'public utility' of these forces, about the 'national police' and about Fascist 'equality' must be relentlessly combated with particular energy, and every effort must be made to rouse a passionate hatred among the people towards these forces and to expose their real character. But every effort must be made to stimulate social differentiation even among those forces and to win over the proletarian elements in them.

Revolutionary work in the army must be linked up with the general revolutionary movement of the masses of the proletariat and poor peasantry. If an immediate revolutionary situation prevails, and if the industrial proletariat is beginning to establish Soviets, the slogan – 'Establish Soldiers' Councils' – assumes immediate practical importance and facilitates the work of uniting the masses of the soldiers with the proletariat and the poor peasantry in their struggle for power.[6]

[6] ibid., section 47–9.

The promoters of revolutionary activity within the army and navy must be *the clandestine communist and young communist cells* (who as the revolutionary situation approaches will become legal or semi-legal), *or, in units where there are no communists, the groups of revolutionary soldiers.*

The establishment of these bridgeheads within the fundamental units of the army and the fleet (companies, squadrons, batteries, artillery-parks, support units, headquarters, warships, etc.) *demands of every communist party the most serious attention.* To this end, it is necessary before the call-up of recruits or reservists to draw up a list of all communists or young communists among them, and to give these detailed instructions on how to act in the army, on how to maintain contact with the Party, etc. *Without the creation of a solid military organization of the Party in the army and navy, there can be no question of revolutionary work among the soldiers and sailors.*

Even more attention must be paid to agitation among the troops, and to the creation of communist cells in the areas and garrisons *whose influence will be decisive* for the victory of the revolution (capital cities, great industrial centres, etc.) – i.e. wherever power will have to be seized at once and wherever it will be necessary to create bases or revolutionary centres from which the revolution can be spread to other areas. The Party will have to send a larger number of militants and more resources into these regions than into the others.

It must be borne in mind that the success of agitation in the army will to a large extent depend on the social composition of each unit. In every army there exist units and services into which, because of their social composition, the Party can never hope to inject elements of class struggle. These are the officer-cadet schools, the special forces, often the cavalry – which in many countries is recruited exclusively from the rich peasant strata – and other similar units. These units can and must be smashed purely by the force of arms of the insurgent proletariat. By contrast, in its military propaganda the Party should aim above all at the artillery and the technical services, in which the proportion of workers is normally higher than in the other units. The same is of course true for the infantry and the sailors.

As for the possibility of winning junior officers over to the revolution, experience has shown that in peacetime the hopes of doing this are very slender. It goes without saying that the Party must never renounce the possibility of using revolutionary officers to subvert some particular unit. Nevertheless, its activity in general must be aimed at the mass of ordinary soldiers.

Here is what the resolution of the 1906 conference of military and combat organizations of the Social Democratic Labour Party (Bolshevik) stated about Party agitation among the officers:

Whereas: (1) the class, social composition of the corps of officers and their interests as a professional military caste compel them to strive for the retention of the regular army and the underprivileged position of the people; (2) in view of this, the officers, as a body, play a reactionary part in the present bourgeois-democratic revolution; (3) the existing oppositionally-minded groups of officers do not play an active part and (4) at the same time it is possible that individual officers may come over to our Party and they may, in view of their specialized knowledge and special military training, render considerable services during an uprising of the army and its defection to the side of the people, and also in technical preparations for an armed uprising –
the conference of military and combat organizations recognizes: (1) that they cannot build up an independent Social Democratic military organization among the officers: (2) that it is essential to use the existing oppositionally-minded groups of officers for purposes of information and in order to draw into our Party military and combat organizations individuals who can serve as instructors and practical leaders.[7]

The cells of communists and young communists inside army units – just like the cells in factories, firms, trade unions and in general in the various mass organizations of the proletariat – are representatives of the Party, and in their activity within the unit in question must apply the Party line on all questions without exception. The communist military organization in the army does not and cannot have a political line of its own; it is simply a fraction of the Party, and must put into practice the latter's general political line.

In an immediate revolutionary situation, at the moment at which the Party calls on the masses to rise and seize power, the basic objective of the communist cells in the army *will be to present an open opposition to the reactionary commanding officers, and to draw the mass of soldiers behind them to carry out revolutionary tasks together with the proletariat.*

The 1906 conference of military and combat organizations of the Social Democratic Party (Bolshevik), in a resolution on the aims of the military organizations within the army, defined these aims in the following way:

[7] *The Communist Party and the Army,* Moscow, 1928, p. 49. Quoted in Lenin, *Collected Works,* vol. 12, p. 414, in 'Apropos of the Minutes of the November Military and Combat Conference of the Russian Social Democratic Labour Party'.

The aims of the military organizations at the present time are: (*a*) the creation of solid social-democratic cells in each troop unit; (*b*) the grouping of all revolutionary elements in the army around these cells and by their agency, with the aim of securing their active support for the popular demands and of persuading them to pass over openly to the side of the people in arms; (*c*) a perfect coordination of their own activity with that of other proletarian forces, including the combat organizations; the subordination of all their work to the general requirements of the moment, and to the political leadership of the collective organizations of the proletariat. Furthermore, the conference considers: 1) that the actual character of agitation in the army must be determined by the objectives being pursued by the proletariat (as vanguard of the people in arms); 2) that these objectives, and the very composition of the army units which are susceptible of being won over to the revolution, indicate the path to be followed in order to obtain *maximum results for social democratic propaganda and agitation within the army, and to ensure the Party's ideological and organizational influence*; 3) that only combined work by all the military organizations of the Social Democratic Party, carried out in the way indicated above, can guarantee that broad democratic strata of the army will pass over to the side of the people in arms.[8]

The military organization, if it is to be capable of carrying out its functions, must be in close liaison with the local organization of the Party. In view of the special conditions of its work, this liaison will be carried out by delegates appointed by the Party authorities to organize work in the army. The Party's delegate (organizer) will receive from the military cells, from the communists and young communists and from non-Party but politically reliable soldiers, all necessary information about the state of the unit in question (where its various sections are positioned, how many officers it has, what the morale of the troops is like, how its daily routine is organized, etc.). He will then in turn give the cells and the individual comrades instructions about what they should be doing and the methods they should employ, and will supply them with literature (Party newspapers, leaflets, appeals), etc.

The specific conditions of agitation in the army (clandestinity) make it essential for the Party authorities to assign an adequate number of militants to this work. These must be absolutely reliable politically. It will sometimes be necessary to put them through special crash courses, in which they can be taught all that is necessary about methods of work in the army (about the techniques of clandestine work). The Party organizations, in their turn, must organize training sessions on the subject for communist or young communist soldiers. Strict observation of the rules governing illegal activity in normal (non-

[8] *The Communist Party and the Army*, Moscow, 1928, p. 47.

revolutionary) periods is of considerable importance in view of the police inquisition and the terror wreaked by government authorities on individuals or organizations who carry out propaganda in the army.

With respect to work in the army, the sections of the Communist International can draw useful lessons from the history of the Bolshevik Party.

Here is what Yaroslavsky said about Bolshevik work in the army before the Revolution in his speech to the Sixth World Congress of the Comintern:

Amidst severe conditions of illegality we had in the years 1905–7 *twenty illegal papers* devoted to revolutionary propaganda in the army. Every big garrison town like Reval, Riga, Dvinsk, Batum, Odessa, Ekaterinoslav, Warsaw, Sveaborg, Kronstadt, St Petersburg, Moscow and other places had its *soldiers' paper* which was distributed by the members of the illegal organizations in those districts as well as by workers who had contacts with the army. As far as the number of *leaflets* published is concerned, I must say that there was hardly a single political event of any importance upon which we did not issue a leaflet for the soldiers. These leaflets were printed in large numbers, several thousand each. These were not only distributed in garrison cities but throughout whole military areas, and every single opportunity was taken to get them distributed.

Our form of *organization* was as follows: we had in mind the fact that the army was not homogeneous in character, and we did not set out at all costs to get all the sections of the troops over to our side but selected those sections which by their class position were best able to accept our revolutionary propaganda. We selected those units in which there were large numbers of workers, as for example the artillery, the engineers, technical troops, seamen in the navy, and concentrated our attention upon these. In modern armies these military units, the artillery, the technical troops and the navy are of extreme importance. We can expect to have the least success among the cavalry, which consists mainly of well-to-do peasants especially in western Europe where the cavalry is recruited principally from among the rich peasants.

Wherever possible we established in every military unit a small *secret group* which represented the *illegal regimental and battalion committees*, which maintained contact with our secret *military nuclei* outside the barracks. Needless to say all contacts between the military organizations were maintained in strict secrecy. We selected the members very carefully, never being concerned about numbers, and these organizations were never regarded as a complete force capable of undertaking independent action. We regarded them rather as an organized force which, at the necessary moment, could win over to our side the sympathetic soldiers and sailors. Although we never set out to get large numbers I must say that we had organizations in Kronstadt, Sebastopol and other places in which we had several hundred men. . . .

Notwithstanding the extremely severe illegal conditions, we managed to organize a number of *military conferences*. In the spring of 1906 we convened such a conference in Moscow. Although nearly all the delegates were arrested at the first session, the conference had some effect. In November 1906 we convened a rather large conference of military organizations in Tammafors in Finland. Lenin wrote a special article on this conference in which he deals very fully with the resolutions passed at the conference and with the significance of the conference itself.[9]

The other communist parties (France, Germany, etc.) have also acquired in recent years a pretty extensive experience of agitation in the army and navy. Unfortunately, for very understandable reasons, this experience cannot become the patrimony of the entire international proletariat (it is impossible, for security reasons, to print information about the Party's illegal work in the army and navy). It should, however, be stressed that in certain countries this work in the army has given and continues to give very significant results in those garrisons and military units where it has been organized seriously.

As for this kind of work in an immediate revolutionary situation or in wartime, we must look at the history of the struggle organized and carried out by the Bolshevik Party after the February Revolution to win over the army to the revolution. Describing that work is no part of our plan here – it has already been done in numerous pamphlets, newspaper articles and books. It should only be pointed out that the sections of the Communist International possess here an inexhaustible supply of previous teachings on the methods of political and organizational work to be applied in order to win the mass of soldiers to the revolution, and in order to incorporate them in the common front in the struggle to overthrow the power of the bourgeoisie and the big landowners.

The attitude of the proletariat towards the armies of colonial or semi-colonial countries will be very different from its attitude towards imperialist armies. There exist different types of army in the colonies and semi-colonies: imperialist armies of occupation; national democratic armies fighting for the country's independence; reactionary armies of military units marching with imperialism against movements of national liberation, etc.

In order to determine the attitude to be taken towards the military system in colonial and semi-colonial countries, consideration must be given to the political

[9] Speech during discussion on the reports on methods of struggle against the dangers of imperialist war – Comrade Yaroslavsky (CPSU), in *Proceedings of the Sixth World Congress of the Communist International*.

role being played by the given country at the given moment, i.e., whether it is an ally or a foe of the Soviet Union, of the Chinese Revolution, etc. On the whole, the proletariat, and the revolutionary masses among the oppressed nations, must demand the democratic system of armaments in which all the toilers are able to learn the use of arms, which will improve the defence of the country against imperialism, secure the influence of the workers and peasants in the army, and facilitate the struggle for the hegemony of the proletariat in the democratic revolution.

Unlike the position in regard to the imperialist states, the slogans: universal military service, the military training of the youth, a democratic militia, a national army, etc., must be included in the revolutionary military programme in colonial and semi-colonial countries. In the present historical epoch, however, the tactics of the national revolutionary movement must be subordinated to the interests of the world proletarian revolution. Revolutionaries cannot advance such a programme in oppressed countries which are themselves oppressors and act as the vassals of the imperialists in a war against proletarian or national revolution. In such countries, Communists must unfailingly combine their propaganda in favour of revolutionary war for the defence of other revolutionary countries, and their propaganda in favour of a revolutionary military policy, with a defeatist position in relation to the given war or army. Such a position must be taken up at the present time in those provinces in China which are under the rule of Kuomintang generals.[10]

In the colonies or semi-colonies, where imperialist armies or those of reactionary political groupings allied with or subject to the imperialists are concerned, we must aim to disintegrate them totally, and in the case of the former to expel them from the country in question. On the other hand, where armies of national liberation are concerned – i.e. armies which are not in all aspects revolutionary but which none the less struggle against foreign imperialism and local reaction for the victory of national independence and the democratic revolution (for example, the national armies of China during the Northern expedition in 1926 and early 1927, or before that the armies of Kwangtung) – we must aim *to democratize them and win them to the revolution by strengthening proletarian influence within their ranks*. In the case of these armies, the partial demands put forward by the communists must principally aim at this goal. The Party's work in these national democratic armies has colossal significance. The speed with which the democratic-national revolution will be transformed into a socialist revolution will to a large extent depend on the revolutionary spirit of the national-democratic armies, and on the political and material influence exercised within them by the proletariat and its vanguard the Communist Party. The negative experience of the Chinese

[10] *Theses and Resolutions of the Sixth World Congress of the Communist International*, 'The Struggle against Imperialist War and the Tasks of the Communists', section 55.

Communist Party in this respect should be put to good use by all communist parties in colonial and semi-colonial countries.

While we are on the subject of failings in the work carried out in the army by the various sections of the Communist International, it is necessary to indicate briefly the errors committed by the Chinese Party. In the period of its bloc with the Kuomintang (up to July 1927), the Chinese Communist Party *had exceptionally favourable conditions for carrying out political work in the national revolutionary army and for winning the mass of soldiers to the revolution*. In spite of this, the Party, or more accurately the Central Committee which led it prior to the August 1927 Conference, as a result of its policy of opportunism and capitulation on all the essential and decisive questions of revolution, did almost nothing to win the soldiers of the national army to the revolution. Here are the instructions given in the Kwangtung military commission's theses on work in the Kuomintang army (the theses date from the autumn of 1925):

If we work in the revolutionary army, it is not to subvert the Kuomintang troops, but to strengthen the army of the national revolution and preserve its unity. We must not carry out political propaganda in the army which differentiates our views from those of the Kuomintang or risks provoking divisions in its ranks.

This line with respect to the national army was the one followed by the Chinese Communist Party from the beginning of its bloc with the Kuomintang to the end. It corresponded to the 'conception' of one of the most prominent members of that party before the August conference, Ch'en Tu-hsiu. This conception was expressed as follows: 'First spread the revolution; radicalize it later' – i.e. before destroying the national army of the Northern warlords (Chang Tso-lin and the rest) and occupying Peking, it is *inadmissible* to spread the agrarian revolution, develop the revolutionary movement of the working class in opposition to the Kuomintang's policies, or carry out revolutionary work in the national army (at the risk of destroying its unity and weakening its fighting value). All this would only become necessary after the end of the Northern expedition.

In making a bloc with the Kuomintang, the Chinese Communist Party never seriously faced up to the fact that its partner was bound, sooner or later, to betray it. Thus, *it never carried out any agitational work in the army other than what was strictly legal*, and forebore to organize *clandestine* cells. This is why the Kuomintang, when it passed over to the camp of counter-revolution, had no difficulty in expelling *all* the communists from the army, and in thereby depriving the Party of all influence of a concrete and organized kind. The Communist Party thus *lost* the army.

During the Northern expedition, the Communist Party never even attempted to win positions of command in the national army, although conditions were extremely favourable for them to have done so. There were therefore only a handful of communist commanding officers, and even these were in the lower grades: squadron and section leaders, company and very rarely battalion commanders. The nomination of the communist Yeh T'ing to the command of a regiment, at the end of 1926, was more the result of an intrigue by Li Chi-shen than of any conscious activity by the Party. And even Yeh T'ing's regiment did not distinguish itself from the other militarist units in any essential way, although it contained a considerable number of communists. There was no purge of reactionary officers, no political work was carried out among the soldiers, and no political apparatus was created. The only difference was that the regiment had a communist at its head instead of a militarist. *Throughout this entire period, the Communist Party never thought of enlarging Yeh T'ing's regiment and making it into a division, nor did they think of organizing any political agitation within its ranks.* It was only shortly before the Nanchang rising (August 1927) that this regiment was transformed into a division. *The absence of political work and political slogans was one of the main reasons why this division commanded by Yeh T'ing (and Ho Lung) was defeated outside Swatow in October 1927.*

Although the Communist Party had increased its numbers during the Northern expedition, the number of communists in the army remained insignificant. Thus, at the beginning of October 1926, the national army contained some 74,000 fighting men. This total included a mere 1,200 communists, and of these 900 were in the units left in Kwangtung province. By the middle of 1927 the number of communists in the army was certainly larger, *but their activity was not directed in any way, for want of an appropriate organ.*

Political work among the soldiers was *almost non-existent.* (In so far as it did exist in places, this was purely due to the initiative of the communists in those particular units.) The leaders, it is true, from time to time used for form's sake to stress the need to strengthen the Party's influence in the units of the national army. But most of the soldiers did not even know of the existence of the Communist Party, and those who did know of its existence could not see any difference between it and the Kuomintang.

Instead of undertaking any serious revolutionary preparation in the army, the leaders of the Party involved themselves in all kinds of deals at the top with the militarist generals, under the pretext of preserving unity in the army; they attempted to persuade these generals to remain faithful to the principles of the 'left' Kuomintang.

This attitude of the Party leadership, as we know, was condemned by the conference of August 1927.

Here is how the theses of that conference express themselves on the conduct of the old leadership of the Chinese Communist Party:

Everybody knows that the army of the Wuhan government is overwhelmingly – with the exception of its small communist fraction, and of those workers or peasants who entered its ranks in response to the Communist Party's directives – a mercenary army, just like the armies of all the other Chinese militarists. Everyone knows too that the commanders of this army, in their overwhelming majority, come from landowning or bourgeois strata and only follow the revolution provisionally, in the hope of drawing some advantage therefrom and of thus advancing their military careers. The leadership of the Communist Party should of course have realized that, confronted with an army of this sort, its policies should have been aimed solely at the mass of soldiers and not at the reactionary commanders. It should have understood that its task was to carry out active propaganda among the soldiers and junior officers, in order to acquire solid backing against the counter-revolutionary manoeuvres of the higher command.

However, the leadership of the Communist Party thought and did exactly the opposite. Its entire policy and 'work' with respect to the army was limited to flirting with generals, and entering into deals at the top with the reactionary command. In practice, no agitation was carried out among the soldiers; indeed no attempt even was made to organize such agitation. The Fifth Congress of the Party did not examine this question separately, despite its importance, and the military commission of the Central Committee, after dragging out its examination of the problem of work in the army for four months, in the end left it unresolved.[11]

On the other hand, time was always found for dealing with the generals and doing them little favours.

This attitude of the Party leadership, on so fundamental a question of the revolution, was a direct consequence of its opportunist tactics on every aspect of the Chinese revolution.

It was natural enough, in view of all this, that when the Chinese bourgeoisie withdrew into the camp of counter-revolution, only the little force under the command of Yeh T'ing and Ho Lung remained

[11] *Theses of the August 1927 extraordinary conference of the Chinese Communist Party.*

on the side of revolution. All the rest of the national army docilely obeyed the counter-revolutionary generals; carried out their orders to crush the class organizations *of the proletariat and peasants; shot the revolutionary leaders, etc.*

And yet, it would have been difficult to imagine conditions more favourable for agitation in the army than those which existed in China at the time. Today, agitation is extremely difficult in the militarist armies – though by no means impossible. The methods to be employed will be appreciably different from what was possible when communists were legally serving in army units as private soldiers, subaltern officers, or political commissars.

In addition to their work in the army and navy, communist parties must seek to disorganize the volunteer organizations of the bourgeoisie which now exist almost everywhere. The basic objectives of these associations, which in many countries greatly outnumber the regular armies,[12] are mobilization of public opinion in favour of war, the military training of their own members, and above all, as history shows, *the defence of the bourgeois order*, i.e. the struggle against the revolutionary proletariat inside the country.

In their social composition, certain of these associations are in large part proletarian. The communist parties of the countries in question must find the means to wrest these proletarian elements from the influence of the bourgeoisie.

In a general way, the communist parties must demand the dissolution of these volunteer associations. But while waging a political campaign on these lines, they must simultaneously seek to subvert them from within. Experience shows that a very powerful weapon for this purpose, i.e. a good means of separating out the proletarian elements, consists in creating semi-military proletarian organizations, like the Red Front in Germany. Thus *wherever possible communist parties must strive to create organizations of this kind;* they must give high priority

[12] Thus in Finland, the Defence Corps and other military organizations number 140–150,000 members, including women; the Estonian League of Defence has some 37,000; the Latvian Defence League 30,000; in Poland, various military and semi-military organizations contain over half a million members. In Germany, the various military organizations (Steel Helmets, National Flag association, the Young German Order, etc.) have four million members. There are similar associations in almost all countries. In Latvia, Estonia, Finland and Poland they receive sizeable government subsidies and arms supplies, are commanded by reservist officers during their military training, etc.

to work (both political and organizational) designed to subvert the military associations of the bourgeoisie.

The Red Front in Germany, a mass organization of mixed character (i.e. working class but not purely communist) with over 100,000 members, and containing communist cells within its ranks, is one of the main centres for revolutionary mobilization of the proletarian masses. It serves to detach the latter from the bourgeois reformist National Flag association, influenced by the Social Democrat Party and the Centre. But not only does it seek to inject a revolutionary spirit into the National Flag by creating a left opposition inside it; it also wages a political struggle against reaction in general, particularly as manifested in the activity of the bourgeois-monarchist military associations (Steel Helmets, etc.). The Red Front also carries out propaganda against new imperialist wars, and against the idea of a war against the USSR.

The revolutionary party must also pose, and resolve in a suitable manner, the question of work among the police. By its social nature the police is often largely composed of proletarian elements, and consequently revolutionary activity among ordinary policemen is objectively possible. The experience of the German revolution in 1923 is a proof of this. The police in Saxony, Thuringia and other regions sympathized in part with the communists – even though the Party has carried out almost no special agitation within its ranks. Certain policemen translated their sympathy into deeds. For instance, there were frequent cases of the police giving communists advance warning of searches, arrests, etc.

The German police is not exceptional. Revolutionary work is both necessary and possible among the police in other countries too. In view of the importance of the police as an instrument of constraint in the hands of the ruling classes, and in view of the results which such work can produce even in a 'peaceful' period (not to speak of the extent to which the political leanings of the police will influence the proletariat's struggle for power in a revolutionary period), this branch of Party work has an importance which cannot be exaggerated.

8

The Organization of
the Proletariat's Armed Forces

One of the main objectives of the party of the revolutionary proletariat in an immediately revolutionary situation is *the creation of proletarian armed forces*, i.e. the formation of a combat organization. The need for this combat organization is indisputable.

The experience of the armed insurrections which have taken place in numerous countries in the past teaches us that however excellent the Party's work in the bourgeois army (and armed forces generally) may be, it will *never be possible* to have subverted the entire army by the time the insurrection is launched. It will never be possible to win over all the army to the revolution, nor even to neutralize it entirely simply by the political work carried out within it. There will always remain units and groups loyal to the reactionary high command, who will fight actively against the proletariat. In his 1906 article: 'Lessons of the Moscow Uprising', Lenin wrote:

We have carried on work in the army and we will redouble our efforts in the future ideologically to win over the troops. But we shall prove to be miserable pedants if we forget that at a time of uprising there must also be a physical struggle for the troops.[1]

Every army possesses many tested units, recruited from the offspring of social elements loyal to the bourgeoisie (officers' and NCOs' training academies, special detachments of the police or the army, 'Mauserists' as in China, etc.), and well paid. There are also all kinds of volunteer organizations (very widespread in the West) which are specially designed for waging an active struggle against the revolutionary proletariat. Moreover it must be borne in mind that the bourgeoisie, during the insurrection, will employ all methods (corruption, lies, drink, repression, etc.) to keep the wavering troops in its grasp. It can therefore be asserted quite categorically that the proletariat will never succeed in wresting the army completely away from the influence of

[1] Lenin, *Selected Works*, vol. I, p. 580.

the ruling classes, or in winning away from the counter-revolutionary command all those soldiers who are wavering, and bringing them over to the revolution. *The subversion and neutralization of these units will only be possible after they have been disarmed by the armed forces of the proletariat. Whence the absolute necessity of constituting in good time adequate proletarian armed forces, capable of allying themselves with such army units as come over to the revolution, so that together they can annihilate the military basis of the old regime definitively.*

In future insurrections, above all if the immediately revolutionary situation does not occur in the aftermath of a war, it will often happen that the entire weight of the first decisive battles must be borne by the red guard detachments, without any help from revolutionary soldiers.

The revolutionary army is needed for military struggle and for military leadership of the masses against the remnants of the military forces of the autocracy. The revolutionary army is needed because great historical issues can be resolved only *by force*, and, in modern struggle, the *organization of force* means military organization.[2]

The structure of the proletariat's combat organization varies from country to country. Only one thing is certain: the detachments of that combat organization must base themselves on the masses (factories, plants, big firms, etc.) and must be numerically strong. Their structure must more or less resemble that of the red guard in Russia, the Proletarian Hundreds in Germany in 1923, the combat squads in China, etc.

The red guard cannot simply be formed in any political situation whatsoever:

The Red Guard is an organ of rebellion. It is the duty of the Communists to agitate for the establishment of such a Red Guard and to organize it when an immediate revolutionary situation arises.

Under no circumstances must it be forgotten that the existence of a proletarian militia or a Red Guard, in imperialist countries, under a bourgeois State and in a state of 'peace', is absolutely impossible.[3]

The mass military organization of the proletariat (the red guard) must be created as soon as the Party puts the question of dictatorship of the proletariat on the immediate agenda, and reorients itself towards direct preparation for the seizure of power.

[2] Lenin, *Collected Works*, vol. 8, p. 563, in 'The Revolutionary Army and the Revolutionary Government'.

[3] *Theses and Resolutions of the Sixth World Congress of the Communist International*, 'The Struggle against Imperialist War and the Tasks of the Communists', section 50-1.

The lessons of Petrograd, Moscow, Germany in 1923, Canton, Shanghai, etc., show that, in an acute revolutionary period, it is relatively easy to create a vast combat organization. Ordinarily, several months will be available for this. But a really combat-worthy military organization can only be formed as quickly as this if there already exists a sufficiently large number of cadres with adequate military and political training. Without these cadres, who will provide the skeleton of the combat organization, i.e. its commanders, the military organization will not be worth much in fighting terms.

In Petrograd, Moscow and the other Russian towns in 1917, the situation was extremely favourable from this point of view. As commanders and instructors, the red guard had communist soldiers and often officers. These instructors, who commanded the red guard detachments during the October fighting, had previously taught the combatants to use their weapons, and had also taught them the principles of tactics and of military science in general.

The situation which we have observed in Germany in 1923 was a quite different one. Here some 250,000 red guards, grouped in Proletarian Hundreds, had been organized in the space of a few months. But there were not enough cadres with military training (the whole mass of red guards only had a handful of communist ex-officers). Moreover, the commanders were ignorant of the fundamentals of street-fighting tactics, indeed of tactics in general, and knew nothing about the organization or tactics of the government's armed forces. The result was that the military value of these Hundreds left much to be desired. This was all the truer in that they only had a very limited quantity of arms at their disposal.

The same could be said for Canton. The red guard, as we have seen, had little idea how to use the arms available to it, and was consequently unable to utilize them in the fighting. It suffered heavy losses and a whole series of its operations failed because it was led by untried comrades who knew little of military science. For the number of communists in Canton who had any military training was extremely limited.

Communist parties, in practice, pay too little attention to the formation of cadres. Yet this is a question of the utmost significance especially in countries like China where the proletariat has few possibilities for forming its cadres inside the existing armies.

As a result of various specific features discussed below and which distinguish it from the ordinary tactics of regular armies, the tactics of insurrection and street fighting (all insurrections in towns take the form of street fighting) is extremely complicated. Its study requires prolonged effort and perseverance. Thus a revolutionary party which remains Marxist through and through – i.e. which treats insurrection as an art, and propagates the idea of armed uprising in the working class – must confront in practice the question of how to train the cadres of the future insurrection, and must resolve it in one way or another. Every proletarian party must set about resolving this question without waiting for an immediately revolutionary situation (when it will be too late); it must do so independently of the current political situation. The problem, despite its apparent difficulty, is not an insoluble one. Side by side with the study of Marxism-Leninism, the Party leadership must organize the study of military science, with particular emphasis on the lessons of past insurrections – especially those of Russia, Germany and China. This study can take place in communist circles and Party schools (legal, semi-legal or illegal depending on circumstances); by recording the lessons of proletarian armed struggle in the Party's publications; by studying military science in practice (sending comrades into the army); by creating legal or illegal military organizations ('Red Front' in Germany, 'Revolutionary Ex-servicemen's Association' in France).

A knowledge of theory is naturally not enough to form tried military leaders for the red guard detachments. *However, it is a precondition for doing so, and should under no circumstances be neglected.*

The great semi-military organizations of the proletariat (like the Red Front and the Revolutionary Ex-servicemen's Association) play an immense role in forming the military cadres of the future insurrection, and providing the proletarian masses with training in military science. These organizations can in no sense be identified with the red guard; they are not instruments of direct struggle for the dictatorship of the proletariat. Their basic purpose, as we have shown in the preceding chapter, is to mobilize the proletariat and educate it in the spirit of class struggle, and to wage a political struggle against the military organizations of the bourgeoisie. But, in addition, they allow tens of thousands of proletarians to obtain a military training, and a preparation for civil war. As the combat organizations of proletarian self-defence, these groupings are simultaneously champions of the idea of civil war and a powerful means for propagating this idea throughout the working class.

The military training of the masses can also to some extent be carried out in various legal organizations: sporting associations, rifle clubs, etc. The Communist Party, wherever possible, must make use of these societies to give the revolutionary youth a military education.

When the immediately revolutionary situation arrives, the military training of the masses (the handling of weapons; the basic tactics of insurrection and street fighting; reconnaissance and liaison work; studying the organization and tactics of the army and police, etc.), the arming of the people and the formation everywhere of red guard detachments must reach their peak. Special attention must be paid in this respect to the decisive centres of the country's political and economic life (the capital, the great industrial centres, the railway junctions, etc.). To neglect these questions means exposing oneself, in the critical moments of the revolution, to extremely fateful consequences.

In the Canton insurrection, about three quarters of the workers who took an active part in the fighting did not know how to fire a rifle and were incapable of making any use of such weapons as they had captured in the initial stages of the rising. There were cases of workers shooting their own comrades by mistake because they did not know how to use the rifles they had been given. And precisely because the insurgents did not know the elementary rules of handling weapons or of street fighting; because they were ignorant of the techniques of reconnaissance and liaison; because they did not know the strong and weak points of the militarists' army – for all these reasons, they suffered heavy losses. In this respect, the Canton insurrection showed up the inadequacies of the Communist Party in military matters, and the errors which it had committed in that field throughout the preceding period.

In July 1905, in his article 'The Revolutionary Army and the Revolutionary Government', Lenin wrote as follows on the need to study military science:

No Social-Democrat at all familiar with history, who has ever studied Engels, the great expert on this subject, has ever doubted the tremendous importance of military knowledge, of military technique, and of military organization as an instrument which the masses of the people, and classes of the people, use in resolving great historical conflicts. Social-Democracy never stooped to playing at military conspiracies; it never gave prominence to military questions until the actual conditions of civil war had arisen. But *now* all Social-Democrats have advanced the military questions, if not to the first place, at least to one of the first places, and they are putting great stress on studying these questions and bringing them to the knowledge of the masses. The revolutionary army must apply the military knowledge and the military means on the practical plane for the determination of the further destiny of the Russian people, for the determination of the most vital and pressing question – the question of freedom.[4]

The previous Central Committee meeting of the Chinese Communist Party (i.e. the one preceding the August conference) had followed an extremely opportunistic line with respect to arming the masses and creating a powerful proletarian armed force, and with respect to work in the national army:

The Central Committee of the Chinese Communist Party never thought seriously about arming the workers and peasants or about the need for any such action; nor in general did it consider how peasant units or truly revolutionary military cadres might be formed. Its military commission displayed a total lack of activity in this respect. Nothing was done about military training for all Party members, which should have been the Party's first duty. No attempt was made to unite the various isolated worker or peasant detachments systematically into an organized force capable of defending the revolution effectively as it developed. Almost no measures were taken to procure arms (even where they were actually available), or to distribute them to the workers and peasants. The Central Committee judged the problem of arming the workers and peasants to be a non-existent one, and even considered it as a threat to its political accommodation with the Kuomintang high command. And then all of a sudden, after this long period of inaction, it did manifest a certain activity – but in the opposite direction, by proposing to the Wuhan pickets 'in order to avoid conflicts and provocations' that they should voluntarily surrender their arms. How is it possible to characterize such an attitude of the Central Committee, in the face of vital requirements of the revolution, as anything other than open liquidationism?[5]

These errors of the old Party leadership – errors which to a certain extent had fatal consequences at the critical hour of the 1927 revolution – are at present being corrected.

One difficult problem to resolve when preparing for insurrection is that of arms. It has great political importance. Under the dictatorship of the bourgeoisie (in 'peacetime'), the proletariat is ordinarily deprived of any possibility of arming itself. And yet, despite the difficulties, this problem is not insoluble. In any political situation in which the

[4] Lenin, *Collected Works*, vol. 8, p. 565.
[5] Theses of the August 1927 emergency conference of the Chinese Communist Party.

seizure of power presents itself as a practical question (i.e. in the event of a rapid growth of revolutionary tendencies among the workers, significant waverings on the part of the petty bourgeoisie and a weakening of the bourgeois machinery of government), the proletariat, given proper leadership from the Party, will be able to obtain arms. It will be able to do so by buying them; by disarming the fascist leagues; by capturing arms depots; or by manufacturing them (at least primitive ones). It will then be in a position to arm the combat organization sufficiently to more or less *guarantee, when the insurrection breaks out, the success of such actions as may be undertaken to procure further arms.* When working out the plan of insurrection, the leadership must pay serious attention to this question of capturing weapons, and of arming such combat squads as have no arms and such revolutionary workers as are willing to fight.

In 1905, in his article 'Tasks of Revolutionary Army Contingents', Lenin wrote:

The contingents . . . must arm themselves as best they can (rifles, revolvers, bombs, knives, knuckle-dusters, sticks, rags soaked in kerosene for starting fires, ropes or rope ladders, shovels for building barricades, pyroxylin cartridges, barbed-wire, nails against cavalry, etc., etc.). Under no circumstances should they wait for help from other sources, from above, from the outside; they must procure everything themselves.[6]

And Lenin goes on to stress that 'under no circumstances should the formation of the group be abandoned or postponed on the plea of lack of arms'.

In reply to the account of the Combat Committee of the St Petersburg Committee, which noted the slowness with which the combat contingents were being formed and the shortage of arms, Lenin urged:

Go to the youth. Form fighting squads *at once* everywhere, among the students, and *especially among the workers*, etc., etc. Let groups be at once organized of three, ten, thirty, etc., persons. Let them arm themselves at once as best they can, be it with a revolver, a knife, a rag soaked in kerosene for starting fires, etc.[7]

Lenin's instructions on how to form the revolutionary army contingents and how to procure arms remain valid to this day.

It must be reckoned that in future insurrections, in the East as much as in the advanced capitalist countries, the proletariat (or at least

[6] Lenin, *Collected Works*, vol. 9, p. 420.
[7] Lenin, *Collected Works*, vol. 9, p. 344–5, in 'To the Combat Committee of the St Petersburg Committee'.

certain elements of it), until it has managed to seize an adequate quantity of modern arms (i.e. at the outset of the insurrection), will often have to content itself with the most unsatisfactory weapons. But it would be quite wrong to make this a reason for abandoning the whole enterprise, since with these primitive and unsatisfactory weapons the fighting contingents can and must obtain real, modern arms.

The insurrection is led by the Party, and each Party member is a soldier in the civil war. This principle makes it obligatory for every communist to have a weapon. This is most of all true in those parts of the country where the class struggle is most turbulent, and where all kinds of specific conditions make a revolutionary explosion more likely.

Returning to the formation and structure of the red guard (revolutionary army), the following main factors emerge from such experience as has been acquired in this field in various countries.

When an immediately revolutionary situation arrives, the red guard must be formed in all factories and cities, while the Party issues ever more radical fighting slogans, and invites the masses openly to prepare the armed uprising. The red guard detachments must be composed in general of non-Party workers, students and poor peasants. The Party must make the most strenuous efforts to ensure its *leadership* in these detachments; to have reliable men in position of command; to supervise their military training, etc. In many countries, it is not impossible that red guard detachments will have to be formed illegally, at least initially. The degree of legality of the red guard will depend on all kinds of conditions: above all on the depth of the revolutionary movement among the oppressed classes; on the extent to which the ruling class apparatus of government has disintegrated, etc. The Party's duty is to take account of the real political situation in each region, and to propagate among the masses slogans whose realization will ensure the legal existence and the progress of the working-class organizations, including the Party and the red guard. It must never be forgotten that *the question of the red guard's legality will ultimately be resolved by the struggle of the working-class masses, and only by that*. The Party must make every effort to explain to the masses that a successful struggle to create the revolutionary army will, to a considerable extent, determine the possibility of a successful outcome to the struggle during the insurrection. For this battle for the creation and legal development of the red guard *is in fact a battle for the principal means of access to the decisive positions, i.e. it is the beginning of the direct struggle for power.* In this period, skirmishes with the armed forces of the bourgeoisie (troops, police, gendarmerie, fascist units) will be inevitable. And partial defeats will be equally inevitable.

In the light of past experience, the basic organizational structure of the red guard detachments can be resumed as follows. As long as they have to operate in conditions of illegality, the armed forces of the proletariat will consist of small groups (of three, five or ten men) organized in each factory, etc., and subordinated via their commanders to the higher instances (factory or neighbourhood red guard commanders, etc.). The formation of larger units (companies, battalion) is not to be recommended in this period, for security reasons.

With the development of the campaign to create a red guard, as soon as the idea has fired the working-class masses to the point where they are bursting all the bounds of legality, and as soon as the formation of revolutionary army contingents takes on a mass character, the Party will have to provide the red guard with an appropriate organizational structure, based on the requirements of street fighting and on the weapons available. This structure must be simple and comprehensible to every worker. It is a mistake to aim for a complicated structure, or to form large units. The Party should rather strive to group together the small base units in a really solid fashion: squads and groups (from ten to twenty men), sections (from thirty-five to forty-five) and companies (two or three sections). In certain cases it will be possible to combine two or three companies into a battalion. The formation of still larger units (regiments or divisions), as was done in Germany in 1923, is not advisable – indeed is even dangerous. For it obscures the importance of the smaller red guard units in street fighting, and is symptomatic of a failure to understand the nature of this kind of combat, all of whose weight falls on groups and detachments corresponding numerically to the squad, section or company. The formation of large-scale units will only become necessary after power has been seized in the city, when conditions exist for the struggle to be extended outside – i.e. for warfare in open country.

In the formation and military training of the red guard, great attention must be paid to the preparation within base units such as the squad or company, of men or groups with special functions: couriers, scouts, nurses, machine-gunners, artillery-men, engineers, drivers, etc. This is extremely important, for the presence of all these specialized skills (even when the weapons in question are not available) will in the first place allow a better defence against those weapons when they are used by the enemy, and in the second place, when such weapons have been captured, will allow them to be used effectively. Couriers (on bicycles if possible) and scouts will always be indispensable in street fighting. It is therefore absolutely necessary to train certain comrades or groups of comrades in each section and company to carry out scouting and liaison work.

In appointing and training the commanders for these detachments, it must be borne in mind that during the fighting they will be required to display great independence and initiative; the ability to orient themselves in the complex conditions of street fighting; personal courage; the ability to take independent responsibility for solving any tasks which may arise during the fighting; and, lastly, a limitless devotion to the revolutionary cause.

The selection of the red guard's leading personnel must take these requirements into account. It must not be forgotten that in street fighting and during insurrections, the ability of the individual commander plays an immense role.

9

Direction of the Party's Military Work

Military work in general is naturally a task for the entire Party and Young Communist League, and for each single individual communist.

However, in view of the specific features of military work, it is necessary for a special apparatus, manned by competent militants, to be made responsible for it. It is a mistake to believe that this work can be organized properly without a specialized apparatus. This is true not only in immediate revolutionary situations, when military objectives take on special importance, but in so-called peaceful periods too. For instance, it would be impossible to conceive of military work in the army without specialized cadres to carry it out, or without a special apparatus to direct it. Experience everywhere shows that if the relevant Party committee is made responsible for directing all work among the troops, this in practice very often means renouncing such work altogether. (What is true of trade-union work, or of agitation within the great proletarian organizations – co-operatives, sporting associations, etc. – is all the more true with respect to work in the army.) All this is particularly relevant for legal communist parties. For before the emergence of an immediately revolutionary situation, the Party's military work, from an organizational point of view, is basically an illegal activity. It requires total security, and also expertise, imagination, etc. It therefore requires a specially selected personnel.

In the absence of an immediately revolutionary situation, the military apparatus might have the following composition: (*a*) the military commission attached to the Central Committee of the Party, made up of three comrades, one of whom, the chairman, will be a member of the Central Committee; (*b*) the military commissions attached to the Party's provincial or equivalent committees, made up of two or three comrades – depending on the scale of their responsibilities; (*c*) the military delegates attached to the district committees; (*d*) the military commissions or delegates (depending on the size of the town and the scale of their responsibilities) attached to the town committees.

One member of the military commission must always be a member of the Party committee to which the commission is attached. In addition the commission must include among its three members a member of the appropriate committee of the Young Communist League.

A certain number of militants (depending on the objectives involved and the Party's resources) must be made available to the military commissions, to carry out tasks for the latter as their basic Party work. These must include members of the Young Communist League.

The functions of the military commissions consist in organizing and directing work in the army, police, fleet and bourgeois military associations, under the orders of the respective Party committees; organizing the Party's intelligence service; training the military cadres of the future red guard; procuring arms; publishing and distributing all kinds of printed material (leaflets, pamphlets, military journals), in accordance with the decisions of the Central or provincial committees; supplying the military editors of the Party press with material, etc. Functions must be allocated to the various commission members accordingly.

The military commissions must be supplied (by the appropriate Party committees) with the financial resources necessary to carry out properly the work assigned to them. Where funds permit, the commission members of military delegates, at least in the main towns and provinces, will have to be maintained at the Party's expense and thus be free from all other work to earn their living.

As the class struggle intensifies and the revolutionary situation approaches – with the Party launching ever more radical fighting slogans, reorienting all its political activity towards immediate preparation for the seizure of power, calling for the creation of a red guard, etc. – the military commissions must be complemented by a new influx of properly trained cadres. In this period, new commissions must be created in all regions where they do not yet exist. In the main political and economic centres (capitals, great industrial cities, ports) where, in addition to the town committees, there exist ward committees as well, military commissions or delegates must be attached to these too. At the same time, the strength of the military commissions must be increased considerably. The formation of red guard detachments; the provision of military training for these; the subversion of the bourgeois State machine, and especially of the army and police; the creation of an intelligence network in the enemy camp; the procurement of greatly increased supplies of arms, etc. – all this will require a far more numerous personnel than is necessary under normal circumstances.

The commissions will also have to draw up the military part of the plan of insurrection for each city or province, or for the whole country, in accordance with the general lines laid down by the relevant Party committees. During the insurrection, each commission will become transformed into a military command, i.e. into a technical organization attached to the equivalent revolutionary committee directing operations.

The overall direction of the Party's military work throughout the country – as of its work in every other specific field of activity (trade unions, press, parliamentary group, co-operative movement, etc.) – *is the responsibility of the Central Committee*, as the supreme authority of the Party between congresses. *Locally, this work will be directed by the appropriate local committee (provincial, district, etc.), on the basis of the Central Committee's directives.*

The Central Committee determines the character and content of Party work among the troops. It formulates the slogans for each stage in the revolution's development; indicates how these should be linked to the Party's political work as a whole; decides which centres and regions are most important from the point of view of subverting the armed forces of the ruling-class; strengthens the relevant committees accordingly by sending them additional funds and militants; exercises control over all this work. The Central Committee decides when the formation of the red guard should begin, gives advice on how to procure arms, judges how opportune or inopportune any given diversionary action is, etc. In short, all important initiatives of general political significance undertaken by local Party organizations or by the Central Committee of the Young Communist League *must be submitted for approval by the Central Committee of the Party*. The military commissions do not have a line of their own, i.e. one not laid down by the general line of the Party. They function under the directives of the collective Party organizations.

These principles may appear to be elementary and universally known. Nevertheless, it is worth reiterating them for they are often forgotten.

In the Canton insurrection, as we have seen, even the date of the insurrection was fixed not by the Central Committee, but by the Kwangtung provincial committee. The Central Committee only learnt of the insurrection when the whole world was already talking about it. The absurdity of this is self-evident. In the second Shanghai insurrection, the start of the strike and the armed uprising were decided on by trade-union officials, with the participation of a large number of Party members but without the Central Committee's knowledge. And insurrections were organized without the higher levels of the Party being informed in various Chinese provinces during 1927.

Sometimes, for all kinds of reasons, autonomist tendencies appear in the military organization. It refuses to obey the decisions of the Party committees; seeks to take political decisions independently of the appropriate Party organs, etc. Tendencies of this kind appeared in the military organizations of certain Russian regions after the February revolution, and even later. Apropos of the differences between the Central Committee of the Bolshevik Party and the Pan-Russian Bureau of the Bolshevik military organizations, the Central Committee was obliged in its session of 29 August to raise the question of relations between the military organization and the Party as a whole. The following decision was taken:

The Military Bureau is the organization which carries out propaganda among the soldiers. . . . According to the Party statutes, no two Party organisms can exist in parallel with the same functions of leadership. This is as true of Pan-Russian bodies as of local bodies. Thus the Pan-Russian Bureau of the military organizations cannot exist as an independent political centre.

There was friction between the Party leadership and the military organizations, because of the latter's autonomist tendencies, in Tomsk, Ekaterinburg and other towns during 1917. Similar tendencies appeared in the German combat organization in 1923.

The organizational principles of Bolshevism demand the strict subordination of the military organization, like any other Party organization (parliamentary group, trade-union fractions, etc.), to the overall Party leadership. This principle is the sole guarantee of discipline, and of unity of action and doctrine. It increases the fighting capacity of the Party, and multiplies the chances of victory during the decisive battle for the dictatorship of the proletariat.

10

The Character of Military Action
at the Beginning
of the Insurrection
General Tactical Principles

GENERAL REMARKS

Armed struggle aimed at destroying the government machine and at a seizure of power by the proletariat takes the form of an implacable armed struggle between the militarily organized fraction of the proletariat and its allies on the one hand and the military strength of the ruling classes on the other. *In the first period* of this open civil war, the struggle will take place principally in the cities, i.e. it will take the form of street battles – which of course will differ in nature and duration according to circumstances. It is upon the outcome of the battle in this period, and upon the speed with which the proletariat succeeds in creating a sufficient number of Red Army units in fighting trim, that will depend to a very considerable degree the outcome of the struggle to consolidate the revolution and to extend it territorially. Subsequently, when power has been solidly secured by the proletariat in the main economic and political regions (capitals, great economic centres), armed struggle will assume the character of a war in the countryside between the regular Red Army and the remnants of the indigenous counter-revolution or of foreign intervention forces.

Civil war (and hence armed insurrection), just like the operations of regular armies, is subject to the rules of military science. Nevertheless, in view of the specific character of the operations involved in insurrection, the tactics of the proletariat's armed struggle for power – i.e. of the first phase of the civil war – differs *markedly* from the tactics of regular armies.

In a duel between two regular armies, whether this takes place in open country or inside a town, they are separated by some kind of front line. The struggle of the proletariat, *at least in the first moments of an armed insurrection*, is waged in quite different conditions.

In the first place, *there is no definite front line between the belligerents.*

The front, for the proletariat as for the ruling classes, is *all round and everywhere*. Friends and enemies, on both sides, *are not separated territorially*. On the one hand, the revolutionary proletariat will inevitably have hidden or open supporters in the ruling-class camp (in the army, the police, the various organizations under the political and material influence of the ruling-class parties, etc.). On the other hand, in the ranks of the proletariat there will be a number of hidden or open supporters of the old order (the full-time officials of the social democratic party; the fraction of the proletariat and petty bourgeoisie which is under social democratic influence, etc.).

In the second place, at the moment of the armed struggle for power, the proletariat will *not yet possess* a genuine regular Red Army, adequately organized and equipped for modern warfare. The red guard detachments are only the embryo of the future Red Army. *The regular army of the proletariat is created, and must be created, in the course of the struggle for power.*

In the third place, experience shows that the state of the armed forces of the ruling classes is appreciably modified in the course of the insurrection, and that for this reason the army *is very different* – with respect both to *its inner cohesion* and to its fighting quality – from that which, in normal times, fights against an enemy State. Within its ranks, under the influence of the struggle itself and of the revolutionary party's agitation, processes of social differentiation will inevitably begin; these will introduce the seeds of disintegration, and will affect its fighting quality. Ultimately, the army (and police) will come to contain, side by side with units ready to fight actively against the revolutionary proletariat, other units large or small whose soldiers will hesitate between revolution and counter-revolution. Cases of troops refusing to obey their reactionary officers, mutinying and defecting to the revolutionary camp will multiply.

In the course of its struggle for power, the revolutionary proletariat *creates its own regular army and* – *by its agitation, and also by direct physical conflict* – erodes the armed support of the ruling classes, i.e. the army itself, the police, the fleet and the various fascist associations.

The three specific features of the proletariat's struggle for power enumerated above put a certain stamp *on the tactics* which have to be employed; as a result, the war tactics of the proletariat during the insurrection differs at many points from the tactics of regular armies. Hence not only must the organizers and leaders of the insurrection have a general knowledge of military science – they must also know how to apply the rules of military theory and tactics to the specific conditions of insurrection.

The particular features of insurrectionary tactics will be brought out when we examine the various elements involved in organizing and carrying out an armed uprising.

One of the key questions of every proletarian insurrection in future will be how to *ensure the superiority* of the organized military forces of the insurrection over the armed forces of the enemy.

The proletarian insurrections of Canton, Hamburg, Reval, etc., were ultimately defeated because their leaders, for various objective and subjective reasons which have already been discussed, were unable to resolve this key problem in favour of the insurgents. Because they did not have military superiority over the enemy, because they did not succeed in increasing their armed forces rapidly during the uprising, the insurgents were obliged – almost as soon as they had gone into action – *to fall back onto the defensive and to abandon all active operations*. But defensive action, in an insurrection just as in a war between two regular armies, *does not and cannot decide* the outcome of an operation.

The experience of the proletarian insurrections of the last decades permits us to conclude that the proletariat will very rarely enjoy military superiority over the armed forces of the ruling-class before the insurrection begins. On the contrary, it will usually be much weaker militarily at the beginning of the uprising. *Superiority over the enemy's armed forces must be won during the insurrection* – and this is quite possible. The very situation of the proletariat as *the attacking force*; the general political situation, which favours revolution and cannot but influence the bourgeois army, the police, and in general all the armed forces of the enemy classes; these factors *objectively help towards winning that superiority*. The plan of insurrection and other organizational measures adopted by the proletariat should keep sight of this need to increase the revolutionary armed forces steadily and as fast as possible during the insurrection – so as to win superiority over the enemy, and crush him beneath the concentrated blows of the revolution's powerful armed forces.

There is another question related to this: how to ensure that the combat organization will receive the active support of the revolutionary masses during the insurrection. How to draw the revolutionary masses into the active struggle, and how to make proper use of them (within the framework of the plan of insurrection), in such a way as to secure their collaboration in accomplishing the insurrection's aims. *To neglect this question* means condemning the proletarian combat organization to failure. As we know, the main reason for the defeat at Reval on 1 December 1924 was the fact that the military organization, once the attack had been launched, *found itself isolated*; for the Party *had not* proved able to organize the mass of the proletariat and draw them into the active struggle *at the moment* when the combat organization moved into action.

How to involve and make good use of the revolutionary masses during the uprising constitutes *one of the most complex and at the same time most crucial problems for the insurrectionary leadership.*

These general considerations must, of course, be kept in mind when establishing the strategic plan for an insurrection. But it is still more important to take them into consideration when drawing up tactical plans on the actual spot (in a city, district, or any inhabited place in general).

ARMED FORCES OF THE RULING CLASSES

The ruling class has at its disposal the following categories of armed force, which will be directed against the proletariat during an insurrection: (*a*) the regular army; (*b*) the maritime and river fleets; (*c*) the police and gendarmerie; (*d*) the volunteer military organizations.

The Regular Army

The regular army, if it has not been subverted (or those of its units which have not been subverted), is the most powerful weapon against the revolutionary proletariat at a time of general revolutionary ferment. With commanding officers who are highly-trained and totally devoted to the government, and with all the most modern equipment for both attack and defence (machine-guns, artillery, armoured vehicles, gas, air power, etc.), the regular army today is *an extremely serious force.* The proletariat's first task during the insurrection will be to fight against, and for possession of, this force.

The strength of the regular army is revealed at its best during fighting in open country, and in daytime operations. Fighting inside cities, particularly at night, appreciably reduces the possibilities for it to make full use of its equipment, and impedes direction of the various units in their operations. For this reason, the tactics of operations inside cities, especially in the case of insurrection, is very different from the normal tactics of the regular army.

The fighting qualities of the various military arms, and the uses to which they may be put in street fighting, can be generally characterized as follows:

Infantry. In almost all military arms, infantry provides most of the manpower and constitutes the main weapon both in open country and in street fighting. It can fight either with firearms or with bayonets, seize buildings and districts, clear the ground of insurgents, and hold captured positions.

The strong points of infantry in street fighting are its organization; its ability to fight either in small or in relatively large units (squads, sections, companies or battalions); its military training; the way in which its units give each other mutual support; its capacity to maintain liaison with neighbouring units. Infantry is admirably armed for street fighting (machine-guns, rifles, revolvers, hand-grenades, artillery, etc.). Because of its mobility, it can fight not only in the streets, but in courtyards or on rooftops.

The weak points of infantry are the following: (*a*) inside towns, its arms can only be used at relatively close range; (*b*) its units have difficulty in deploying in streets, once they surpass a certain size (regiments, brigades, divisions); as a rule it can only fight in small or medium-sized detachments (up to battalion); (*c*) initially at least, infantry has little detailed knowledge of the town to use in its operations (it has difficulty in finding its way about); (*d*) there is always the risk of being ambushed by insurgents hidden in cellars, on roofs, in courtyards, at windows, in attics, etc.; (*e*) when the infantry is in barracks, particularly at night, the insurgents with good organization can take it by surprise (as indeed they can all regular troops), and deprive it of any possibility of using its weapons; (*f*) the infantry (like the entire regular army) is mainly made up of peasants, workers and proletarian elements in general (the mercenary armies, e.g. in China, Germany, Bulgaria, etc., also include *lumpen* elements); objectively this mass *has no interest at all* in defending the ruling classes or the bourgeois or feudal-bourgeois order. By coming into direct contact with the working-class population of the towns during the fighting, the infantry cannot avoid to some extent being influenced by the revolutionary proletariat. If fraternization and agitation are carried out properly by the revolutionary proletariat, the troops can be demoralized and won over to the insurgent side.

The need, in street fighting, for the troops to operate in small groups which can no longer be directly controlled by the reactionary command, combined with the contact of these groups with the population, means that certain soldiers or groups of soldiers cease to be reliable. Given good work by the insurgents, it is then relatively easy to bring them over to the side of the people. *Whence the necessity for the insurgents to put the enemy command out of action* (sharpshooters; bold attacks by small groups of insurgents on military headquarters or on particular officers, etc.), and to carry out active agitation among the soldiers wherever possible.

Artillery. Artillery, especially howitzers, mortars and trench-mortars (high-angle guns), comprises a powerful weapon in the enemy's hands.

The use of heavy artillery (15·2 cm. and over) and light artillery (low-trajectory and field pieces) is limited in street fighting. Nevertheless, it can often be used with great success where there is a free field of fire for it.

The key objective of artillery in street fighting is the destruction of the various obstacles (barricades) or buildings held by the insurgents. Artillery-fire can exert a great psychological effect; it has a demoralizing influence on the population and often on the combatants themselves if they are badly trained and do not know the properties of artillery – i.e. how to protect themselves from its fire, and how to combat it. Yet the material damage it causes, for insurgents who know how to take cover, is normally negligible. This is a truth which must be driven into the heads of the insurrectionary forces during their training in order to neutralize the unfavourable psychological effect exerted by enemy artillery during the fighting.

The insurgents can disorganize and demoralize artillery units (by sudden charges and surprise attacks) in precisely the same way as they can infantry, or any other branch of the modern army.

Armoured vehicles. Armoured cars and tanks, armed with machine-guns and light artillery, are powerful weapons in street fighting and can play an important role in it. They possess armour which protects their crews and armament from the bullets of normal rifles and machine-guns, and can manoeuvre rapidly in the conditions of street combat. The insurgents, with rare exceptions, cannot procure special anti-tank weapons. In addition, tanks can destroy and overturn barricades, if these have been erected hastily. Consequently, if the insurgents do not take proper measures, the armoured cars and tanks which every modern army has at its disposal will be able to penetrate their defences with impunity and inflict heavy losses on them, spreading panic in their ranks and causing them great material damage.

To resist tanks and armoured cars, the insurgents have the following means at their disposal: artillery, if they have any; concentric charges (i.e. hand-grenades tied in bundles of five or six) and high-explosive bombs thrown under the tanks and armoured cars; wide, deep trenches dug across the streets (depending on the type of tank, they must be from 1·5 to 3 metres wide, and from 1·5 to 2 metres deep).

The way in which the Hamburg insurgents dealt with armoured cars (isolating them by means of barricades, etc.) provides an excellent example of good defensive action against these devices.

Cavalry. Cavalry is of all arms the most vulnerable inside a town, for it can only move about on the actual streets and offers a large target. Thus its role in street fighting is insignificant. It is normally used against unarmed crowds; to guard districts which are not yet occupied by the insurgents; to isolate the insurgent districts; or for liaison purposes. Foot-cavalry can fight in the streets more or less as infantry can.

Air power. Air power can be used in street fighting for reconnaissance (including aerial photography), and for carrying out bombing and machine-gun attacks from the air. If however the insurgents use even the most elementary forms of camouflage (simple adaptation to their location), air reconnaissance will give no really significant results. The psychological and material damage caused by an air attack can only be serious if the insurgents are grouped in large masses and do not take the proper camouflage and defence measures. Aeroplanes can be used with great success to disperse open-air meetings and demonstrations, and to reconnoitre the layout of barricades (by aerial photography).

Chemical weapons. These have not yet been employed in the struggle against the insurgent proletariat. However, it is necessary to envisage *the very real possibility* that, in future insurrections in the West, they will be employed by the ruling classes, in spite of certain negative results from the point of view of those who employ them (poisoning of the whole population, including women, children and old people, and hence embitterment of the masses against the old order).

The best defence against chemical weapons is *the capture by the insurgents of the devices involved* (gas containers, projectiles, etc.) and the destruction (physical annihilation) of the personnel operating them. If there is any chance of capturing and using such devices, this must of course be taken advantage of.

Maritime and River Fleets

The power of the war fleet consists in its armament – i.e. its guns. The use of heavy naval artillery is ruled out in street fighting. The fleet's guns can only be used to shell particular buildings or districts in ports (e.g. the cruiser *Aurora*'s bombardment of the Winter Palace during the days of October 1917). The same can be said with respect to the river fleet. However, the crews of warships, if they are politically reliable from the government's point of view, can be used (in the form of small infantry detachments) against insurrections in ports (e.g. the attempt to use the crew of the cruiser *Hamburg* during the 1923 Hamburg insurrection; the red sailors' detachments during the Civil War in Russia).

Police and Gendarmerie

The fundamental purpose of the police and gendarmerie is to repress 'internal disorders'. Their armament varies from country to country. In China, for example, and in other countries too, the police does not constitute a serious force against insurgents. The insurrections in Shanghai, Canton and other towns showed that the insurgents were able very rapidly and at relatively low cost to put the police out of action. The same thing happened in the October revolution in Russia. In China and in Russia, the police was in reality nothing more or less than a stock of arms for the insurgents to take and use.

The low fighting calibre of the Chinese police is due to its poor armament (revolvers, relatively few rifles, no machine-guns or armoured cars); its lack of military training; its not being housed in barracks; its lack of military organization and its wretched material condition. All this, combined with its permanent contact with the population (influence of the revolutionary population upon the police), greatly reduced its fighting calibre.

Nevertheless in certain countries, Germany for example and some others, the police and gendarmerie differ little from the regular army in their military qualities. They are admirably armed (sub-machine-guns, machine-guns, armoured cars); well-trained militarily; commanded by officers who have an excellent tactical preparation and who are politically devoted to the existing order. The German police is organized in semi-military fashion (sections, companies, etc.) and housed in barracks. It is mainly recruited among the members of the nationalist (or the republican 'National Flag') ex-servicemen's organizations, i.e. among people who are politically reliable. Its close contact (like that of every other police force) with the population does weaken its fighting quality to some extent; nevertheless the insurrections of 1919–23 showed that it constitutes a pretty serious force which the German proletariat must under no circumstances disregard. Even if the Communist Party carries out intensive political work within it to eliminate the influence of its counter-revolutionary officers, a part of the German police will fight actively against the insurgents during the revolution – at least in the first period of the struggle.

It is unnecessary to characterize the police forces of all the various countries individually. We have only dealt (and that in broad outline) with the weakest in military terms, i.e. the Chinese, and the strongest, i.e. the German police. Allowing for inevitable differences, the police forces and gendarmeries of all countries can be assimilated to one or other of these.

The police and gendarmerie, by the nature of their service, and unlike the regular army, are *well-acquainted with the city*.

In the light of the various insurrections which have occurred in Germany and elsewhere, the commanding officers of the German police and gendarmerie receive special instruction in the methods and tactics to be used in combating insurrections. For this purpose, there exist rule-books and special manuals in which the history and tactics of struggle against the proletariat can be studied, like *Combat Methods of the Security Police in Internal Disorders*, 1926, by police-colonel Hartenstein, and *Police Tactics*, 1928, by captains B. Elster and H. Vilski, respectively of the police and the gendarmerie.

Volunteer Military Organizations of the Ruling Classes

There is almost no country in Europe where there do not exist various military and fascist organizations – entitled Rifle Clubs, Defence Leagues or Corps, Veterans' Associations, Youth Organizations, etc., or straightforwardly Fascist Leagues. Characteristically, social democracy takes an active part in creating and developing these (e.g. the National Flag association in Germany). In certain countries, like Germany, Poland, Finland, Latvia, etc., these organizations contain many more members than the regular army has soldiers. The key purpose of these various organizations, as has already been said, is the defence of the existing order.

In a period of revolutionary upheaval, these organizations cannot remain unaffected by the situation, thanks to the presence within them of a large proportion of proletarian and semi-proletarian elements. Nevertheless, certain units and groups will actively fight against the revolutionary proletariat – of this there can be no doubt. The régime will use them in various ways. In the form of independent armed units under the command of the police and the military, one part of them will be incorporated into the police force and used for certain tasks of a secondary character, while another part (as was the case in Germany in 1923) will be incorporated into the regular army.

The fighting qualities of these irregular formations are *not very high*. But since during operations they will benefit from a fairly competent military leadership – in the person of reservist officers, or even serving officers – and since they will be equipped with modern weapons (rifles, machine-guns, etc.), they can and will act as an auxiliary force for the army and police during the fighting. Consequently, the revolutionary proletariat must take these forces too into account in its struggle for power.

ARMED FORCES OF THE PROLETARIAT

The main weakness of the insurgent proletariat is its lack of arms at the start of operations. Rare are the cases in which the military organization will have been able to accumulate sufficient reserves before the insurrection. The experience of past insurrections (Hamburg, Shanghai, Reval, etc.) shows that – as a result of ruling-class terror, and its own lack of financial resources – the military organization of the proletariat is often unable to procure enough arms and ammunition before the insurrection even to arm itself, let alone the broad proletarian masses. Arms are normally acquired in the course of the insurrection itself.

Another weakness of the proletariat is the fact that most of the insurgents – with rare exceptions (e.g. when the seizure of power occurs in wartime or immediately after a war, and the proletariat thus has the chance of learning to use arms in the army) – do not have any adequate knowledge of how to handle weapons, especially machine-guns and artillery. This was particularly evident in the insurrections of Canton (when only five of the thirty captured cannon could in fact be used – and that very poorly) and Reval (when the insurgents, as was mentioned earlier, were not able to use their three Thompson machine-guns because they had never learnt to handle them).

Insurgents are generally badly trained from a military point of view. This is due above all to objective causes (lack of arms, ruling-class terror, etc.). Nevertheless, most communist parties devote too little attention to the military training of the workers. The proletariat usually has no tactically or operationally trained commanders for its combat organization (e.g. at Reval, the actions of the unit which captured the airborne corps, or of the one which was supposed to free the prisoners, etc.).

Insurgents for the most part are highly impressionable. Small temporary setbacks often have a disastrous influence on them, so that their morale and fighting quality decline suddenly. On the other hand, success raises their courage to an extraordinary extent, and encourages them to undertake further daring actions. Hence, it is imperative during an insurrection to seek constant successes – even if only minor ones. This is especially true during the first period of the uprising.

On the other hand, the armed forces of the proletariat (the combat organization) *possess many valuable fighting qualities* – qualities which give them great advantages over the armed forces of the bourgeoisie. These are: their level of consciousness; their vital interest in the victory of the insurrection; their permanent contact with the working masses who support them; and, lastly, the idea that chaos is reigning among the ruling classes, that the government is bogged down in insoluble contradictions, and that the only way of escaping from the chaos and improving the wretched material and cultural condition of the workers is to wage an implacable struggle against the exploiters – a struggle to follow the example of the Soviet Union and install the dictatorship of the proletariat. Here are *the prerequisites* for each combatant to display a maximum of initiative, enthusiasm for the struggle and readiness for sacrifice – thus making it possible to order the most desperate of attacks on the enemy, and to wage street combat equally well in big units (100, 300 or 500 men) or in small combat squads.

Insurgents, as inhabitants of the city, know it well; they can find their way around, are familiar with conditions there, etc. It is therefore easy for them to launch surprise attacks, appearing suddenly where the enemy least expects them; to carry out effective night raids and, in case of failure, to slip away unnoticed to begin operations anew, in a fresh district and with fresh objectives.

All this – when added to the revolutionary struggle of the masses, who, both before the combat organization has begun operations and also during the insurrection itself, have shaken and disrupted State power by their growing activity; and to the constant flow (provided that the workers are really in a fighting mood) of new workers ready to fight and of army units coming over to the camp of revolution – *will compensate to a certain degree* for the technical and tactical weaknesses discussed above, and ensure that the action will be successful.

Thus, resuming what has been said about the ruling-class and proletarian armed forces respectively, the following conclusions can be drawn – and must inspire the plan of insurrection.

1. The troops of the regular army are a serious military force, not only in open country but also in street fighting. If some units at least do not sympathize with the revolution, i.e. if the insurgents do not succeed in winning over certain units of the army, *the insurrection is doomed to failure*. To ensure success the proletariat, before it ever moves into action, must fight a determined struggle to win the army and bring it over to the ranks of the revolutionary proletariat, or at least neutralize it. The Party, and whatever part of the proletariat follows the Party, must pay maximum attention to this task.

The insurrection in the broad sense of the word should be seen as beginning not with the entry into action of the combat organization, but in fact several days or weeks before the outbreak of armed struggle, at the moment when the date for the uprising has been fixed and when the Party is (or should be) carrying out its work of winning over the troops, arming the proletariat and mobilizing growing numbers of proletarian and semi-proletarian elements for the decisive battle. In short, it begins when the masses of their own initiative embark upon a struggle against the government forces. In this preliminary period of preparation for the attack, the Party must fix its attention on the subversion and political conquest of the army. It must assign its best militants to carry out agitational work in the army; it must organize fraternization between the workers and soldiers; it must distribute Party literature; it must strengthen the communist cells in the various units and give them regular instructions; it must work on each man individually, etc.

This work must on no account be interrupted during the insurrection itself; it must on the contrary be stepped up, despite the sacrifices and failures which this may involve.

2. Troops of a counter-revolutionary disposition must be disarmed *by surprise attacks carried out by armed worker detachments*, before they are ready for battle or can make full use of their equipment.

In units where there exist fairly strong communist cells with some influence over the mass of troops, mutinies must be organized to eliminate the reactionary commanding officers, so that it will then be possible to use these troops against other units who have not yet been subverted. It is a good idea to incorporate a certain number of workers into units, or isolated groups of soldiers, who have come over to the side of revolution. Moreover, in street fighting it is generally expedient to reinforce such units as have been won over to the revolution with detachments of red guards.

3. In the event of the initial surprise attack not being crowned with success, the troops must be surrounded in their barracks and prevented from entering the city. Barricades must be set up around the barracks and military quarters, and they must be blockaded until the insurgents have been able to create their own armed forces in the other districts, consolidate the positions which they have won, and organize their forces to attack the trapped enemy. During the siege, strenuous efforts must be made to stop all communication between the enemy and the outside world (i.e. nearby units and headquarters); to cut off his water and light; to harass him physically (by multiplying bold and sudden attacks) and psychologically (by spreading rumours to alarm him), etc.

4. If regular troops have entered the city to combat the insurrection,

barricade tactics must be adopted to hold them off frontally, while attacks are simultaneously organized in their rear from windows and rooftops. The aim must be to exhaust them by ceaseless and daring actions, to organize fraternization and political agitation, and to shake the soldiers' morale and win them over to the side of the revolution.

COMBAT OBJECTIVES DURING THE INSURRECTION

Once the insurgents have seized power in the town in question, their basic objective will naturally be to remove what is now the main obstacle to consolidation of their power and its extension to new fields – i.e. such regular army units (or counter-revolutionary detachments of any other kind) as may have been brought in from other regions to crush the insurrection, or as may have remained intact by leaving the city temporarily during the actual uprising. Under such circumstances, it is relatively easy to determine the most favourable line of attack against this single target: the counter-revolutionary armed forces. The need to concentrate all the strength and resources of the new régime against an enemy who is not yet definitively beaten is self-evident.

A quite different, and far harder, question concerns the choice of targets to attack and seize initially, when the combat organization first goes into action during an insurrection in a city. The leaders of the insurrection are then confronted by a whole number of objectives which it is indispensable for them to capture if they are to win a definitive victory: government buildings (ministries, police stations, administrative centres, etc.); economic establishments (Chambers of Commerce, banks, the management blocks of factories, the head offices of firms and trusts, etc.); railway stations; telegraph offices; army units and military headquarters; arms depots, fascist organizations; the leading bodies of parties and associations hostile to the revolution; newspaper offices and printing works, etc.

Naturally, all these targets must be occupied and either destroyed (police, counter-revolutionary parties and associations, etc.) or utilized by the proletariat to achieve its aims. There is no question about this. The problem is to decide *the order in which* they should be occupied. How can the best use be made of the combat organization and such arms as are available to it? Experience shows that before the seizure of power the proletariat will be badly in need of arms. In Canton, for instance, although the combat organization numbered some 2,000 men it only had 200 bombs and 27 revolvers. The combat organization of Shanghai, with 6,000 members, could only arm 150 of them. In Germany, the Proletarian Hundreds contained 250,000 workers in 1923, but there were only arms for a few thousand of these. In future insurrections – if these do not take place in wartime (which is possible and indeed likely in various countries) – the question of arms will be just as crucial, and the proletariat, with rare exceptions, will never have an adequate supply of modern weapons.

Consequently, in view of the extremely small quantity of arms available, one of the key tactical problems in an insurrection is *how to make effective use of these when the combat organization first moves into action.*

Any attempt to spread the armed squad members out evenly with the aim of seizing all possible objectives simultaneously (as occurred at Reval) *lead inevitably* to the defeat not simply of certain units but of the entire insurrection. If they spread out their men and resources evenly in this way, the red guards will succeed in capturing secondary objectives which have no really decisive influence (from either side's point of view) on the general course of the insurrection: railway-stations, government buildings, municipal offices, telephone and telegraph exchanges, etc. On the other hand, in the struggle for the essential, decisive targets (the army, stocks of arms, the police, the counter-revolutionary leaders, etc.) the proletarian detachments will be defeated as a result of their numerical weakness (and because they do not have arms for the mass of workers), and the chances of victory will *appreciably decrease.* This is why the principle of partial victory ('Be stronger than the enemy at the decisive time and in the decisive place'), which is one of the key principles governing the tactics of regular armies, becomes *doubly* important in an insurrection.

The leaders of the insurrection must decide which of all the various targets is the most important – the one whose capture will swing the balance of forces in favour of the insurgents – and must accordingly concentrate the maximum available manpower and resources (arms) to take it. They should not therefore be afraid of ignoring initially certain secondary targets or districts, but should bear in mind that once the key objectives have been captured it will be easy to deal with the secondary ones.

Depending on circumstances, the key objectives will differ. Generally they will include: firstly, the army; secondly, the police (in the absence of the army, or if the army has gone over to the side of revolution before the insurrection itself); thirdly, the capture of arms depots – so that the workers can be armed; and, fourthly, the elimination of all counter-revolutionary leaders (government, chiefs of staff, central organs of reactionary parties and associations, etc.).

In selecting which of these should be their principal target, the leaders of the insurrection must take into consideration the political and military importance of each of them. Depending on circumstances and the strength of the insurgents, the main target might consist of all these objectives collectively, or merely of certain of them. The armed forces of the proletariat must then be deployed accordingly. Only minimal forces should be kept back at the start of the insurrection for all the secondary objectives; if their capture does not contribute directly to accomplishing the principal task, they should be left temporarily on one side. It should be borne in mind that many objectives for whose capture armed squad members are set aside (at Reval, twenty-five armed men were sent to occupy the railway-stations) *could very well be taken by detachments of workers armed with only improvised weapons* (iron bars, axes, knives, pistols, etc.), under the command of a small number of energetic and experienced Party members from the combat organization.

With respect to the army units, there are two kinds of task which may confront the insurgents: on the one hand, the organization of a revolt inside a unit (or in parts of one), if the mass of soldiers is already under communist influence; on the other hand, if it is believed that a part of the soldiers might march against the insurgents, the organization of a sudden armed attack to eliminate the commanding officers, with the aim of thereby swaying the mass of soldiers and winning them over. In both cases the red guard detachments must be accompanied by responsible Party functionaries who are well known to the soldiers.

To illustrate these observations on how to select the main target, let us take a few historical examples.

In Petrograd in 1917, the revolutionary military committee chose the government and the *junkers* (officer-cadets from the nobility) as the main targets to be attacked by the red guard and the revolutionary units of the garrison. In the given situation this was the most rational solution; for once the government, the most prominent generals and the leaders of counter-revolutionary parties had been arrested, and once the *junkers* (and the counter-revolutionary women's battalion attached to them) had been crushed, then the revolution could be considered as effectively accomplished. And that is what in fact happened. It was possible to achieve the revolution so easily in the capital of Russia because, fundamentally, power had already passed into the hands of the proletariat and the revolutionary garrison, which were both under the influence of the Bolshevik Party, well before the Second Congress of Soviets had proclaimed the dismissal of the Kerensky government. The entry into action of the red guard and the arrest of the government were only, so to speak, the ratification of a *fait accompli*. Even several weeks before the revolution, the Kerensky government could already no longer rely on the Petrograd garrison or on the Baltic fleet (with the exception of a few units: *junkers*, women's battalion, etc.), not to speak of the proletariat. Needless to say such a situation had not created itself but was largely the result of the organizational work and political agitation carried out by the Bolshevik Party, both in the working class and among the soldiers and sailors.

In Moscow, however, the main target *during the October insurrection was the conquest of the army*. For reasons that were specific to that town (the Bolshevik Party was less strong than in Petrograd, the centre of the revolution; the bourgeoisie, for historical reasons, was stronger), agitation in the army had not attained the same scale, the red guard was worse trained and far worse armed than in Petrograd, and in general no extensive organizational or political preparation of the Party and the working class for insurrection had been carried out. For this reason the fighting lasted for eight days in the streets of Moscow.

The main objective of the Canton insurrection was initially the organization of the mutiny in the training regiment. In the prevailing conditions, as has already been shown (see Chapter 5), this choice was absolutely correct. Given the very limited quantity of arms available and the presence of a strong communist cell in this regiment, no conceivable objective could have been more important than the organization of the mutiny in the training regiment, and the disarming of the nearby artillery and infantry regiments and infantry battalion – all units which were already wavering. But the leaders of the insurrection, after correctly choosing the main initial target, committed a great blunder by leaving the arms depots untouched. After the organization of the mutiny in the training regiment and the disarming of the above-mentioned units, these were undeniably far more important targets than the headquarters of the 2nd and 12th Divisions and the 4th Army Corps, against which a long struggle was engaged.

In Hamburg, the fundamental and most urgent task of the insurgents was to obtain arms both for the combat organization itself and for the working-class masses. In the given situation, this could only be achieved by disarming the police – which the insurgents therefore proceed to do.

In Reval, as we saw when we studied the plan of the rising (*see map, p. 69*), there was clearly no main objective upon which the insurgents concentrated the mass of their forces. They seem to have accorded more or less equal importance to all the various targets. In order to occupy a whole series of different objectives, they split their forces into an equivalent number of small groups. But with such limited resources, in terms of both men and equipment, it would have been infinitely more rational to concentrate the main body (i.e. almost all) of their forces either on capturing the *junker* academy, or on winning the 3rd Battalion of the 10th Regiment over to the revolutionary side. Once the main objective had been secured, it would subsequently have been possible for them to redeploy their forces for the next tasks in order of importance.

It is indispensable to respect the principle of a partial victory, not only when forces are being deployed at the start of an insurrection, but equally throughout the entire period of struggle. Non-observation of this basic rule of military science prevents the insurgents from achieving a rapid shift in the balance of forces to their advantage, and thus results ultimately in the crushing of the uprising. Once a particular task has been accomplished, the available forces can be redirected to the next in order of importance – while on the way eliminating isolated enemy groups, and capturing such secondary objectives as constitute obstacles to the achievement of their main objective. Furthermore, this same principle of military science must be observed by each group commander when deploying his forces to execute the specific mission assigned to him.

It has already been stated above that one of the first objectives of the insurrection (whose accomplishment will immediately give the insurgents big advantages) may be the liquidation of counter-revolutionary leaders: the occupation of military headquarters, the arrest of high government officials (ministers, police chiefs, etc.), the liquidation of reactionary commanding officers and of the leaders of counter-revolutionary parties, etc. This objective will often dominate all others from the very first moment of the uprising, as happened in Petrograd in 1917. Moreover, the experience of past revolutions compels us to stress that this objective must not be lost sight of during preparations for the rising and when the plan of action is being worked out, even in cases where the insurgents will initially have to devote the major part of their forces to other objectives of predominant importance (the organization of mutinies among the troops; the disarming of counter-revolutionary units; the capture of arms, etc.). The liquidation of the old régime's top leaders, and of its active defenders during the insurrection, is of the first importance. Yet certain experts in the tactics of street fighting in time of insurrection consider that the liquidation of counter-revolutionary leaders and the organization of diversionary actions of this kind are matters of little interest. Thus, in the symposium *On Street Fighting*, the Russian author Anulov writes as follows: 'As for *terrorist acts*, these cannot produce any great results in street fighting between classes, *for single individuals play an absolutely negligible role under such conditions.*'[1]

Further on, in the course of criticizing the field regulations of the Red Army, according to which '*the personal capacities of the officer placed in command of the troops are of the first importance with respect to the successful repression of an insurrection*'[2], Anulov repeats: 'as for terrorist acts, their importance in the struggle of organized masses is minimal'.[3]

This assertion cannot be accepted, for it is absolutely wrong and anti-Leninist. Anulov confuses two different notions of individual terror. He takes the judgement passed by Marxism on individual terror in a non-revolutionary, 'peaceful' period, and transports it into the struggle of the proletarian masses for power. But the Marxist's attitude in these two cases must be different. While rejecting the individual terror which the Narodniks saw as a panacea against social evils in general, Marxism allows terror in a revolutionary period, during the immediate struggle of the proletariat for power.

[1] F. Anulov: 'A Brief Study of Street-fighting Tactics', in *On Street Fighting*, p. 77, Moscow 1924. Anulov's emphasis.

[2] *Field Regulations of the Red Army*, section X, p. 10.

[3] Anulov, op. cit., p. 88.

This is what Lenin wrote on the subject in his 1906 article: 'Lessons of the Moscow Uprising':

It is not passivity that we should preach, not mere 'waiting' until the troops 'come over'. No! We must proclaim from the housetops the need for a bold offensive and armed attack, the necessity at such times of exterminating the persons in command of the enemy, and of a most energetic fight for the wavering troops.[4]

Besides, Anulov contradicts himself. Quoting a passage from *Rote Fahne* on the immense movement of the masses and the fighting spirit of those masses during the Spartakist uprising of January 1919 in Berlin, and on the inaction and passivity of the leaders who 'were sitting discussing' while 200,000 workers were desperately waiting for leadership and directives for action, he draws the following conclusion:

The Spartakist insurrection of January 1919 in Berlin provides a classic example of a defeat caused by passivity and indecision on the part of the masses in revolt, and above all on the part of their leaders.[5]

If the masses were defeated because of the passivity of their leaders, it follows that the role of leaders is important in an insurrection.

In all insurrections in which the insurgents have not succeeded, or not succeeded in time, in liquidating the leaders of counter-revolution, they have been defeated; for they have been obliged to fight in conditions infinitely more difficult than if they had eliminated the enemy leaders in time. Precisely such insurrections as the Hamburg rising or the example of the Spartakist rising quoted above by *Rote Fahne*, in which leadership was lacking and the masses left to their own devices, are doomed to failure. The victorious insurrections are those in which, in addition to the other factors necessary for success, there is a firm and experienced leadership and in which the insurgent proletariat, for its part, has 'decapitated' the counter-revolution early on. This decapitation can be effected by means of carefully prepared diversionary actions, including terrorist acts (executions or arrests).

This is a fundamental principle, about which there can be no doubt. It must be applied wherever the opportunity arises, both with respect to political leaders and military or police chiefs, and with respect to the commanding officers of enemy troop units or of small detachments during street fighting. Thus the field regulations of the Red Army

[4] Lenin, *Selected Works*, vol. I, p. 581.
[5] Anulov, op. cit., p. 83.

of the USSR are absolutely correct in according great importance to the person of the leader who has command of the troops.

It should be borne in mind that achieving this objective – i.e. the suppression of the enemy leaders, or at least of some of those who, by virtue of their official or social standing, can have a direct and active influence in hampering the insurrection initially – normally only requires a small number of squad members. If their whereabouts has been carefully ascertained in advance, small isolated groups of squad members, well trained both in general and for this specific mission, will be able to capture them in their houses or wherever else they may happen to be. It is thus important when preparing an insurrection to consider, as a matter of course, the problem of how to liquidate the enemy leaders, and, at the outset of the general proletarian uprising (i.e. from the moment the proletariat moves into action), to resolve it – if not completely, at least in part.

If, in the Canton insurrection, carefully trained groups had been given the task of suppressing the most prominent leaders of the Kuomintang and of the reactionary camp in general, including Chang Fa-k'uei (such a task would have been perfectly feasible), this would not have failed to have an immense influence on the outcome of the conflict. As we know, the counter-revolutionary authorities of Canton, as soon as the proletariat rose, fled to Hong Kong and to Li Fu-lin's headquarters on Honam island, and from there directed the repression. Again, if the Estonian comrades had had sufficient forces and had prepared diversionary actions in advance with the aim of capturing the most actively reactionary government officials, and if this mission had been carried out even partially, then the Reval insurrection would have taken place in appreciably more favourable conditions. However, given the limited forces of the insurgents, there was of course no possibility of such an undertaking in the first stages of the insurrection.

Among the key targets must also be mentioned the means of communication: telephone, telegraph, and radio communications (i.e. wireless offices in the city, on the railways, in the various military headquarters, etc.). The leaders of the insurrection must make certain to occupy all these installations in good time, and to make the best use of them. If the forces are lacking for this, measures must be taken to neutralize them so that the enemy will not be able to use them. It is considerably easier to disrupt these services than to capture them: it is enough for a few individuals to cut the wires of the main telephone and telegraph lines.

In most cases, the insurgents initially devote sizeable forces to occupying the various municipal centres: the post office, railway-stations, banks etc. By so doing they weaken the forces sent to carry out essential missions, i.e. those which are initially the most important. This represents a faulty deployment of forces. Installations such as railway-stations, post offices, town halls, etc., are not of crucial importance for the insurrection. It will always be easy to capture them, but hard to hold them if the enemy's main strength has not been destroyed. Thus, occupation of these centres, when the insurgents only have limited manpower, must be demoted to the second rank of objectives, or at least entrusted to workers' detachments without modern weapons.

In working out the plan for an insurrection, the liberation of political prisoners must not be neglected. As the experience of Canton and Reval showed, this too is an objective of the greatest importance. The prisoners should, if at all possible, be freed at the very outset of the insurrection.

THE ELEMENTS OF SURPRISE AND 'TIMING' AT THE OUTSET OF THE INSURRECTION

In our survey of the insurrection's targets, we have constantly stressed the first moment, the first minutes when the combat organization of the proletariat goes into action. Since it is far weaker than the enemy in military terms, the combat organization is obliged to compensate for this inferiority by its activity and by the unexpectedness of its operations. Only thus will it be able on the one hand to seize the arms which it lacks, to win new armed forces into its ranks (e.g. by provoking mutinies among the troops, or by arming fresh workers' detachments with captured weapons); and on the other hand to weaken and disrupt the enemy as far as possible. From this point of view, *the first instant of the insurrection is of decisive importance*. The subsequent evolution of the conflict will depend in large measure on the success or failure of the operations undertaken in the first hour or two.

In the struggle for power in a city, surprise is of the utmost importance. The insurgents, as attackers, must draw the maximum advantage from this, above all *in the first moments when they move into action*, and must take the enemy by surprise before he has had time to prepare his resistance. Such surprise attacks are best carried out at night or early in the morning, when the troops and police (whether these have been specially mobilized, or are permanent police units as in Germany) are sleeping, and it is therefore easiest to capture arms depots and suppress the counter-revolutionary leaders. However, the surprise attack must be organized in such a way as to ensure that at the right moment the working-class masses will enter the fray.

The element of 'surprise' has been utilized in most past insurrections, and, with rare exceptions, surprise attacks by insurgents have been extremely successful. As we have seen, it was only by surprise attacks that poorly armed and numerically insignificant groups of revolutionaries in Hamburg were able to disarm seventeen police stations, and in each case to capture some thirty rifles or machine-guns. If the Reval insurgents failed in their surprise attack on the *junker* academy, this was due to the lack of coordination and synchronization between the two groups sent to attack respectively the ground and upper floors of the building. If it had not been for this blunder, the fifty-six insurgents would certainly have captured the entire academy and disarmed *junkers* who outnumbered them by eight to one. Attacks on several other objectives were fully successful, thanks to the element of surprise.

In the Canton insurrection, considerable use was made of the element of surprise, and this invariably had favourable results: disarming of the infantry and artillery regiments and an infantry battalion; disarming of the police force, etc. In the third Shanghai insurrection (21 March 1927), the insurgents carried out a surprise attack on the police in broad daylight, with total success.

On the other hand, in the 1923 peasant insurrection in Bulgaria, the elememt of surprise was rarely adopted: the peasant detachments went into action singly against the troops and gendarmerie and were ultimately crushed.

But surprise operations, apart from the courage and decision which they demand of the insurgents, can only succeed given certain preconditions: (*a*) careful reconnaissance of the targets to be seized; (*b*) an extremely detailed plan of action, and perfect *coordination* (*with respect to the timing and allocation of missions*) between the various units or individuals taking part in the attack; (*c*) support for the detachment or detachments at the appropriate moment from the mass of workers, so that the initial success can be consolidated.

The role of reconnaissance in armed insurrection is immense. Before drawing up the plan of action, a careful and complete reconnaissance must be carried out; it is only on this basis that the available forces should be allocated to their respective targets. Since it is the proletariat which holds the initiative and can decide on the moment for the action to begin, and since the targets in a city are usually fixed ones, it is fairly easy to carry out a complete and thorough reconnaissance in good time. Exceptions may of course occur – cases in which some circumstances or other will oblige the proletariat to attack at a particular moment regardless of its degree of preparation. But such cases will never be the rule. It must also be recalled that the smaller the scale of an operation, the more detailed the reconnaissance must be. The leadership of the insurrection in a large city will not need, for example, to know the layout of the rooms in such and such a police station; the approaches to every single police station; nor the degree of tactical training or the personal qualities of individual officers commanding minor police or army units. It will not need to know details of how particular units are disposed in their barracks, how their guards are posted, where the soldiers keep their weapons, etc. All it will need will be more general information, such as: the degree to which the officers influence the rank and file in the various military units; the mood of the mass of soldiers; the location of the arms dumps; the addresses of top officials and leaders of counter-revolutionary parties, etc. But the leaders of the insurrection in any given district of the city, and the commanders of each detachment of the red guard, will on the contrary need to possess extremely detailed information on the enemy, and on the locality which will constitute their field of operations.

In street fighting, personal reconnaissance by the commanders of units and squads assigned specific missions during the insurrection plays a greater role than it does in the conditions of a war of manoeuvre in open country. Such personal reconnaissance by military commanders is, in any case, infinitely more feasible in a city before the launching of an insurrection than it is either in open country or during the actual course of an uprising. Thus, in addition to the work carried out by specialized scouts, whose task it is to collect regular information about the enemy as required by the red guard commanders, all leaders from the highest to the lowest should seize every possibility of carrying out personal reconnaissance of the planned objectives.

The disarming of the police stations in Hamburg would have been absolutely impossible if the insurgents had not previously carried out a careful reconnaissance of the buildings which they had to attack; if they had not studied the approaches to them, the layout of their rooms, the location of the arms-magazines, the positions of the sentries, etc. The surprise attack on the *junker* academy at Reval was only possible because, the week before, the commander of the assault unit and his immediate aides had systematically reconnoitred the approaches to the building, the daily routine of its occupants, and the layout of the academy and the officers' mess. It will be absolutely impossible, for example, to eliminate the main individual counter-revolutionary leaders properly and in good time if the groups charged with the task do not possess extremely precise information about the whereabouts of the individuals in question and how to gain access to them, or if they only have information of a general character: e.g. such and such an official lives in X street, at number Y, etc. In addition to the street and the number of the house or flat, they must also know the time at which the person in question comes home, how to get into his quarters, and, if there is no way of killing him in the street, details of how his residence is guarded, etc. The rescue of the German communist Braun in 1928 from the Moabit prison in Berlin shows that operations of this kind are by no means impossible given meticulous reconnaissance and good organization – that they are indeed perfectly feasible.

In addition to the information provided by reconnaissance, the insurgents, if they are to succeed, must have *a detailed plan of action in which every particular is spelled out*. This plan must specify the precise allocation of forces for the various missions; the way in which good coordination is to be ensured; the hour at which mobilization of the insurgent forces is to begin, and the hour by which it is to be completed; the precise moment at which each specific target should be attacked, etc. *In the initial surprise operations* (and in surprise operations generally, at any stage of the fighting) *timing plays a considerable role*. It is therefore essential for the insurgent groups to be most scrupulous in keeping to the times specified in the plan for the operation to start and for each of its phases: this is *one of the most crucial tactical requirements in these initial surprise actions*. The least infringement of this principle will often result in the failure of the operation and the death of the insurgents themselves.

A few examples:

At Reval, the attack on the *junker* academy failed because the group detailed to capture the upper storey arrived a minute or two later than the group detailed to take the ground floor.

In Hamburg, the leaders of the insurrectionary groups attached the greatest importance to strict observation of the times laid down in the plan. Thus the Barmbek commander instructed his subordinates to see that each group was present and ready at its assembly-point at 4.55 a.m. precisely. These assembly-points had been chosen so that they were exactly five minutes away from the police stations to be attacked. The attack on the police stations was to begin at 5 a.m. precisely. To ensure simultaneity of action, the watches of the group commanders were checked and synchronized immediately before the attack. Thanks to this strict timing, the operation was brilliantly successful as far as most of the groups were concerned.

What has been said concerns the execution of specific missions during the insurrection. But 'timing' also plays an important role in insurrections generally, whether in a single city or in a region containing several cities. What is involved here is the whole question of simultaneity of action. Simultaneity is necessary whether the uprising is taking place in a single big city or throughout an entire province (or even an entire country, if it is not too large in area). It allows the insurgents to utilize all their available forces for a concerted blow, thus limiting the enemy's freedom of action and preventing him from concentrating his forces to defeat them separately, one by one. The insurrection should always be launched simultaneously in the largest possible number, and with all the forces available. It is relatively easy for the proletariat, as the attacker, to launch operations simultaneously – at least within the context of a single city. However, experience has shown that the insurgents are not always capable of fulfilling this essential tactical requirement.

A comrade who has studied the Bulgarian insurrection of 1923 from precisely this point of view writes:

The same comrade adds:

Four peasant detachments with a combined strength of about 10,000 men were sent to capture the provincial capital of Stara Zagora. They were to take up position secretly at the exits to the town, in order to be able to attack it simultaneously from every side. The government forces were estimated at about five hundred men, with thirty machine-guns and twelve cannon. The signal for the attack was to be given by a raid on the prison, which was to be carried out by workers armed with hand-grenades. This raid took place at the appointed time, but the peasant detachments had not yet all taken up their positions, so that the simultaneous attack did not take place. The enemy was thus able to defeat the insurgents one by one.

The same comrade adds:

For the night attack on the provincial capital of Kazanlyk, armed peasant detachments totalling over one thousand men were mustered from the surrounding district. The government forces in the town consisted of some six hundred men, with twenty machine-guns. The signal for a concerted attack was to be given by a power failure. This signal was never given; as a result, the insurgents began their operations at different times.

The experience of the first two Shanghai insurrections (23 October 1926 and 21 February 1927) shows that it is sometimes impossible, for purely material reasons, to achieve simultaneity of action. Thus, on 23 October, it had been fixed that the combat organization would move into action at 3 a.m.; but the operations were supposed to begin at a signal, to be given by a cannon-shot from a gunboat which had gone over to the insurgents. This signal in turn depended on a rocket which was supposed to be fired from the house of Niu Yung-ch'ien, the representative of the national government. But the signal was never in fact given, because the gunboat did not notice the rocket.

In the second insurrection, as we have already seen, a misunderstanding of a similar kind occurred. Since the shelling of the arsenal by a gunboat, which was to serve as a signal for the entire insurrection, for various reasons did not take place, the insurrection was put off from 21 to 22 February. This time, the gunboat opened fire on the arsenal precisely at the appointed time (6 p.m.). The insurrection began, but only in the southern part of the city. The squads of the northern part (Cha-pei) had not heard the cannon-fire, and for this reason took no part in the rising.

The third Shanghai insurrection, as we know, started at a fixed hour (1 p.m.) without any kind of signal, and did so simultaneously in all districts of the city.

It is thus clear that the start of operations must not be made dependent on any auditory, visual or other kind of signal which, for some material and sometimes accidental cause or other may fail to be given, or if it is given may not be noticed by the people concerned. *The best signal is a prearranged time.* Operations must be fixed to begin *at a precise hour.* From a technical point of view, this is the best way of guaranteeing that the insurrection will begin simultaneously at all points.

Attacks by peasant detachments too both can and must be synchronized and precisely timed. All that is necessary is to make certain beforehand that the detachments have in fact arrived at the assembly-points where they are supposed to form up for the attack. In this respect, the Bulgarian experience and that of Canton (a detachment of 1,500 peasants was supposed to arrive in Canton for the start of the insurrection, but only 500 in fact turned up) are conclusive.

Simultaneity is far more difficult to achieve over a wider area (throughout an entire country in the West; throughout a province or group of provinces in the East, e.g. in China). Nevertheless, it must be aimed at as far as possible. It is a mistake to order, as in Germany, an insurrection in a single town like Hamburg, without planning any action to coincide with it in other towns and regions (at the very least in the neighbouring ones) where conditions were no less favourable than in Hamburg.

Every communist party organizing and directing the preparations for an insurrection should know that the more centralized the State apparatus, and the more highly-developed the transport system and communication network, the more important it will be to attack simultaneously and the more the leaders of the insurrection must strive to achieve this.

The initial surprise attacks by the insurgent forces on their various targets must be backed up at the right moment by the proletarian masses entering the active struggle. If this does not occur, the combat organization will be unable to consolidate its initial successes, and there will be a loss of contact between its operations and the movement of the broad proletarian masses. In view of the poor armament of the combat organization and its relatively limited manpower (as a result of the shortage of arms), the attacking units, immediately they have won their first successes, must be in a position to distribute the arms they have won to such workers as are willing to fight; thanks to these reinforcements, they will then be able to develop the initial victories.

Armed insurrection is not exhausted by the military operations of the insurgent units – even where these are relatively large in numerical terms. When there is a situation favourable for an insurrection (see the conditions enumerated by Lenin, and the instructions given in the Programme of the Comintern), the combat units have the task of striking the initial, unexpected blow at the enemy; but, thereafter, the broad masses of the proletarian population must be drawn into the armed struggle. In this sense, the revolutionary mass movement of the proletariat is at the same time the basis upon which the operations of the red guard (the combat organization) must be organized, and serves directly as a reserve force for the latter. The leaders of the insurrection must at all costs ensure that the masses are drawn into the conflict at the same time as the military organization moves into action. This is one of the most crucial tactical principles of armed insurrection. In no circumstances must exclusive reliance be placed upon the initiative of the revolutionary masses. The Party must, immediately before the combat organization goes into action, take the necessary measures to guarantee the participation of the masses when the moment arrives.

Numerous participants in the Reval insurrection have indicated that one of the tactical errors of their leaders was their failure to provide for reserves. This accusation is not justified. In the case of Reval, it was impossible for reserves to exist because of the extreme numerical weakness of the combat squads. But this was not the only reason. It is our view in general that it will very rarely be necessary to have reserves at the moment of the first surprise blow (start of the insurrection). At any rate, such cases will be the exception. As a rule it is not at all expedient to provide for reserves in the first phase of the insurrection. The insurgents must devote all their available forces to dealing the enemy an initial surprise blow. The role of reserves in consolidating the victory should be filled by such workers as have no weapons; these must secure arms in the course of the insurrection, as soon as the combat units have succeeded in disarming the enemy or in capturing arms depots. Reserves will be necessary later, in the event of prolonged fighting in the streets, or of operations in the surrounding countryside. But to keep armed detachments in reserve at the start of the insurrection can only weaken the revolutionary forces. Reserves should be created and grow in size during the actual course of the fighting, by the addition of new workers' detachments. If this is impossible, and if the leaders of the insurrection are not capable of achieving during the battle a constant growth of the active nucleus of its combat forces, then there can be no question of their emerging victorious from the struggle.

Furthermore, from a tactical point of view, to set aside reserves at the start of the insurrection has no sense. If the initial attacks are planned in accordance with the principle of surprise (and this will be so in ninety-five per cent of cases), the operations of the insurgents in this initial period can obviously not be of any great duration. They will be swift raids, which in most cases will end either in the total defeat of the enemy or else in failure. In the event of victory, the attacking unit becomes available to carry out the next mission, i.e. in a sense it becomes a reserve, since it can be moved wherever its presence is most needed at that particular moment. For example, the detachment which had captured the airborne corps at Reval found itself in possession of machine-guns, rifles, plenty of ammunition, cars, trucks, and some forty additional men; it thus became a sort of reserve, which could and should have been used to carry out new missions.

If, on the other hand, the unit carrying out the surprise attack fails, no reserve will be able to restore the situation. In view of the instantaneous character of such operations (organized according to the principle of surprise, with a minimum of forces involved), and in view of the absence in this phase of the insurrection of any technical liaison between the leadership – at whose disposal reserves would be kept – and the commanders of the fighting units, reserves could hardly arrive in time to be of any use.

ACTIVITY AND DETERMINATION IN COMBAT
DURING THE INSURRECTION

'Let us remember,' wrote Lenin at the end of August 1906, 'that a great mass struggle is approaching. It will be an armed uprising. It must, as far as possible, be simultaneous. The masses must know that they are entering upon an armed, bloody and desperate struggle. Contempt for death must become widespread among them and will ensure victory. The onslaught on the enemy must be pressed with the greatest vigour; attack, not defence, must be the slogan of the masses; the ruthless extermination of the enemy will be their task; the organization of the struggle will become mobile and flexible; the wavering elements among the troops will be drawn into active participation. And in this momentous struggle, the party of the class-conscious proletariat must discharge its duty to the full.'[6]

Immediately before the October revolution (9 October 1917) in his letter 'Advice of an Onlooker', Lenin wrote as follows about the activity that is necessary in an insurrection:

Armed uprising is a *special* form of political struggle, one subject to special laws to which attentive thought must be given. Karl Marx expressed this truth with remarkable clarity when he wrote that '*insurrection is an art quite as much as war*'. Of the principal rules of this art, Marx noted the following:

  1. *Never play* with insurrection, but when beginning it realize firmly that you must *go all the way*.
  2. Concentrate a *great superiority of forces* at the decisive point and at the decisive moment, otherwise the enemy, who has the advantage of better preparation and organization, will destroy the insurgents.
  3. Once the insurrection has begun, you must act with the greatest *determination*, and by all means, without fail, take the *offensive*. 'The defensive is the death of every armed rising.'
  4. You must try to take the enemy by surprise and seize the moment when his forces are scattered.
  5. You must strive for *daily* successes, however small (one might say hourly, if it is the case of one town), and at all costs retain 'moral superiority'.

Marx summed up the lessons of all revolutions in respect to armed uprising in the words of 'Danton, the greatest master of revolutionary policy yet known: *de l'audace, de l'audace, encore de l'audace*'.[7]

Having formulated these key tactical principles, Lenin drew from them practical conclusions with respect to Petrograd, and gave the Party all kinds of advice about the military and political measures to be taken in order to seize power in that city. In particular, he drew its attention to the need to display the greatest courage and decision in the struggle – the 'triple audacity' of which Danton speaks.

The experience of all past revolutions has confirmed in the most categorical fashion the tactical principles of Marx and Lenin. The insurgents must display total courage, must be active to the point of rashness, must not allow a single chance of dealing a blow at the enemy to escape them. Each detachment, each individual combatant, after carrying out their assigned missions, must strive to seek out the enemy and finish him off, until he has been utterly annihilated. This is as necessary a precondition for victory as a well-organized, concerted

[6] Lenin, *Selected Works*, vol. I, p. 583, in 'Lessons of the Moscow Uprising'.
[7] Lenin, *Selected Works*, vol. II, pp. 426-7.

initial attack, correct timing for the insurrection to begin, or firm leadership from the Communist Party and its combat organization.

We have seen the failure of precisely those insurrections (we are not referring here only to definitive victory, but rather to the conduct of all proletarian armed struggles, including such insurrections as the 1905 Moscow rising, the Paris Commune, the German insurrections of 1919, 1920, 1921, etc., which as a result of all kinds of unfavourable conditions could not possibly have succeeded) in which insufficient energy, courage, contempt for death and determination in combat were displayed, or in which all these qualities were only displayed early on in the struggle and subsequently declined.

In the 1921 March Action in central Germany, the insurgents in the area round the Leuna-Werk (totalling tens of thousands – the Leuna-Werk alone had some 22,000 workers at the time) had every chance of capturing the neighbouring towns, above all Merseburg (some four kilometres away from the Leuna-Werk), destroying the government apparatus and the police barracks, and extending the territory held by the insurrection to join up with the insurgents from other regions (Mansfeld, etc.). After organizing fifteen Proletarian Hundreds and some auxiliary forces (an engineer unit, a cycle detachment, etc.) and capturing huge arms stocks (we have no accurate figures on the insurgents' armament, but when the Reichswehr and police occupied the Leuna-Werk, they found some 800 rifles, three machine-guns and various other arms; the insurgents certainly had many more, since a great part were hidden after the insurrection), the insurgents then merely remained passively in their own area until the Reichswehr advanced on them from three sides at once with artillery and police auxiliaries, and crushed this, the most important centre of the March insurrection. Things might have turned out differently throughout central Germany if the leaders of the Leuna-Werk worker detachments had displayed the energy required in such cases.

This passivity of the Leuna-Werk workers should not of course be viewed as a lack of energy on the part of the thousands of workers who had already proved their energy by rising. Those who were guilty here were the leaders of the insurrection, who did not prove capable of giving the masses practical slogans and directives. The blame falls squarely upon the 'action committee', which was made up of representatives of the Unified German Communist Party and of the Communist Workers' Party of Germany (an ultra-left party with strong anarchist tendencies, which has now degenerated and lost all influence on the masses).[8]

One could find numerous examples in the history of proletarian armed struggle to illustrate and confirm the above-quoted principles of Marx and Lenin regarding the need to display the greatest possible energy during an insurrection. We shall only quote one, the most striking of all, which shows that the proletariat can succeed in seizing power even when the workers are totally without arms, if they have an unshakeable determination to win and display incomparable energy. This example is the Cracow rising of 6 November 1923.

Here is what a Polish communist who has studied that insurrection writes:

The events of November and the Cracow rising are an instructive example of proletarian class struggle. On 4 November, the government published a decree forbidding open-air meetings. On 6 November, a crowd began to move in the direction of the People's House, situated in the centre of the city. The streets which led there were blocked by strong police cordons. Behind the police, there was a company of infantry. The crowd broke the police cordon and disarmed the soldiers. The arms which it used, as the official indictment acknowledges, were sticks, bottles and cabbage-stalks! Now some of the workers had arms. Most, however, continued to fight with sticks. No shot had yet been fired. Police reinforcements arrived and formed a square. The crowd promptly opened fire, and the police was obliged to withdraw into the back streets, where it was once again met with gunfire. The police took flight and hid inside the houses. At this moment the cavalry came into action. One after another, four cavalry squadrons plunged into the battle under cover from a machine-gun group, and were followed by three armoured cars. Under a hail of bullets which met them from windows and cellars, they were unable to advance and were picked off like rabbits. The horses could not move easily on the asphalt, preventing those behind from advancing. The armoured cars came to a halt, because their crews had been put out of action. One of them fell into the hands of the insurgents. After fighting for only three hours, the working class found itself master of the town. From a purely military point of view, the Cracow proletariat had triumphed. The political and administrative authorities had lost their head, and the military commander (*wojwoda*) of the city had taken to his heels.[9]

The Cracow workers, absolutely without arms at the start of the battle, armed themselves in the course of the struggle and defeated a half-battalion of infantry, a regiment of cavalry supported by armoured cars, and the entire police-force of the city. If the insurrection was

[8] This information is taken from an anonymous article 'German Struggles' in the communist military/political journal *Der Bürgerkrieg*, no. 2, 1923.

[9] Article by 'Ludwig' in *Der Bürgerkrieg*, no. 13, 1924.

subsequently crushed, this was due to the treachery of the Polish Socialist Party (PPS) and to the poor use which the Communist Party made of the revolutionary situation at that time.

The Cracow insurrection figures in the history of the armed struggle of the international proletariat *as a model example of mass struggle for power*.

'The defensive is the death of every armed rising.' This is an incontrovertible truth. Victory can only be won by offensive action, by active operations on the part of the insurgents. Even the temporary defensive tactic to which the insurgents may be forced in some particular sector should have an active character. Defensive action taken not for its own sake, but with the object of speedily returning to active operations and putting the enemy out of action: such must be the insurgents' watchword.

If an unfavourable balance of forces at a particular spot obliges the insurgents to fall temporarily back onto the defensive, they must show the greatest possible determination, hold down the largest possible number of enemy troops, and inflict the heaviest possible losses upon these by good use of their fire-power. At the same time they must take advantage of even the slightest possibility to counter-attack (at least partially), by carrying out sudden raids on the enemy's flank or rear; by organizing unexpected running fire; by harassing the enemy forces; and, finally, by returning to a general offensive to liquidate the enemy definitively.

Insurgents forced back onto the defensive, if they display enough determination and make proper use of the advantages of their situation (houses, windows, attics, rooftops, and all cover in general – including barricades), can inflict serious damage on the enemy, both materially and in terms of morale.

Trotsky, in his book *1905*, recounts a characteristic episode during the defensive action of the Moscow insurgents in December:

A group of thirty men, which had installed itself inside a building, for four hours resisted the fire of 500–600 soldiers with three cannon and two machine-guns. After using up all their ammunition and inflicting heavy losses on the troops, the squad members moved away unscathed. The soldiers had demolished several blocks of houses with cannonfire, burned down several wooden houses and exterminated a considerable number of panic-stricken inhabitants – all this in order to force a small group of revolutionaries to retreat.

Such episodes were frequent in the Moscow insurrection.

By way of contrast, the Reval insurrection of 1924 provides a negative example in this respect. The insurgents, as we have seen, did not display the least determination. After the first setbacks, they at once dispersed without organizing any resistance. This was certainly to some extent due to the fact that the insurgents did not feel that they had the support of the masses: whence their demoralization. The insurrection had not been preceded by large-scale working-class actions, strikes, meetings, demonstrations, etc. During the insurrection itself, the masses did not have time to join the battle, since the rising was crushed in three or four hours. It would, however, have been possible to draw them into the struggle if the key working-class cadres had known that an insurrection was planned and had prepared for it. But this was not the case. The insurrection was not expected even by the Reval proletariat.

THE PLAN FOR THE ARMED INSURRECTION

The need to have a plan is obvious. Not to draw up a plan and to count solely on improvisation means voluntarily renouncing any possibility of exerting a conscious and rational influence on the course of the insurrection.

The plan, in its general outline, must be an overall strategic plan covering the whole country. In accordance with this overall plan other detailed plans must be drawn up (i.e. tactical plans) for each town or centre.

The overall strategic plan must define *which* centres or towns (the capital, the big industrial towns, such and such a province), in the prevailing conditions, are of decisive importance for the planned action. It must study all regions or centres which could be the sites of revolutionary insurrections, and from which the revolution could radiate out towards the other regions. It must, at least in broad outline, provide for mutual collaboration between these various revolutionary centres, both in terms of synchronizing the time at which the insurrections are to begin and, subsequently, during the actual fighting, in terms of the material and political help which they may be able to afford each other and of the coordination of their operations. The strategic plan must give an answer to the following question: should the insurrection be preceded by a general strike, from which it will emerge as a natural consequence, or does the prevailing situation allow the launching of an insurrection without a general strike (as, for example, in Russia in October 1917)? In working out its plan, the leadership of the armed insurrection must decide whether the rising should be timed to coincide with some congress of proletarian organizations (trade unions, Soviets, factory councils), as was the case in Petrograd in 1917 (the Second Congress of Soviets) and in Germany in 1923 (the Congress of Factory Committees at Chemnitz – which, in the Central Committee's plan, was supposed to declare a general strike whose outbreak would be the signal for insurrection); in other words, whether it should coincide with the congress of some political organism which will announce that the old order cannot be allowed to exist any longer, and declare itself the supreme authority of the new revolutionary régime. Alternatively, does the Party consider it more rational, in the given conditions, to organize the seizure of power and the overthrow of the old government by an armed action on the part of the proletariat, even before there is any authoritative proletarian organism in the decisive centres of the country capable of playing the role of supreme legislative authority of the revolution?

Finally, the strategic plan must lay down in broad outline the measures to be taken by the Party in the event of outside intervention, and must provide for the formation of a regular Red Army as soon as revolutionary power has been consolidated in any given region or big city. It goes without saying that the leaders must also plan the fundamental political measures (nationalization of the land; expropriation of heavy industry; legislation on the working day, wages, housing, etc.) which the new régime must at once put through in order to consolidate its power.

The strategic plan (the basic elements of the planned insurrection) must of course be established, at least in broad outline, quite a long time before the insurrection itself. Later, if circumstances change, it can be particularized and improved. In accordance with this plan, the Party must in good time take all the necessary political and organizational measures to create favourable conditions for revolution, above all in the decisive regions.

When drawing up a plan for insurrection in a centre, town, or inhabited place in general, it must be recognized that it is impossible to foresee all the fluctuating circumstances of the coming conflict, or, therefore, all actions to be taken by the insurgents during the entire duration of the uprising. The tactical plan for insurrection in a town must be as detailed as possible, and concern itself solely with the first phase of the insurrection, the initial actions, the first missions to be assigned to each main detachment of the red guards. As far as the subsequent stages are concerned, the leadership of the insurrection can and must give instructions of a general kind in good time; these will then be made more precise in the light of such circumstances as may arise during the conflict, in the town itself and in the surrounding regions.

The plan for insurrection in a town must include: (*a*) an evaluation of the situation and the balance of forces in the town itself; (*b*) the date when the insurrection is to begin; (*c*) an indication of the main objectives which the insurgents absolutely must take, and whose capture will exercise the greatest influence on the course of the operation; (*d*) an indication of the secondary regions and objectives to be occupied in the second phase of operations (if they cannot be captured by detachments of unarmed workers); (*e*) details of how the insurgent forces are to be deployed against the various objectives – with the maximum manpower being reserved for the main targets; (*f*) an indication of the most likely tasks which the various detachments will have to undertake after their first missions have been successfully accomplished; (*g*) instructions on the course to be adopted in the event of the failure of any given unit; (*h*) an indication of the measures to be taken to prevent the arrival of government troops from other towns or regions (sabotage of the lines of communication, guerrilla actions, etc., etc.); (*i*) an indication of the measures to be taken to ensure that the mass of workers is drawn into the armed struggle, and that arms are distributed to them; (*j*) provision for the elimination of counter-revolutionary leaders; (*k*) provision for the formation of regular Red Army units during the fighting; (*l*) instructions on the organization of liaison during the insurrection; (*m*) the location of the overall military commander and the other military and political leaders, including the members of the Revolutionary Committee, at the start of the insurrection; (*n*) directives on the political measures to be enacted by the Revolutionary Committee, as representative and organizer of the new régime.

The plan should be drawn up on the basis of the following data: (*a*) a social map of the city, showing which districts are friendly by virtue of their social character; showing the degree of organization and fighting spirit in the districts which will be the centre of the uprising, i.e. in the districts which will strike the initial blow and later fuel the insurrection with a flow of new recruits; and showing which districts are socially hostile and should be destroyed during the insurrection; (b) details of the deployment and degree of disaffection of the police units, and of the counter-revolutionary military associations if these are on a war footing (mobilized); (c) the addresses of all high officials, all leaders of parties and associations hostile to the revolution, and all commanders of army and police units; (d) the location of arms depots, and details of how they are guarded; (e) a tactical evaluation of the city, indicating positions, buildings, groups of buildings, etc., which are suitable for offensive or defensive action; (f) information on the location of cars, trucks, motorcycles, etc. (whether belonging to the State or to private individuals), which are to be appropriated; (g) the technical information necessary to enable the urban transport system, telephone, etc., to be used during the insurrection; (h) detailed information concerning the personnel and armament of the revolutionary forces and the tactical judgement of the various red guard commanders.

The plan for insurrection, or at least its various individual parts, must be drawn up in such a way that both the commanders of the insurgent detachments and sub-units and the active, reliable nucleus of the Party are able to study their first objectives in sufficient time to make the necessary preparations; in such a way that the leadership itself is able to take the political and organizational measures required in sufficient time to ensure that the first actions of the combat squads will be as successful as possible.

It goes without saying that the plan of insurrection and all parts of it are secret, and that the leaders must take the greatest precautions against the plan or any part of it falling into the enemy's hands (via provocateurs, comrades gossiping, etc.).

11

The Character of
the Insurgents' Operations
during the Insurrection

PRELIMINARY REMARKS

In the last chapter we only dealt in the most general way with the problems of street fighting in the real sense of the word. The whole weight of the chapter lay in an attempt to set out the main tactical principles which must govern the drawing up of the plan for *the proletariat's first, surprise actions at the start of the insurrection*.

But it is hard to imagine a situation in which the proletariat could, with a single rapid blow, however powerful, smash the state machine of the moribund ruling class and annihilate its armed strength – the regular army, the police, and the volunteer military associations which support them. At all events, such a situation could only occur as a rare exception – even in a single isolated town, let alone a whole country.

The initial actions of the proletarian armed forces, confronted by an enemy who is not yet completely bogged down in his own internal contradictions and who still retains some ability to defend his dominant position, can and must deal the class enemy as telling a material and psychological blow as possible. This means capturing arms for the mass of workers (and proletarian elements in general) willing to fight and die for the revolution; organizing mutinies among the troops and winning them over to the revolution; seizing key tactical objectives; and eliminating some at least of the counter-revolutionary leaders. The aim must be to achieve the most favourable possible balance of forces for the proletariat, and to create the conditions for a successful struggle to consolidate proletarian power definitively.

The experience of past armed insurrections confirms the correctness of this principle categorically. Tempting as it may be to believe that one can destroy the enemy with a lightning blow, in practice this is quite unattainable. For the enemy too is getting ready for a desperate struggle, and the experience of past conflicts has not been wasted on him either. When preparing for insurrection, the proletariat should be aware of the fact that it will have to sustain a more or less prolonged armed struggle before it can hope to break the resistance of the ruling classes completely.

The conditions of struggle which will emerge *after* the initial surprise attack by the combat organization will be *essentially different* from those which obtained before the attack. Provided that it has been well prepared, the initiative *when the insurrection is first launched* (opening of hostilities by the armed forces of the proletariat) will be held by the proletariat. The ruling classes will naturally suspect that some action is being planned. But even though they are aware that decisive conflicts are imminent, if the insurrection has been properly prepared and organized with the requisite security they will not know *when* it will break out, nor *where the first blow will fall*. However, after the first blows struck by the combat organization at its planned objectives, this situation becomes totally changed. *Henceforward, the two sides are in a state of open and implacable civil war*. From now on, all other categories of class struggle are entirely subordinated to armed struggle. All the normal everyday life of the city is temporarily suspended, and public attention is fixed solely and exclusively on the military operations of the belligerents.

Depending on the circumstances, the tactical methods to be adopted will vary. Armed struggle, in a proletarian insurrection, means fighting in the streets of a city. The tactics of street fighting are only *a variation* of military tactics in general: in the main, they obey the same principles as the tactics of regular armies.

The object of the present chapter is to set out the main tactical principles which govern the various kinds of operations in street fighting – bearing in mind the specific features of such a tactic as employed by insurgents, i.e. by irregular armed forces during an insurrection. In the last chapter, we dealt in considerable detail with a number of general tactical factors – such as the principle of surprise; the principle of partial victories, i.e. of concentrating one's main forces against the main target; the principle of energy, decision and perseverance in combat, etc. We shall therefore not need to concern ourselves any further here with the general importance of these tactical rules.

The duration of street fighting in a proletarian insurrection depends on a whole number of conditions, but above all on the balance of forces involved. The duration will vary according to circumstances. Experience shows that it is wrong to count on street fighting being over quickly. In Moscow in 1917 fighting went on in the streets for about a week; in Hamburg and Canton it lasted for over two days, and in Shanghai for twenty-eight hours. In Reval it only lasted for three or four hours, but this was basically because the balance of forces actively involved was markedly unfavourable to the insurgents.

In the conditions we are considering, street fighting is utterly pitiless in character; its aim is the physical extermination of the enemy. Any humanity towards its class enemy shown by the proletariat during the armed struggle only creates needless difficulties, and may, in un-favourable conditions, cause the defeat of the entire insurrection. The bourgeoisie has grasped this principle thoroughly. Without exception, all insurrections in which the proletariat was defeated have demonstrated the inhuman cruelty with which the ruling classes treat their class enemies; and they are equally brutal during the armed struggle itself.

Basing himself on the experience of the proletarian revolutions in Germany and Russia, W. Balk, the military theorist of the German bourgeoisie, writes on this subject as follows:

Mass arrests of insurgents present great disadvantages, since there is usually nowhere to put them. Appropriate orders must be given, indicating how insurgents taken carrying arms should be dealt with. In any case, the rebels cannot expect any excessive tenderness at the hands of officers and soldiers enraged by the street fighting (especially by house-to-house combat).[1]

Everyone knows what these 'appropriate orders' on how to deal with the insurgents consist of. What happens is that all combat members taken prisoner (and indeed anybody else who has even the slightest connection with the revolt) are simply shot out of hand.

The lesson which the bourgeoisie has drawn from the experience of past civil wars must be learnt by the proletariat too.

Street fighting is a particularly terrible form of conflict:

There is no category of warfare requiring greater personal talent and courage in commanding officers of lower rank [states an English manual on street fighting] than operations carried out in a limited space, or hand-to-hand combat in street fighting. Street fighting abounds in difficulties not found in the more normal types of combat; any commander who takes part in it without prior training may easily suffer a defeat.[2]

[1] W. Balk: 'Street-fighting Tactics', in *Monatshefte für Politik und Wehrmacht*, 1919; quoted in the symposium *On Street Fighting*, p. 115, Moscow, 1924.
[2] *British Army Manual for Junior Officers*, quoted in *On Street Fighting*, op. cit., p. 117.

This rule laid down by the training manual for British army officers can and must be taken to heart by commanders of insurgent detachments.

CHARACTERISTICS OF THE CITY

The difficulty of street fighting is conditioned by the specific character of the city, its layout, its architectonic features. For somebody who does not know it, the city is like a vast heap of buildings piled together higgledy-piggledy – a labyrinth of streets, alleys and squares in which planned operations are inconceivable and everything must be left to improvisation and chance.

Such a person is therefore absolutely unfit to direct operations in the streets of a large modern city. These operations require: a perfect knowledge of the city as a whole and a good tactical appreciation of its various districts, streets, squares, buildings or blocks of buildings, from the point of view of offensive or defensive action or of the construction of artificial defences, etc.; a knowledge both of the urban transport system (surface, underground or elevated railways, tramways, etc.) and of communications with other parts of the country; a knowledge of telegraphic and telephonic links, both within the city and with the outside world; an ability to judge the class composition of the city's population, etc.

The economic history of the city objectively determines from the first the balance of forces between revolution and counter-revolution, and their territorial disposition. In industrial towns, the proletarian population predominates over the other social strata. It is installed mainly in the suburbs. Here too (or immediately outside the city, in military camps) the troops who make up the garrison are normally stationed.

The government institutions, the transport authorities and the post and telegraph offices, and the economic organizations (banks, chambers of commerce, employers' federations) are mainly situated in the city centre.

This structure of social life in the city and this class distribution of its population to some extent historically determine from the outset the nature of proletarian action during an insurrection: the insurrection will begin in the suburbs, with simultaneous diversionary actions in other districts, and will culminate in a concerted general assault on the city centre.

The age, geographic situation and size of the town will exercise considerable influence on the tactics of fighting inside it. Towns situated in hilly country are more decentralized, and there layout of buildings and streets is more irregular, disconnected and chaotic than in cities lying in plains. Towns divided by a river also have their special tactical features which commanders must take into account during street fighting. In large cities the conflict will be infinitely more complex than in small ones.

The broad, central thoroughfares of a great modern city are suitable for offensive operations carried out by relatively large units. On the other hand, the narrow streets and alleys of ancient cities (or of the ancient quarters of modern towns) are more favourable for defensive action and small units.

The buildings in a city present a whole series of awkward problems from a military point of view. In large towns, it is more difficult to survey the terrain, observe the enemy, direct one's own troops, organize liaison, deploy one's forces for battle, ensure that the various units will give each other mutual support, etc.

On the other hand, the stone buildings of a city offer perfect protection from infantry fire; provide some defence against artillery and (so long as certain precautions are taken) against gas; shelter the garrison from the inclemencies of the weather; mask it completely from aerial reconnaissance, and thereby allow the element of surprise to be exploited more fully.

The layout, architecture and cultural level of a city and the physical relief of its site will all influence the character of street fighting. In each town, the conflict will have its own individual stamp. The complexity of operations will increase as a function of the city's dimensions.

One highly characteristic feature of street fighting is the influence of the population on the general nature of the military operations. The population's intervention in the struggle may be the decisive factor – depending on which side its most active elements join.[3]

The transport and communications systems of a modern city can, if the situation arises, be utilized to great advantage by the insurgents. Underground electric railways, for example, provide a convenient means for the insurgents to deploy and concentrate their forces; tramways, elevated railways and motor-cars can similarly serve to transport forces from one sector to another. Trucks can rapidly be transformed into armoured cars (by covering them with sufficiently thick iron plating and equipping them with machine-guns), and railway wagons can similarly be transformed into armoured trains.

[3] *Provisional Field Regulations of the Red Army*, section 1321–4.

The city's communication system, especially the telephone, can and must be made full use of for the military needs of the insurgents.

In the conditions of street fighting, artificial defences can be erected very quickly and easily, thanks to the participation of the population and to the variety of materials available for constructing barricades, etc.

The conditions of street fighting afford single insurgent units a broad degree of manoeuvrability. They can pass rapidly and unexpectedly from the defensive to the offensive or *vice versa*, and can make extensive use of camouflage, diversionary actions, etc.

For the units of the regular army, night operations against the insurgents present immense difficulties. W. Balk, in the article quoted earlier, writes that 'at the approach of darkness, fighting normally comes to a halt'.[4] This view was supported by the famous Russian military writer V. Muratov (an expert on combat in inhabited areas), in a comment on Balk's article.

Although this observation by W. Balk is relatively correct as far as the regular army is concerned, it does not apply at all to insurgents. The experience of past insurrections shows the precise opposite. The initial operations of the combat organization are normally launched at night or in the early hours of the morning (Reval, Canton, Hamburg, etc.). If night operations can be carried out effectively at the start of the insurrection, then they can be carried out equally well at any other stage of the fighting. The insurgents must certainly *take advantage of the darkness, their knowledge of the town and the population's support to carry out night operations. In the course of these they must launch surprise attacks of the utmost daring, harass the troops, destroy their system of liaison, eliminate their commanding officers,* etc. The insurgents should view night operations as a normal, routine type of action offering certain specific advantages. The city, as a theatre of operations, by its nature favours night action by the insurgents.

The conditions of combat inside a city require each unit commander, and indeed each individual combat-squad member, to display the highest degree of initiative and self-reliance. The difficulty of maintaining close liaison between commanders and their subordinates in street fighting often obliges the latter to act on their own initiative – within the spirit of the overall plan. Consequently, the most serious attention must be paid both to the selection of the commanders and to the composition of the squads.

[4] W. Balk, op. cit., p. 116.

RECONNAISSANCE IN STREET FIGHTING

The revolutionary party must always continue to carry out reconnaissance and intelligence work. The objectives to be reconnoitred change according to circumstances. Without good intelligence, the Party is not only incapable of leading the proletarian insurrection, it cannot even regulate its activity properly in time of peace. The information gleaned from the national press, the parliamentary group, working-class correspondents or the base-groups of the Party, and then analysed by the intelligence sections attached to each Party committee, is not always sufficient. Even in 'peaceful' periods, it is always in the Party's deepest interest to obtain secret or semi-confidential information about all decisions taken by the leading organs of enemy parties (especially the social democrats); about such measures as the government may be planning, especially those which concern the Party or its members; about the decisions and intentions of the employers' federations, etc. It is impossible, for example, to carry out any agitational work in the army, navy, police or volunteer military associations without such reconnaissance.

If this intelligence service is to be organized properly, the Party must have a whole series of secret and regularly-functioning agencies at its disposal. When the situation becomes immediately revolutionary, this existing apparatus must be further enlarged. New personnel with a clear idea of their mission must be recruited; the number of agencies must be increased; subsidies must be stepped up, etc.

The role of reconnaissance in a time of insurrection is immense. Unless the planned targets have been carefully reconnoitred, no success is conceivable in the combat detachments' initial attacks. Nor is success conceivable in any of the subsequent street fighting. Reconnaissance constitutes the insurgents' eyes.

The colossal importance of reconnaissance during the insurrection is evident in the examples we have quoted. If, during the Canton insurrection, one of Li Fu-lin's detachments were able to approach to within 150 metres of the revolutionary committee's headquarters, this was because the insurgents had neglected entirely to provide for reconnaissance. On the other hand, the success achieved in disarming the police stations at Hamburg was largely due to the careful reconnaissance which had been carried out before. The other insurrections too demonstrate precisely the same thing.

As soon as the Party and its military commissions set about forming red guard detachments (combat squads, Proletarian Hundreds, etc.), they must simultaneously create special, suitably trained intelligence sub-sections for each unit. These intelligence sections must be attached to every single red guard unit. In addition, the military commissions must have at their disposal a special intelligence department (they normally take over an existing one which is then augmented as the directly revolutionary situation approaches).

The main intelligence technique of the proletarian combat organization prior to the insurrection is its network of *agents and observers*. Reconnaissance by the combat organization can be subdivided as follows: (*a*) the gathering of information about the enemy's armed forces (army, police, gendarmerie, navy, fascist and other volunteer military organizations of the ruling classes); (*b*) reconnoitring the locality (the city), including special reconnaissance carried out for engineers, artillery, etc.; (*c*) political intelligence.

A special category of intelligence work is constituted by counter-espionage.

As far as gathering information about the enemy's armed forces before the insurrection is concerned, the aims of intelligence work carried out by the proletarian armed forces are:

A. To establish in detail how the troops are deployed in the city and its immediate surroundings; to locate arms and ammunition dumps, headquarters and guard-posts, and discover how to get through to them and destroy them; to determine where the enemy commanders live and what chance there may be of isolating them in their homes when the insurrection begins; to study the telephonic and telegraphic links connecting the various headquarters with their troops and with the outside world. Particular attention should be paid to living conditions in the barracks, to relations between the soldiers and their officers, and to the prevalent political mood in the various enemy units.

All objectives must be reconnoitred in the minutest detail, as meticulously as possible.

The commanders of red guard detachments must also be familiar with *the principles of troop tactics and with the fighting and tactical properties of a regular army's various arms*.

The following means are available for reconnoitring the regular army: soldiers who are members of the Party or Young Communist League (and revolutionary soldiers in general); personal reconnaissance by the commanders of red guard detachments; information from agents specially trained for this purpose.

B. With respect to the police, reconnaissance must determine the location of every single police station; the numerical strength of the various police forces; the whereabouts of arms stocks; where the armoured cars are garaged; where the high-ranking officials live; the mood of the police as a whole. As far as the individual police stations are concerned, it is essential to know the exact layout of the rooms; how to get inside; where the sentries are posted; where the police keep their weapons; and where the reserve arms stock is kept.

Means available: individual policemen sympathetic to the Communist Party; personal reconnaissance by the commanders of red guard detachments; specially-trained agents.

C. As far as the fascists and other military associations of the ruling classes are concerned, reconnaissance must locate their arms depots; identify their leaders and discover where they live; evaluate the morale of their members, etc.

Means available: sending communists as undercover agents into these associations; making use of such proletarian elements as may exist within them, etc.

As far as reconnoitring the locality is concerned, the intelligence services of the combat organization must find out about: (*a*) the communications system in the city, and between the city and the outside world: the central and local telephone and telegraph exchanges and radio offices; the location of underground cables and telephone lines; the telephone extensions leading to the homes of high state officials, and top-ranking army and police commanders. These data are necessary if the communications system is to be taken over or put out of action; (*b*) the urban transport system, and links with other regions: where the stations are situated; the layout of the railway network; the system of underground or elevated electric rail services within the city; how these can be taken over or destroyed; where motor-transport vehicles are garaged or parked, and how they can be captured; the layout of the city's tramlines, and where the trams are garaged; (*c*) the water supply, lighting grid, power stations, gas works, etc.; (*d*) bridges and ferries, if the city is divided by a river; where the ferries are moored; the landing-stages for river traffic; how the bridges are defended; the ways of crossing the river, if the bridges are held by the enemy; (*e*) the layout of the main thoroughfares and squares and of key buildings and groups of buildings – which must be assessed from the point of view of defensive or offensive action; (*f*) the addresses of newspaper offices, printing presses, paper warehouses, etc.; (*g*) the location of government institutions, employers' federations, banks etc.; (*h*) where the prisons are situated, and the possibilities for releasing the inmates; (*i*) arsenals, arms factories, workshops, and how these can be captured.

The means available for reconnoitring these objectives are as follows: specially trained scouts and intelligence agents; employees sympathetic to the Communist Party; personal reconnaissance by the combat-squad commanders, etc. The use of official handbooks, guides, descriptions and plans of every kind can greatly facilitate the task.

The objectives of *political reconnaissance* in the period immediately preceding the insurrection are the collection and classification of information concerning: the political situation of the various strata of the population (trade unions, co-operatives, sporting associations, societies of every kind, etc.); the mood in the factories, among the railwaymen, among the troops, among the police, in the navy, etc. One further objective of political reconnaissance will be to discover the addresses of the main counter-revolutionary leaders, the key members of the government and the leaders of the various parties – in order to be able to isolate them as soon as the insurrection begins.

All this information must be concentrated in the appropriate Party sections, and carefully studied and classified. On the basis of this, it will be possible to draw up in advance an overall plan (which can be modified, added to or corrected in the light of circumstances) for operations throughout the town and in each of its districts.

Counter-espionage has the task of uncovering police provocateurs and spies in the ranks of the Party and its combat organization. The Party is surrounded by enemies; police spies, agents and hostile elements in general may easily slip into its ranks. Thus counter-espionage is part of the duty of every Party member, and constitutes a fundamental obligation. Nevertheless, in view of the specific character of such work, it will be appropriate in large mass parties to entrust it to a special apparatus, or at least to a group of the most reliable and experienced comrades in the intelligence department as a whole.

During street fighting, intelligence work is somewhat different in character than it has been prior to the armed uprising. Before the insurrection begins, the element of time often plays a fairly limited role. The combat organization can reconnoitre the requisite objectives without taking time particularly into account. In contrast, during street fighting time plays an exceptionally important role. Even the very best intelligence information will have no practical value if it is not transmitted in time to the appropriate troop commander. This fact must constantly be borne in mind while intelligence work is being organized in street fighting.

Most reconnaissance in street fighting consists – as before – of intelligence work. The various categories of intelligence work remain the same as before the insurrection: political reconnaissance; reconnaissance of the enemy's forces; reconnaissance carried out on behalf of engineers, artillery, etc. Nevertheless, during street fighting, *straightforward military intelligence can play an essential role too.*

Here is what the provisional field regulations of the Red Army say on this subject:

Military reconnaissance is extremely difficult. The main weight must fall on the intelligence network.

Inside the city, reconnaissance work is carried out by armoured cars, cyclists, motor-cyclists and scouts on foot. Trucks armed with machine-guns reconnoitre enemy positions (barricades, houses, etc.) and quickly warn the assault columns which follow them. In the key sectors, internal courtyards too are reconnoitred by the same means. Sometimes the reconnaissance parties will even be able to occupy some important point or other before the main forces arrive.

Great advantage can be drawn from observation carried out from the tops of tall buildings, if the configuration of the neighbouring streets permits this.[5]

What is said here about reconnaissance in street fighting refers to reconnaissance by regular units. However, it applies just as well to insurgent detachments.

In street fighting, active reconnaissance (diversionary activity) is of great importance. Its aims are: (*a*) to destroy supply depots, bridges and ferries, railway embankments, military trains, etc., in the enemy's rear; (*b*) to destroy the communications system in the enemy's rear; (*c*) to organize attacks on small groups of soldiers to disarm them; to organize terrorist actions against the leaders of the forces fighting against the insurrection; (*d*) to organize mutinies among the enemy troops; (*e*) to mislead the enemy by spreading false information (rumours favourable to the insurgents, etc.); (*f*) to intercept the enemy's telephone calls, by linking a telephone receiver to his communications system.

[5] *Provisional Field Regulations of the Red Army*, p. 411.

By operating behind the enemy's lines, small diversionary groups – from three to five men with a good general and technical training – can be of great assistance in street fighting against troops and police.

Active reconnaissance to some extent also involves organizing revolts among the proletarian elements in districts held by the regular troops (and drawing them into the fighting generally) – particularly in areas where the local communist organization is not strong enough.

The other types of reconnaissance (political reconnaissance, reconnaissance of the enemy's armed forces, reconnaissance of the locality), discussed earlier with respect to the period preceding the insurrection, also have the job in street fighting of giving the leaders of the insurrection and the commanders of the combat units all necessary information about the enemy: his numerical strength; the political condition of each individual unit or subdivision thereof; the intentions of the enemy command; the mood of the population behind the enemy lines; the special features of the locality, etc.

In street fighting, however, reconnaissance will only be able to provide the required information in time *if* its organization is impeccable; *if* the commander of the red guard detachment has properly trained personnel at his disposal; *if* he knows very well himself what he wants from reconnaissance, and gives the intelligence sections and individual agents their instructions accordingly. When an intelligence mission is being assigned, the time required for its execution must be taken into consideration. Thus every commander must pay serious attention to the organization of impeccable reconnaissance. No red guard commander or leader of the insurrection is exempt from this duty.

Reconnaissance is obligatory in all circumstances and at all times. Only then will the possibility of being taken by surprise be reduced to a minimum – thus allowing the insurrectionary command to prepare and carry out its operations in a well-planned and efficacious manner.

In a proletarian insurrection, the entire population takes part in reconnaissance. This greatly facilitates the work of the combat organization's intelligence section. It is the task of the red guard commanders and of the insurrectionary leadership in general to direct effectively the reconnaissance work both of the intelligence sections and of the population as a whole (wherever the latter takes part in the fighting), and to coordinate their respective efforts.

Experience shows that there are great advantages in using women and children for reconnaissance work, and that all missions of a less complicated kind should be entrusted to them. Here are some examples of such missions: to discover whether such and such a street, square or building is occupied by troops; to discover where the artillery is positioned; to find out whether such and such a unit has passed by such and such a street, and if so when, etc.

LIAISON IN STREET FIGHTING

Liaison is very important in every type of warfare, but in street fighting during a proletarian insurrection it is especially crucial. Without good liaison, the leadership of the combat units has no way of directing the insurgents' endeavours or coordinating their operations properly. Without liaison, or with faulty liaison, events will develop spontaneously, in a disorganized and improvised fashion, and the leadership will be unable to exercise effective control over them.

Liaison is the collective name given to all the various means which make it possible to lead troops. Good leadership is impossible if liaison is missing, or if it functions badly.

Liaison must function reliably (with no blockages or breakdowns); it must transmit the necessary orders, reports, etc., accurately and rapidly, and must be organized in such a way that it is possible to check how it is functioning.[6]

The plan and physical configuration of the city, and the need to fight in small, decentralized units, make it extremely difficult to organize liaison well during street fighting. For the insurgents, further complications are caused by the fact that they do not always have at their disposal the necessary material means; or do not have them in the quantity required; or do not have sufficient technically and tactically trained personnel.

In street fighting, in differing circumstances, the same liaison methods can be used as in field warfare, i.e. technical means, ordinary means, and military postal systems.

Among the technical means must be numbered: the telephone; to a limited extent (in big cities like Berlin, London, Paris, etc.) the telegraph; radio communications; various other types of visual, auditory or mechanical signal.

The ordinary means of liaison comprise: personal contact between commanders and their subordinates; liaison personnel circulating

6 ibid., pp. 40–1.

between the units and the various headquarters; messengers; observation-posts and vocal transmission of information.

Military postal systems include the various types of courier-service and communication by carrier-pigeon or messenger-dog.

The means of liaison listed above can only all be used in large units, which possess both the means themselves and the appropriate liaison personnel. The insurgents will frequently find themselves in a very much weaker situation from this point of view. At the moment of the first blow (the start of the insurrection), they will only possess very limited technical means for liaison. The main liaison means available to them at this time will be: foot-messengers; cyclists; motor-cyclists; messengers with cars; liaison personnel attached to the various units; and the personal presence of the commanders in their own combat zones.

It will only be possible to make very limited use of the urban telephone system at this stage. More extensive use of the telephone, which is a most effective means of liaison even in street fighting, will only be possible after the central and local telephone exchanges have been occupied, and after certain military units, especially communications units, have come over to the insurgent side.

As for the use by insurgents of means of liaison such as the telegraph, radio communications, and dogs or pigeons, the possibilities for this – at least in the first phase of the insurrection – are infinitesimal. Before being able to use them, it is necessary to have them; and even if it were possible to capture them at the outset of the insurrection, it is doubtful whether there would be any personnel capable of operating them. No doubt the telegraph and wireless can be used for liaison with other insurgent areas, but the possibilities for using them as a means of liaison inside the town are extremely dubious.

It is essential for the insurgents to attempt to seize the city's communications system at the outset: the telephone, telegraph, wireless, air force, motor garages, etc. *For not only do the insurgents need them for their own use, they also need to deprive the enemy of them.*

In Petrograd during the October revolution, the insurgents seized the central telephone and telegraph exchange before anything else; in one blow they deprived the Provisional Government of all contact with the rest of the city and with those units who had remained loyal to them (*junkers*, women's battalion). In Canton, on the other hand, the insurgents were guilty of a serious blunder when they failed to isolate the headquarters of the 4th Corps at the outset, or to sever its contact with the units under its command and with Hong Kong. This headquarters maintained its contact with the outside world throughout the first day of the rising, and a link between Hong Kong and the aristocratic quarter of Tung-shan continued to function throughout the entire insurrection.

Just as the insurgents can and must achieve superiority of numbers in the course of the fighting, they can and must also gain control of the communications system and get it working regularly as the conflict proceeds. They possess the necessary ways and means of accomplishing this; all they need is sufficient initiative, and the ability to organize liaison during the insurrection.

The lack of sufficient technical means during the first operations of the red guards (the start of the insurrection) can and must be compensated for by the organization of direct liaison by couriers, and in general by *the unity of action and aim* of all the forces involved in the fighting. This can be achieved by assigning to the red guard units not only their immediate but also their subsequent missions, and by informing the commanders about the missions of the neighbouring units as well. If each red guard commander knows all about the missions allocated to his own unit, and has been thoroughly briefed on the overall plan of action and the missions of neighbouring units, then (given sufficient initiative) the commanders will be in a position to act in the spirit of the overall plan – even in the event of there being no direct physical liaison among them, or between them and their superiors. Consequently, this aspect (unit commanders being well informed about the overall plan) demands special attention when the insurrection is being organized.

In addition, when the initial operations are being planned, the leadership of the insurrection must endeavour to ensure that it has proper physical contact with the combat units, so that immediately the proletarian forces have moved into action it will be in touch with what is happening and able to take the necessary decisions. This can be accomplished by the following means: (*a*) by providing the combat units with liaison personnel whose function will be to inform the higher instance regularly about the situation of those units. This liaison personnel must be given good tactical training, and must be informed about the insurrectionary command's plans and intentions, so that it will be able, if circumstances require, to give the necessary instructions on the spot in the latter's name; (*b*) by assigning a number of cyclists and motor-cyclists to each detachment, to bring back regular reports to the leadership. There must also be cyclists, motor-cylists and if possible cars at the disposal of the leadership in question (especially the Revolutionary Committee); these can be used to transmit orders to the unit commanders, and for personal visits to the battlefield; (*c*) by using foot messengers for liaison both with superiors and with neighbouring units; (*d*) by setting up 'collection points' known to the detachment commanders, to which the latter can send their reports; several of these can be established (depending on circumstances) in various districts of the town, but preferably not far away from the appropriate central or local headquarters; (*e*) by organizing a courier-service in which a number of ordinary combatants or cyclists (sometimes motor-cyclists) convey orders or reports to their destination by relays.

Given good organization, these five liaison procedures – used in combination, since it is indispensable to provide for dual liaison during an insurrection – will ensure that operations at the start of the insurrection are properly directed.

Nor must the insurgents overlook the possibility of using the city telephone system even before it has been captured. All that is necessary is for conversations to take place in a prearranged code. However, it would be wrong to count on any very extensive use of it; this will only be possible when it has been taken over by the insurgents.

In order to ensure that it will get regular reports on the situation of the various combat units, the leadership must work out a schedule fixing set times at which such reports are to be submitted. At the start of the insurrection, it will obviously be necessary for the leadership to be informed at once of the accomplishment of each specific mission; of the switch to the next mission; or, in case of failure, of the situation in which the unit finds itself.

Later, when the city's means of communication – telephone, cars, motor-cycles – have been taken over; when a number of army units have come over to the people's side; and when communications experts, especially telephone operators, have been recruited from among the population; then the organization of liaison will be appreciably easier.

Liaison must be invulnerable, and absolutely reliable. Therefore, when it is being organized, the following principle must always be borne in mind: the liaison system must as far as possible be camouflaged.

This especially applies to the telephone. It is in fact extremely simple for the enemy, in street fighting, to tap the telephone wires and overhear conversations. To avoid this, no secret information should be transmitted by telephone if there is the slightest risk that it might be intercepted by the enemy – or at least a code must be used. The main telephone lines must be guarded by special guards. The central and district telephone exchanges need to be guarded with special care, to prevent the enemy from recapturing them.

Important reports and directives must be sent in several copies by different channels. If there is a risk of their falling into enemy hands, they should not be transmitted in written form but verbally. There is a great advantage in using women and children for this, since they attract less attention. This is all the more necessary when the message is to be sent from behind the enemy lines.

In every plan of operation, liaison should be given its proper place:

> The commander is always and in all circumstances responsible for liaison in the area where his troop is stationed. He must always know where his troop is and what it is doing, and also what the last orders it has received are. Subordinates, for their part, must always know where their immediate superior is.[7]

This principle laid down in the Red Army regulations must not be disregarded by the leaders of an insurrection either. Both the unit commander and anyone else directing an operation in street fighting must endeavour to establish and maintain regular liaison; for this, if it goes hand in hand with other favourable conditions, is the guarantee of success.

DEFENSIVE ACTION IN STREET FIGHTING:
GENERAL PRINCIPLES

> Defensive action is employed: (*a*) to gain the time needed to concentrate forces and equipment for a return to the offensive; (*b*) to hold the adversary at certain points while striking the main blow elsewhere; (*c*) to hold such lines and positions as have been taken; (*d*) to hold the positions of units which are resting.
>
> The object of defensive action is to oblige the adversary to abandon his attack, by inflicting maximum losses on him.[8]

These principles governing defensive action taken from the Red Army regulations were written for the regular army. Nevertheless, defensive action as a mode of combat is employed not only by regular armies in

[7] ibid., p. 327.   [8] ibid., pp. 326–7.

field warfare (i.e. in open country) – but also frequently in proletarian insurrection within the city.

Both during street fighting in a city, and when a city held by insurgents is attacked by counter-revolutionary forces from outside, defensive action can be used by the insurgents in certain situations and on certain sectors, when, although they have won inside the city itself, they are (for whatever reason it may be) not yet capable of going over to the attack and crushing the enemy in a pitched battle. Thus the principles laid down in the Red Army regulations retain their validity in street fighting during an insurrection.

The historical experience of the proletarian armed struggle is the proof of this. In the Canton insurrection, after the main elements of power had been won, the insurgents found themselves obliged to defend the city against the militarist armies from Kwangtung province until such time as they might be sufficiently organized in Canton to go over to the offensive. The Paris Commune provides a similar example.

As for the use of defensive action in individual sectors during the proletariat's struggle for power in the city – i.e. during street fighting – the history of past insurrections shows by numerous examples (the Moscow uprising of December 1905, and many others) that the insurgents are often obliged to fall back temporarily onto the defensive, even though not abandoning preparations for a decisive offensive.

On the other hand:

In itself, defensive action is not a decisive means of annihilating the enemy. The aim of the operations (crushing the enemy) cannot be achieved by defensive action; the only way to achieve this is by offensive action.[9]

'The defensive is the death of every armed rising' (Lenin). This is absolutely incontrovertible. If, in certain cases, insurgents are compelled to use defensive action as a method of struggle, they must not for a single instant forget that at the first available opportunity they must go over from defence to attack.

Defensive action itself must be considered as *a way of preparing for an offensive* (by weakening the enemy's forces, and concentrating the proletariat's own forces for a decisive blow).

If defensive action is seen as one method which may be adopted by the insurgents during an urban insurrection, more careful consideration must be given to the following problem: proletarian insurrections may

[9] ibid., p. 327.

occur which, historically, cannot succeed and are objectively doomed to failure. Examples: the Paris Commune, the Moscow uprising of December 1905, the Canton insurrection, etc. The fact that the 1905 Moscow uprising objectively could not succeed was something that was only realized some time later. The same was true in the case of Canton: during the fighting, nobody could have foretold that the insurrection was only the final chord in the revolutionary struggle of one particular historical phase, and that it had broken out as a rearguard action at a time when the revolutionary wave in China was ebbing. All this could only be said with certainty several months afterwards.

What is more, even if there had been people in the Party capable of predicting the inevitable defeat of a given insurrection, in a whole series of cases it would still have been impossible to refuse the battle or abandon leadership of the masses, even though the ultimate defeat of the proletariat was inevitable. Mass movements as typical as the 1927 Vienna insurrection, or the Canton insurrection itself – which was really forced on the Party – are good illustrations of this.

Insurrections like the 1905 Moscow uprising, the Canton commune, the Vienna rising and many others – i.e. insurrections which are doomed – will doubtless occur in the future too.

It can be concluded from this that the proletariat, as the attacker in these historically doomed insurrections, after it has struck a series of more or less telling blows at its class enemy, is fatally obliged sooner or later to fall back onto the defensive in an attempt to inflict by this means the maximum physical and psychological damage on the enemy – without abandoning the hope of crushing him by a new offensive as soon as this becomes possible. In such cases, defensive action is the proletariat's only possible method of struggle. It is better to go down fighting, and thereby to inflict a partial defeat on the enemy and disrupt his forces, than to be defeated without a battle. In such cases, the struggle will *take on a defensive character* for the proletariat, not only tactically *but also politically* (strategically).

THE DEFENCE OF A CITY HELD BY INSURGENTS
AND DEFENSIVE OPERATIONS INSIDE THE CITY

The defence of a city by insurgents, as has already been said, may become a real necessity in the event of the insurgents not yet being able to complete the organization of the city's internal forces and the preparation of these to annihilate the enemy outside in the open country. Success will depend on a whole series of circumstances, of which the most important are: (*a*) the support given to the insurrection by the majority of the population, and the will of that population to defend the city whatever the cost; (*b*) the presence of a strong, competent and generally popular political and military leadership, and good tactical organization of the defence; (*c*) the existence of sufficient technical resources; (*d*) the strength of the attackers.

In the type of situation under examination here, the role of the population is enormous. It is still greater if the insurgents do not have at their disposal sufficient numbers of regular troops (won over to their side during the insurrection) who can at once be turned against the enemy – i.e. if the armed forces of the revolution have to be created in the course of the fighting itself. In such cases, the fate of the city depends entirely on the active participation of the population.

Hence the new régime must, by skilful agitation and propaganda and by a judicious system of economic and political measures, prove to the proletarian and semi-proletarian masses that the revolution has been carried through to smash the old régime for ever and create a new order diametrically opposed to it, and that it is therefore up to the proletariat and all the poor inhabitants to defend the city against reaction.

The Communist Party and those in command of the military side of the defence must find concrete ways of ensuring that the masses can take part in the battle for their city, and must issue appropriate fighting slogans.

One of the basic tasks of those responsible for the defence of a city will be to increase their armed forces. This means: forming new armed proletarian detachments; training them; providing them with weapons and ammunition, commanders, victuals, etc.

The entire life of the city must be reorganized to meet the requirements of its defence. All factories and workshops which can be used to manufacture war *matériel* (arms; ammunition; barbed wire; armour-plating which can be used to transform cars into armoured cars or railway trucks into armoured trains; gunpowder; telephone wires, etc.) must be set to work. The former technical personnel (engineers, technicians, etc.) must be involved in this (and, if necessary, obliged to work for the new régime). Given proper leadership, the right priorities, and mass involvement of the workers, this militarization of industry can aid the city's defence enormously.

An inventory must be made of all stocks of food in the city, and these must be concentrated in special warehouses. The distribution of foodstuffs to the population must be organized systematically (using ration-cards if possible), in accordance with class principles and with defence requirements. The bourgeoisie must be rationed most strictly of all. Trading in food must be forbidden, or at least regulated by the authorities.

In the distribution of foodstuffs, priority must be given to the combat units (including those in process of formation) and to those working in factories manufacturing war *matériel*. All health establishments and medical personnel must be registered and utilized for defence. Arrangements must be made to evacuate the wounded from the battle zones into the centre of the city. This is a measure which will have a very good effect upon the combatants' morale.

The leadership must organize mass participation of the population in preparing the city's defences. The combat units – apart from such work as has to be carried out directly at the front – should be freed unconditionally from all obligations of this kind, so that they can devote their time entirely to preparing for military action.

The active part of the bourgeoisie must be isolated. To guard against possible treachery on the part of such bourgeois as have remained in the city, it is a good idea to announce in advance that class terror will be used against it – and first and foremost against such bourgeois party leaders and public figures as are already in detention. The non-active part of the bourgeoisie can be used, if needed, for public works – including the construction of the city's defences.

This must be organized on the basis of a careful reconnaissance of the enemy's forces and line of attack, and must take into account the possibilities which the terrain affords both for defensive action and for counter-attack. The leadership must therefore pay particular attention to organizing its intelligence, and to studying the plan of the city.

If the enemy forces are not very large, and if the defenders feel sufficiently strong and have sufficient material means at their disposal (artillery, machine-guns, etc.), the defence should be organized to halt the enemy's advance in the outskirts of the city; the aim will then be to use fire-power to inflict telling losses upon him, and then to attack and defeat him here without allowing him to carry the battle into the city. It goes without saying that the city itself must still be prepared for defence in case the fighting in the outskirts turns out badly for the defenders.

But even if the enemy attacks the city with large forces, a first line of defence should still be organized in the outskirts – in the direction of the attack – with a second line of defence inside the city. The function of the first line of defence is to feel out the enemy's strength and the direction of his main attack. For this purpose, a system of outposts with fairly strong garrisons must be set up at, or close to, the edge of the city. These must join battle with the attackers and thus oblige them to reveal their forces and line of attack. Once this task has been accomplished, and as soon as it becomes impossible to hold the first line, these garrisons should retreat in good order to the main line of defence inside the city. The outposts must be set up in such a way that they can give each other supporting fire and are themselves covered by artillery positioned inside the city.

Depending on its length, the nature of the terrain and the direction from which the enemy's attack will come (if this is known in advance), the line of defence must be divided into sectors, each with its own headquarters. The overall command of all these sectors is the responsibility of the general headquarters for the city's defence.

The defence forces must be so distributed among the sectors as to permit the combination of covering fire with counter-attacks wherever circumstances demand this. For this purpose (for counter-attacks and counter-blows) the sector-commanders must have shock-troops available in adequate numbers. In this period of the fighting, the leaders of the defence must discover ways and means to influence the enemy and weaken his combat forces. This can be achieved by agitation, or by means of diversionary actions in his rear or along his line of attack. Workers can be sent as agitators into enemy territory to subvert the troops. The distribution among the soldiers of leaflets, revolutionary proclamations and decrees, and newspapers (including dropping them from the air), and the organization of successful diversionary actions and guerrilla struggle behind the enemy lines, can produce extremely favourable results from the point of view of the defenders.

The strength of defence lies in the combination of fire-power with a skilful use of the terrain and with counter-attacks executed by mobile forces brought up from the rear.[10]

[10] ibid., p. 327.

This principle laid down in the Red Army field regulations should be made the basis for the operational plan of defence within the city (second line of defence). The need to combine fire-power with skilful use of the terrain and with the execution of counter-attacks is not hard to comply with, provided that the leaders of the defence are adequate to their task.

And essential part of the operational defence plan is the siting of fortifications. These latter must be conceived of as a system of defence-works which will give the defenders maximum cover from the enemy's fire, and at the same time allow them to keep him under surveillance and subsequently to defeat him by use of their own fire-power and by their counter-attacks. The success of the defence will depend to a large extent on a skilful combination of these three elements; fortifications, fire-power and counter-attacks.

On the occasion of Yudenich's offensive against Petrograd in 1919, Trotsky wrote in one of his orders of the day:

From the strictly military point of view, the most advantageous solution would be to allow Yudenich's bands to break through and advance right up to the walls of the city; for it would then be easy to make Petrograd into a gigantic trap for the white guards.

The Northern capital of the workers' revolution covers an area of forty-one square versts. Petrograd contains almost 20,000 communists, a strong garrison, immense – indeed almost inexhaustible – reserves both of construction material and of artillery. Once they have entered this colossal city, the white guards will find themselves in a stone labyrinth in which every house will be an enigma – either a threat or a mortal danger.

From which side will the blow fall: from a window or attic? Out of a courtyard? From behind a corner? We have machine-guns, rifles, revolvers and hand-grenades available everywhere. We can block certain streets with barbed wire, leave others enticingly open and turn them into traps: all that is necessary is that a few thousand men should be utterly determined not to give up Petrograd.

Holding a central position, we would be able to strike out along the radial avenues, from the city centre right to the periphery, and on each occasion we would be able to place our blow where it was most needed.[11]

Change the city into a trap to annihilate the enemy – that is what the key idea of the defence plan must be.

As with the first line of defence, the city too must be divided into various sectors. Each sector must have its own commander, who is responsible for its defence. In each there should also be created a

[11] L. Trotsky: *How the Revolution was Armed.*

central stronghold (redoubt). This is where the headquarters of the sector and the reserves should be situated.

In the centre of the city, a central stronghold should be established; this should contain the overall defence headquarters and the general services: stocks of arms and victuals, liaison centres, etc. This stronghold should constitute a whole fortified area, capable of continuing the struggle after the collapse of the various individual sectors. Such a fortified area will assume particular importance if it happens to be a high point commanding the surrounding sectors (e.g. the Kremlin in Moscow).

After the stronghold of each sector has fallen, all the available defence forces will withdraw into the fortified area in the centre of the city to continue the struggle.

Fortifying the individual sectors involves fortifying all the main thoroughfares which lead out from the centre towards the enemy. This can be achieved by running barbed-wire barriers right across these streets; by installing firing-positions both directly behind these barricades and on the flanks; by establishing further firing-positions on rooftops, at windows, on balconies, etc.

SETTING UP A BARRICADE (*see diagram opposite*)

Here is how barricades should be constructed. A trench 1-1·5 metres wide and 1·5 metres deep is dug right across the road. The front of the trench is lined with paving-stones, and some 50–70 metres in front of it a barrier is constructed – out of barbed-wire, carts, furniture, barrels filled with sand or stones, or whatever else happens to be available. It is best to install barricades at crossroads so that the approaches to the main street leading to the centre of the city will be blocked from various sides.

The type of barricade depicted in the sketch – i.e. one built at a crossroads, barring access to the main street leading to the city centre – offers maximum advantages to the defenders. If they have machine-guns hidden on the rooftops, on balconies or at the windows of the corner houses, the insurgents have every chance of catching the enemy in a devastating cross-fire.

As few marksmen as possible should remain in the firing-trench behind the barricade, for this offers too easy a target for the enemy artillery. It will be enough to leave a small group of snipers there, while

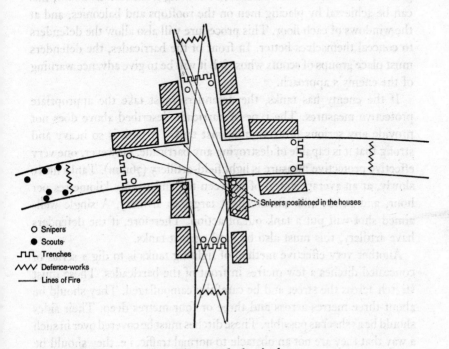

Snipers positioned in the houses

○ Snipers
● Scouts
⊓⊔ Trenches
∧∧∧ Defence-works
— Lines of Fire

5. Diagram of a barricade

the others are hidden on rooftops and balconies, at windows, and in the attics of the corner houses, so that they will be able to machine-gun the enemy from these vantage-points when he attacks the barricade. When positioning snipers and machine-gunners, thought must be given to the need to have parallel fire coming from various floors; this can be achieved by placing men on the rooftops and balconies, and at the windows of each floor. This procedure will also allow the defenders to conceal themselves better. In front of the barricades, the defenders must place groups of scouts whose job it will be to give advance warning of the enemy's approach.

If the enemy has tanks, the defenders must take the appropriate protective measures. The type of barricade described above does not provide any serious protection against tanks. A tank is so heavy and strong that it is capable of destroying any barricade. However, one very effective protective measure is light field-artillery (76mm). Tanks move slowly, at an average speed of between ten and twenty kilometres per hour, and hence offer an excellent target to artillery. A single well-aimed shot will put a tank out of action. Therefore, if the defenders have artillery, this must also be used against tanks.

Another very effective method of fighting tanks is to dig a series of concealed ditches a few metres in front of the barricades. These must stretch across the street and be carefully camouflaged. They should be about three metres across and three or four metres deep. Their sides should be as sheer as possible. These ditches must be covered over in such a way that they are not an obstacle to normal traffic, i.e. they should be able to support a weight of two or three tons. It is best to dig them at night and keep them absolutely secret. It should also be borne in mind that hand-grenades – i.e. a bundle of five, six or seven of them (a so-called concentric charge), or even a single grenade of high explosive capacity – are capable of putting a tank out of action if they are thrown accurately underneath it.

The defenders can successfully use the same methods to fight against armoured cars. These are not capable of surmounting a normal barricade or trench. A high-explosive grenade of the Novitsky type (weighing two and a half kilos) or a concentric charge of ordinary grenades thrown accurately beneath the wheels of an armoured car will put the vehicle out of action.

In general, defenders do not lack the means to fight successfully against armoured vehicles. It is only necessary for them to learn to use such resources as they have and to exploit all the various possibilities open to them.

A weapon of great importance in street fighting, and especially in defensive action, is the machine-gun. Full use must be made of its fire-power, for the success of the defence will largely depend on this. When positioning a machine-gun, care should always be taken to camouflage it carefully. For the enemy's attention will be keenly focused on the disposition of the defenders' machine-guns, and he will seek to knock them out with artillery fire or aerial bombing if they are positioned on rooftops and spotted by his air force. As soon as a machine-gun has been pinpointed by the enemy, its position must be changed. The best solution is to position the machine-guns on upper floors (since this will extend their field of fire).

The defence must be given an active character, for only thus can it hope for success. When defences are being organized and barricades constructed, the defenders must constantly bear in mind the possibility, indeed necessity, of striking swift, decisive blows. To this end, special squads of shock-troops must be formed and placed in well-protected positions; their mission will be to attack the enemy at the first opportunity, under cover of the fire from the houses.

If an enemy attack fails, a part of the defence forces must be left in position, and must continue firing until the enemy has been entirely wiped out; the rest must join the shock-troops in launching energetic counter-attacks.

If the enemy penetrates the defence lines, the defenders must not abandon their positions, but must prepare to fight inside the buildings and houses. In this phase, the shock troops and all the other defenders need to display the maximum energy.

ATTACK IN STREET FIGHTING

We are not concerned here with problems involved in the capture of cities by attack from outside, followed by fighting inside. We shall confine ourselves to studying attack inside a city as one type of military action which insurgents can use against such armed forces of the old régime as have not been wiped out by the first blows of the combat organization.

'By defensive action, it is only possible to weaken the enemy, not

to annihilate him.'[12] Insurgents, once they have begun operations
against the existing régime, must make maximum use of their situation
as the attacking side. After exploiting the initial successes gained by
their surprise attack on the enemy, they must not give the latter time
to organize his defences. Without losing a moment, they must strike
his scattered forces wherever they show themselves. The time element,
as was indicated earlier, is of enormous importance in the first phase
of the insurrection. A mere half hour may sometimes have a decisive
influence on the outcome of the entire operation. No political or other
considerations (e.g. lack of arms, lack of information concerning the
enemy, etc.) which might slow down the insurgents' offensive operations
either can or should be accepted as valid. Energy, offensive action and
attack must dominate all else at this stage – whatever the cost may be.

It is only when the adversary has succeeded in organizing his defences when he has gone over to the attack and the insurgents have
fallen back onto the defensive, that the latter's offensive operations
should take on a systematic character. Attacks must be carefully
prepared:

The main factor determining success in attacks during street fighting [says the
English manual quoted earlier] is their perfect preparation and organization before
the troops are actually sent into action. There is no category of warfare in which
an ill-prepared attack causes such heavy losses as it does in street combat. A
mistake once made can only be repaired with the greatest difficulty, and success
can only be achieved by a systematic study of the methods and tactics of street
fighting. This becomes even more important when the enemy has a certain amount
of cunning, and enough time to prepare his defences.

Before each offensive in street fighting, the attacker must carry out
the most meticulous reconnaissance of the enemy forces, the terrain,
and the approaches to the defenders' positions. This reconnaissance
must provide precise and complete information on the defenders'
system of fortifications; on their strongholds; on their machine-gun
positions; on the possibility of attacking them from all sides at once,
etc. It is on the basis of such intelligence about the enemy and the
terrain that the leadership must work out its plan of attack.

The plan of attack in street fighting must be simple in conception
but at the same time absolutely systematic, and must provide for the
systematic elimination of the enemy's positions. The various detachments must be assigned clear and concrete missions, or else there will

[12] *Provisional Field Regulations of the Red Army*, pp. 245–6.

inevitably be misunderstandings between them and confusion in the operations – which may destroy the whole enterprise.

The plan of attack must provide for the immediate fortification of such houses or streets as may be occupied by the attackers; in this way solid staging-points will be created from which to launch the next advance. Particular attention must be devoted to destroying the defenders' machine-gun nests. In the hands of a defender, the machine-gun is an excellent weapon. If the attacker has artillery or trench-mortars with him, their main function should be to destroy enemy machine-guns. Artillery is normally best positioned either at the edge of the city or on open spaces inside it. In this case the artillery observers must accompany the attackers. Cases may occur in which it will be advisable to allow the guns to be brought right up into the immediate vicinity of the assault column so that they will have an unobstructed field of fire.

This was the case, for example, during the revolt of the left Social Revolutionaries in Moscow in 1918. The red command gave the order to bring up two batteries of artillery in front of the Villa Morozov, which was occupied by the rebels who had machine-guns. One gun was brought up to a position some 300 yards from the hotel, and opened fire on it. The results of this shelling were extremely positive. Vatzetis, who was in command of the operation, has described it as follows:

As was established after the revolt had been put down, at the moment when Berzin (the battery commander) opened fire on the Villa, a meeting of the left Social Revolutionaries was in progress. The first shell exploded in the room next to that in which the session was taking place. The second did the same. Then shrapnel shells were fired at the roof and balconies. The deafening explosions had a devastating effect on the members of the meeting, who rushed out into the street and scattered in all directions to escape the shrapnel. After their leaders had fled, the troops soon followed suit.[13]

Trench-mortars too can play a considerable role in attacks during street fighting. W. Balk, on the basis of the experience of street warfare in Berlin during 1919, reckons that they are more useful than field-artillery. In his article quoted earlier, 'Street-Fighting Tactics', he gives examples of the use of trench-mortars during the repression of the Spartakist uprising in Berlin:

[13] Vatzetis: 'The left Social Revolutionary Rising in Moscow', in the review *Vojna Revolutsia*, 1927, nos. 10–11.

The attackers' main objective was to wipe out the Spartakist positions at the entry to the tunnel. The Alexanderplatz was raked by heavy mortar-fire from the Werder market, and this opened up craters six or seven metres deep. The shells pierced the surface of the street over the underground tunnel and caused huge losses among the Spartakists. As usual, it was the psychological effect which was decisive. The Spartakists withdrew in panic, abandoning their strongholds, and retreated towards the Münzstrasse. The communist garrison holding the teachers' union building and the Café Braun attempted to put up an energetic resistance. As artillery could not be brought into play against these buildings, they were bombarded with mortar-fire. Once again, the effect was admirable. The surviving insurgents promptly abandoned the building, and fell into the hands of the government troops. Similarly, two mortar-shots which hit the Tietz warehouse put out of action a machine-gun position there. ... Trench-mortars are more useful in street fighting than field-artillery.

This opinion on the advantages of trench-mortars as compared to field-artillery in street fighting is shared by the Americans who, in their training manual dealing with the repression of insurrections in towns, draw on the German experience – as indeed they do in all questions of street-fighting tactics in time of insurrection. In attacks on individual targets in a city, in all probability 'trench-mortars will be more useful than light artillery' (American Training Manual).

In attacks on houses, hand-grenades and bombs (which have a higher explosive capacity) are of considerable importance. They can be used to very great advantage against defenders, both as anti-personnel weapons and against machine-guns (provided that these are approached under cover until within throwing range); also to destroy minor obstacles (i.e. to blast open doors, gates, etc.).

The entire responsibility for attack in street fighting falls on the smaller units of the proletarian combat organization: the squads, sections, companies, or battalions (in which several companies are combined). These units normally have to act independently during an attack, and must themselves resolve such problems as may arise. It is therefore important, as far as possible, to provide each unit (each company, battalion and sometimes even section) with one or two guns or trench-mortars. Each of these units must be plentifully supplied with hand-grenades and high-explosive bombs. In addition, it must have an adequate quantity of axes, crowbars, picks and rope-ladders – all of which are necessary for house-to-house fighting (to force doors, break through walls, get from one floor to another, etc.).

Street attack consists in the successive capture of individual blocks of houses, squares and barricades. It can be carried out by a drive along the street, or, if this is blocked, by circling around through the houses, courtyards and gardens. The first method is quicker; the second is more reliable and involves fewer losses, but is slow. The choice of method is left to the individual commander, depending on the general situation and the amount of technical resources at his disposal.[14]

If the attacker has enough artillery at his disposal (field-guns and trench-mortars) to reduce the enemy machine-guns to silence, it is preferable to adopt the first method, since it produces the quickest results – i.e. to advance down the street. If not, the attack will have to be made by circling around by way of the houses, courtyards and gardens. Sometimes it will be possible to use a combined method of attack: to advance simultaneously along the street and to use circling manoeuvres.

The aim of circling manoeuvres is to force a way progressively from one house to the next, and by frequent attacks to disrupt the enemy's defence system and oblige him to abandon his positions. When an attacker enters a building, he must search every part of it with the greatest care. If he discovers that the inmates have fought with the defending troops, he must arrest them and confine them for the duration of the battle in special quarters under guard.

Attacks on barricades are best carried out with the help of armoured cars or tanks. If the attackers do not possess these, they will have to use infantry; the latter must be supported by machine-guns, and above all by artillery – which should aim for the defenders' machine-gun nests, the defenders themselves, and the houses commanding the barricade. The frontal assault should be accompanied by simultaneous flanking movements to take the defenders on the barricade from behind.

When drawing up the plan of attack for a given street or district, special attention must be paid to the organization of liaison. In addition to using the city's technical communications system (telephone), ample use must be made of direct liaison by means of couriers. Only if liaison functions uninterruptedly will the leadership be able to give its orders in time to influence the course of the fighting.

One serious means of influencing the course of events during an attack is the reserve kept back by the commander of the operation. Whence the need, when deploying the assault forces, to provide for a fairly strong reserve which should be kept in the immediate vicinity of the attack zone. Often the commanders of the lesser units too (i.e. the individual battalion or company commanders) will have to have their own reserves. The role of the reserve is (*a*) to consolidate the victory if the attack

---

[14] *Provisional Field Regulations of the Red Army*, p. 414.

succeeds; (*b*) to reinforce the attacking units; (*c*) to guard against the unforeseen.

When a particular building is to be occupied, the first thing to be done is to isolate it from the neighbouring buildings; next it should be subjected to a heavy barrage of fire; and only then should it be stormed in accordance with a detailed plan. The isolation of the building to be attacked should be accomplished by occupying all the surrounding buildings and all routes leading from it to the city.

The barrage of fire should be carried out by artillery, and also by machine-guns. The role of the artillery is to knock out the defenders' machine-guns, destroy the outer doors, etc. The machine-guns must rake the balconies, windows and roofs; the best solution is to organize the firing from the windows and roofs of neighbouring houses which have already been cleared of the enemy. The infantry attack itself must be swift and energetic, and its commander must take measures before-hand to cut off the enemy's retreat. The commander of an attack on a house or block of houses must also provide in his plan for the measures to be taken in case of failure.

12

The Party's Military Work among the Peasants

Revolutionary Guerrilla Methods

Victory of the proletarian revolution is *impossible* in rural and semi-rural countries *if the revolutionary proletariat is not actively supported* by the mass of the peasant population. This is an incontrovertible truth for both the bourgeois democratic and the proletarian revolution. In the period of the bourgeois democratic revolution, no struggle by the proletariat to realize its slogans and develop the bourgeois democratic revolution into a proletarian revolution *can be crowned by success* without a revolutionary bloc of proletariat and peasantry, and without the active participation of the mass of oppressed peasants in realizing the slogans of the revolution. Clear proof of this is provided by three Russian revolutions, by the great Chinese revolution, and by revolutionary struggles in numerous other countries. This fundamental Leninist principle is today an absolutely incontrovertible fact for every genuine revolutionary. In China, in India, in Latin America, in many European countries (Balkan countries, Rumania, Poland, Italy, France, Spain, etc.), the decisive ally of the proletariat in the revolution will be the peasant population. Only if the revolutionary wave sets in motion the rural masses, under the leadership of the proletariat, will the revolution be able to triumph. Hence the exceptional importance of Party agitation in the countryside.

Any serious revolutionary movement among the peasants, as we have seen (and to some extent can still see today) in China, at first takes the form of isolated, spontaneous and uncoordinated revolts by guerrilla groups – against the big landowners, kulaks, merchants and money-lenders; against the authorities collecting taxes; in short, against all the administrative and political powers which exist in country or town and against the existing régime – for the confiscation and distribution of the land, the suppression of rents, the cancellation of debts and the seizure of political power by the peasant organizations. In the first phase of the revolutionary movement, the peasants rarely put forward any very definite slogans of agrarian revolution; they merely protest against 'bad' landlords, and demand reductions in rents and taxes, etc.

The key characteristic of peasant revolution in its first phase is its spontaneous character: isolated, uncoordinated actions; no fixed political programme common to all regions; no settled slogans.

The aim of the proletarian party with respect to the peasants is clear. It must win leadership of the movement, organize it, mobilize the peasant masses around certain class slogans which accord with the character of the revolution, and in short must lead the entire movement towards realizing these slogans. The party of the proletariat must co-ordinate the peasant movement with the revolutionary aims and operations of the proletariat in the industrial centres.

It must be obvious to the revolutionary party that the peasant movement, however large it may be, cannot count on any decisive success if the working class does not move. The same is true for the latter's operations (in rural and semi-rural countries) if they are not accompanied by powerful revolutionary activity on the part of the peasants. To organize and prepare combined actions, if possible simultaneously in the towns and the countryside – such will be the fundamental aim of the revolutionary party in the rural and semi-rural countries.

In China, as a result of the Northern expedition, the peasant movement attained colossal proportions. Towards the time of the Fifth Congress of the Chinese Communist Party (May 1926), there were some ten million peasants organized in peasant leagues in the Centre and South of the country. The enormous majority, mainly in the South, in the Yangtze basin, was already fighting (by 1927) consciously under the slogan of agrarian revolution. The Chinese Communist Party (its leadership of that period) – instead of carrying out agitation among the peasants in accordance with the directives of the Communist International; instead of drawing the mass of the rural population on to the path of revolutionary action, by helping the peasants to organize and to draw up a political programme and a plan of action, and by accelerating social differentiation in the countryside; instead of subordinating the movement to its own influence and directing its strategy towards extending and deepening the agrarian revolution – acted as a fetter on the peasant movement, and in concert with the Kuomintang combatted so-called excesses – i.e. what in reality were the revolutionary initiatives of the peasant organizations. That was the biggest error of the communist leadership of the time.

It is hardly astonishing that this policy of the Communist Party towards the peasants and this bloc with the Kuomintang produced the following result: when the insurgents who had risen under Yeh T'ing and Ho Lung at Nanchang on 1 August 1927 set out towards the South, they could not find a sufficient number of coolies to transport their munitions and other war *matériel*.[1] The peasants abandoned their villages to escape being mobilized. The armies of Yeh T'ing and Ho Lung were thus obliged to leave behind enormous quantities of munitions to fall into the enemy's hands. Similarly in the Swatow area, where the communist and left Kuomintang commanders of the revolutionary army in question tried to persuade the peasants to join their ranks, and wanted to distribute the surplus arms to them. The peasants did not join the revolutionary army, for they made no distinction between it and the militarist armies. Indeed, there was no distinction to be made; for, although in some divisions (the 24th and 25th) all the regimental commanders and twenty per cent of the officers were communists, and although the Revolutionary military committee also included communists, the army's policy towards the peasants (as on every other issue for that matter) did not differ in any way from that of the Kuomintang Left. Instead of the slogans like: 'Down with big landowners!' 'Expropriation of the land!', etc., put forward by the peasant leagues, the Revolutionary committee put forward the following slogans: 'Down with bad landowners!', 'Confiscate estates of more than twenty *mou*!', 'A 50 per cent reduction in rents!', etc. In view of this, it is not surprising that the peasant masses should have turned away from the Revolutionary army and abandoned their villages to withdraw into the mountains at the very news of its approach. It is not surprising either that, in the town of Lin-ch'uan, the army of Yeh T'ing and Ho Lung should have been welcomed by a friendly demonstration of merchants, with a total absence of peasants.

It must be borne in mind that these same peasants, at the beginning of and during the Northern expedition, in the hope that the Kuomintang would bring them social and economic emancipation, had striven with all their might to help it crush the army of the old-style warlords

---

[1] The Southern armies do not possess special convoys: all transport of war *matériel* is carried out by coolies, i.e. by peasants who are either mobilized for the purpose or well paid.

(Sun Ch'uan-fang, Wu P'ei-fu and the rest). They had done so by rising in its rear; harassing it with constant guerrilla attacks, and assassinating officers or big landowners; in short, by disrupting life totally in its rear.

It must be clearly stressed that the Communist Party's bad policy on the peasant question was one of the fatal causes for the defeat of the Chinese revolution in 1927.

Another example of how not to act with respect to the peasant movement is provided by the events of 1923 in Bulgaria. Here, in the autumn of 1923, peasant insurrections broke out spontaneously in a whole series of regions. However, the Bulgarian Communist Party spent a whole week without doing anything to win leadership of the movement. The peasant insurrections – for lack of organization and coordination, because of their isolation, and because of the absence of any correct leadership from the Communist Party – were crushed by counter-revolution.

On the other hand, the victory of the October revolution would have been impossible if the Bolshevik Party had not been capable of mobilizing the peasant masses under its own slogans, and leading them into battle to overthrow the power of the bourgeoisie and to establish the dictatorship of the proletariat. If it had not been for this correct policy of the Bolshevik Party towards the peasants, there could never have been any question of winning the Tsarist army over to the revolution; for it was precisely the Bolshevik Party's bold policy towards the peasants which gave it immense possibilities for winning over the Tsarist army – composed mainly of peasants.

One reason for the defeat of the Canton insurrection was that, at the moment when the proletariat rose inside the city, there was no serious revolutionary peasant movement in the neighbouring areas. On the other hand, the innumerable peasant risings in various provinces of China (e.g. in Shantung) were defeated mainly because they remained isolated from the revolutionary movement of the working class in the industrial centres, and were not supported by proletarian action in the towns.

At the moment of the Russian proletariat's active revolutionary struggle in 1905, the great mass of peasants still showed too little revolutionary activity. The peasant movement in Russia only reached its peak in 1906-7, about a year after the revolutionary wave of the urban proletariat had ebbed. The fact that the revolutionary movement in the towns did not coincide with that in the countryside was the basic reason for the defeat of the first Russian revolution.

To ensure the greatest possible simultaneity of action between the proletariat and the peasants, the party of the proletariat, above all in rural and semi-rural countries, must devote its attention to political and organizational (including military) work among the peasants. This work must not be left to chance, nor be carried out in an unplanned, uniform manner throughout the country. It must rather be geared to the Party's fundamental perspectives with respect to the order and date of the various revolutionary actions which may be possible in any given region or province. Uniform political agitation or organizational work, in a country as vast as China, will inevitably lead to the dispersal of manpower and resources. The differing importance of the various provinces in China's political life (as in similar countries) must determine the varying intensity of Party work among the peasants in each of them. Thus, the political importance of Kansu, Kweichow, Kwangsi and other provinces of this kind cannot be compared with that of Kwangtung, Hupeh, Hunan, Kiangsu, etc., with their great industrial and commercial centres and their numerous proletariat. Naturally, revolutionary agitation must be carried out among the peasants everywhere, but *its main weight* must be directed towards a specific province or group of provinces. This principle derives from the universally recognized truth that in countries like China, which present an infinite diversity of geographical, economic and political conditions, the revolution (the seizure of power by the proletariat, in alliance with the peasants and urban poor) cannot be accomplished as a single act (i.e. in the space of a few weeks or months), but must necessarily fill an entire more or less prolonged period of revolutionary movements in the various provinces or industrial and political centres.

It is beyond a doubt that Soviet power will initially establish itself in China in some province or group of provinces possessing a great industrial or commercial centre, which will serve as a base for the subsequent development of the revolution. The date at which new territories will be added to this revolutionary base will depend on the balance of forces between revolution and counter-revolution, not only in China but in the entire world. This is a question which will only be resolved by struggle. But in any case, the consolidation and revolutionary unification of China will require infinitely more time than was necessary to chase the counter-revolutionary forces out of Russia after the October revolution in Petrograd and Moscow.

Thus when the revolutionary party foresees the approach of an immediately revolutionary situation, it must (while continuing to educate and mobilize the working class), indicate which provinces or districts are most important from the point of view of agitation among the peasants, and must fix its attention and concentrate its resources accordingly upon these provinces. With respect to agitational work among the peasants, the Party must concern itself above all with the areas surrounding the main industrial and political centres. This is equally true for a whole number of European countries (Poland, France, Rumania, etc.).

When a powerful revolutionary peasant movement starts after a defeat of the proletariat (e.g. after the 1905 revolution in Russia, or in China after the defeat of the proletariat in 1927), the Party must undoubtedly place itself at the head of that peasant movement and guide it. The revolutionary struggle of the peasantry, especially if it develops successfully in areas containing important industrial and commercial centres, is a powerful weapon; it can incite the working class, which has been defeated and has fallen once more into the clutches of reaction, to resume the initiative and act.

Given that any serious revolutionary movement among the peasant population necessarily takes the form of armed actions (i.e. actual military operations by peasant detachments) against the arbitrary power of landowners, money-lenders, government officials, etc., it is absolutely essential to discuss the Party's military work among the peasants at greater length.

It is not possible to embark on creating armed peasant detachments simply at any given moment, just as it is not possible to form a red guard in the factories at will. The armed struggle of the peasants, as a form of mass struggle, arises in specific political circumstances – when the yoke of the ruling classes has become intolerable, and the village masses are in a state of revolutionary ferment and ready to fight actively against the established order. Spontaneous actions by armed peasant detachments are symptoms which show that 'the exploited and oppressed masses have become aware of the impossibility of going on in the old way, and demand changes' (Lenin), and that the country is entering an immediately revolutionary situation. No revolutionary guerrilla movement is possible in a 'normal and peaceful' situation, for it represents the beginning of a period of open civil war between two sections of a people.

Historical experience of guerrilla warfare in various countries shows that initially it is characterized by small engagements of only local significance. This is a result of the weakness and limited numbers of the guerrilla units, and the low level of awareness among the peasants of their goals – due to their lack of revolutionary experience, and to the absence of any adequate influence of the proletarian party in the countryside. The essential aim of the guerrilla detachments in this period is to defend the peasants of the area in question against the violence of the reactionary authorities, against the arbitrary requisitions of the army (in wartime), etc. To this end, the struggle of the guerrilla units often takes the form of acts of individual terrorism or sabotage against village officials, merchants, landowners, officers, police, leaders of fascist or black-hundred organizations; of attacks on isolated units carrying out punitive expeditions, or on small bodies of troops, to seize their arms or free their prisoners; of destroying roads and railways; of 'expropriations', and the seizure of sums of money; of burning estates, etc.

Problems concerning the capture of political power, the coordination of guerrilla operations between the various regions, or the adaptation of these operations to the political and economic struggle of the urban proletariat, are not ordinarily posed in this initial period of civil war in the countryside. The slogans of guerrilla warfare do not as yet have an explicit class character.

Subsequently, as the revolutionary upsurge increases in the countryside, as the class antagonisms within the peasant population heighten, and as the proletariat's influence over the peasantry grows, guerrilla actions will begin to multiply. The number of detachments will increase and continually embrace new areas. Their operations will progressively become more ambitious in scale. The armed struggle of the oppressed peasants against reaction will now begin to take on a mass character; it will pass progressively over from defensive to offensive action, and will keep the authorities in perpetual fear of surprise raids by peasant detachments.

In this period, the guerrilla detachments no longer limit themselves to operating in their home area. They venture out from their own villages or districts, gradually transform themselves into flying columns of varying strength, join up with detachments from the neighbouring areas and become emboldened to undertake larger-scale operations.

The range of their objectives now increases markedly. In addition to minor raids on warehouses – executions of big landowners, reactionaries and police officials, the firing of large estates, etc. – they now begin to go in for regular attacks on the police and on the troops and their rearguard units, and for surprise attacks on small towns (sackings, etc.).

The history of peasant struggle throughout the world richly illustrates the way in which the guerrilla movement transforms itself little by little into a serious force; into one that is capable, given proper leaders, of carrying out revolutionary tasks of enormous importance.

During the Northern expedition, in 1926 and early 1927, the revolutionary army of the Canton government, which when it first left Kwangtung province numbered some 90,000 soldiers, defeated the armies of Wu P'ei-fu, Sun Ch'uan-fang and Chang Tsung-ch'ang, which were several times larger – indeed absolutely exceptional by Chinese standards. This great military success of the numerically small, poorly armed and badly equipped Canton army was only made possible *by the active operations of the peasant detachments* behind the enemy's lines. During the entire Northern expedition, and particularly at the beginning, the peasants of the southern and central provinces – who at that time saw the national revolutionary army as the standard-bearer of struggle against the big landowners, gentry, imperialists, warlords, and in general against all reactionaries – gave incalculable assistance to the national army with their guerrilla actions, their revolts, their sabotage of the warlord army's lines of retreat, their surprise attacks on the troops. The warlord armies found themselves obliged to sustain the attack of the revolutionary troops from the front, and at the same time to organize a desperate resistance to the peasant detachments at their rear. Naturally, no army is capable of fighting effectively under such conditions. The army of the warlords of South and Central China, though vigorously supported by imperialism, disintegrated inevitably beneath the combined and coordinated blows of the national army and of the numerous peasant detachments attacking its rear.

The Communist Party and the Kuomintang, through the work which they carried out among the peasants in the provinces held by the warlords, played a considerable part in organizing and leading the peasant detachments which disrupted the warlords' rear.

The history of the revolutionary struggle in China also provides a fine example of the use of guerrilla detachments for counter-revolutionary aims. At the beginning of 1926, the 2nd People's Army of Feng Yü-hsiang, quartered in the province of Hunan, was in a state of war against the army of Wu P'ei-fu. As a result of the ceaseless warfare between the warlord cliques, Hunan province had been completely ruined and the peasants reduced to beggary. The pauperization of the rural population had continued during the 2nd Army's sojourn there – its 200,000 men had of course to be supported by the population. This pauperization had led hundreds of thousands of peasants to enter the bands of the *t'u-fei* (bandits). Others organized themselves in the religious or semi-religious peasant leagues whose number grew enormously in 1925 and 1926.

The discontent of the Hunan peasants was exploited by Wu P'ei-fu, whose agents carried on skilful agitation against the 2nd People's Army. Various peasant organizations ('The Red Pikes', 'The Long Knives', 'The Empty Bellies', etc.) actively fought against the régime imposed by the 2nd Army on Hunan; they attacked and disrupted the latter's rear, carrying out systematic raids upon its smaller units and calling on the soldiers to desert and enter the peasant detachments, etc.

The demoralization of the 2nd Army reached such a point as a result of the hostility of the semi-military peasant organizations that immediately after the first attacks by Wu P'ei-fu's numerically insignificant forces, this army of 200,000 men fell to pieces like a house of cards.

Wu P'ei-fu was able to exploit the revolutionary potentialities of the Hunan peasants for a counter-revolutionary aim. However, when Wu P'ei-fu's own troops entered the province, those same peasants who had recently been attacking the 2nd People's Army now turned their weapons against Wu P'ei-fu. The latter suffered heavy defeats in this struggle against the Canton army as a result of the hostile action of the guerrilla detachments.

It would be possible to find numerous examples of heroic guerrilla actions in the history of the Russian civil war – in Siberia, the Ukraine, the Don region, the Northern Caucasus, etc. – which helped the Red Army clear the country of counter-revolutionary forces: the Tsarist generals, the landowners and the bourgeoisie.

The key to the durable success of guerrilla detachments is the solidity of their contact with the peasant masses. Guerrilla action is inconceivable without a revolutionary situation, a revolutionary ferment among the peasant masses. The guerrilla struggle must mirror the interests of the broad peasant masses, and there must be an immediately revolutionary situation for their victory to be possible. The kulak detachments which were created artificially by the counter-revolutionary parties in various regions of Russia during the civil war did not and could not achieve any durable success, because they did not reflect the aspirations of the peasant population, which absolutely refused to fight against Soviet power. Their temporary successes, for instance in the province of Tambov in 1920, quickly gave way to defeat and to revolts by the peasant masses against their counter-revolutionary leaders.

The conditions of the struggle; the size of the revolutionary movement in the countryside; the objectives which the peasant population sets itself – these are the factors which determine the forms of guerrilla struggle at any given moment, in any given country. From these forms in turn derive the organization and structure of the guerrilla detachments. It is the duty of the proletarian party always to take into account the concrete conditions of the moment, so that it will be in a position to give the guerrilla movement the forms which correspond to that particular situation, and to guide its operations. The guerrilla movement must be given not only political, but also military and tactical leadership.

General recipes and universal formulae for organization and tactics are absolutely inapplicable to the struggle of peasant guerrillas. The forms which this struggle takes in China, for example, are fundamentally different from those which it will take in France. To start with, the very fact that the theatre of operations is different will make this true, not to speak of all kinds of other differences and particularities. If one is not to stray from the terrain of Marxism and risk falling into abstraction, one can only speak in the most general way of the forms and structure of guerrilla detachments, merely outlining questions of principle.

Before recommending such and such a form of organization in guerrilla warfare, a detailed analysis must be made of the political situation in the region under consideration. All the particularities of the population's way of life and culture must be taken into account, together with such experience of class struggle as the peasants already have.

In the overall pattern of class struggle, guerrilla movements play the role of an auxiliary factor: they cannot of themselves achieve historic objectives, but can only contribute to the solution provided by another force – the proletariat. It follows that the specific objective of guerrilla operations is harassment and disruption of the reactionary forces, to facilitate the common victory of the working classes led by the proletariat.

As far as organization is concerned, the basic conditions which the guerrilla movement must fulfil are the following: (*a*) the organization must be supple, and must have several levels capable of acting independently of each other; (*b*) it must be mobile; capable of swift action; able to switch over rapidly as circumstances demand from illegal to legal conditions and vice-versa, and to combine judiciously legal, semi-legal and illegal methods; (*c*) the structure must be such that it allows the Party to exercise its political and operational leadership; (*d*) it must be simple, intelligible to the masses and in accordance with their customs, to ensure a continual accretion of new forces.

In the initial period, in which the movement's aim is to defend the peasants of the locality against the arbitrary rule of the reactionaries, the guerrilla detachments (i.e. the small primary groups) are formed along territorial lines. As a rule they are clandestine. Subsequently, as the class struggle sharpens in the countryside, and as it changes into an open civil war, these primary groups join together to form larger-scale regional detachments (communes, districts).

It goes without saying that the guerrilla detachments must include the most advanced elements in the village (that is what in fact happens anyway). Nevertheless, in the initial period, in view of the need for secrecy, in view of the spying and provocation of the authorities, the recruitment of the primary groups must be very closely scrutinized. Later, when the movement becomes transformed into a vast and powerful torrent, and draws into its ranks all advanced and active elements in the villages, the principle of secrecy and the screening of personnel lose a little of their importance. But a good choice of leaders, who must be politically reliable and adequately trained militarily, will always be a pressing problem; any negligence on this point will invariably have fatal consequences for the entire organization.

Good leadership of the guerrilla movement by the party of the proletariat is only possible if the latter possesses influence over the peasants, and if the peasants accept its slogans and struggle to realize them. In countries where there are mass peasant organizations, the Party must strive to influence these and to guide the guerrilla movement both directly and through them (for the guerrilla detachments are directed precisely by these peasant organizations). Where such mass organizations do not exist, the Party must use the guerrilla organizations as instruments to guide the peasants politically. The guerrilla organization itself must be, indeed is, the vanguard of the toiling peasantry – its active, combative and leading fraction.

The Bulgarian insurrections of 1923 were very unfavourably influenced by the fact that, at that time, the armed forces and leadership apparatus of the guerrilla detachments were not properly organized in Bulgaria. This was why the actions of the various units were so badly coordinated, and why the regular troops which were sent against them had a relatively easy campaign. The Communist Party only started to construct a leadership apparatus at the beginning of 1924. The peasant armed forces were meant to be set up, or rather reconstituted, according to the following pattern: at the base, groups of six (a leader and five armed men); three or four groups of six make up a *cheta*, and from three to five *chety* a *druzhina*. In case of need, from three to five of these *druzhiny* can be combined to form a larger detachment.

The peasant combat organization is directed at the commune level by a commune (political and military) headquarters, at the district level by a district headquarters, to which the *druzhiny* are subordinated.

It should be remarked that the organization of the Bulgarian *druzhina* is based on a fairly clear differentiation of functions: in addition to its fighting units, the *druzhina* includes scouts, machine-gunners, couriers, etc.

If such an organization had been fully realized, and had succeeded in adapting itself to the conditions imposed by the terrain, by its chosen objectives, by the need for security, etc., it would certainly have permitted the Bulgarian insurgents to carry out the missions entrusted to them effectively. Unfortunately, the Communist Party undertook the reorganization of the guerrilla forces along these lines too late, so that in practice it was not realized everywhere. For the Party only began seriously to pose the question of organizing armed forces in the villages at a time when the revolutionary wave, after the defeat of September 1923, was already on the ebb in Bulgaria.

In China, the structure of the fighting organizations of the peasant population (the 'Red Pikes' and the rest) is different from in Bulgaria. The basic unit is the group of ten; these groups join up into groups of a hundred, and the latter normally form up into yet stronger detachments.

In Germany, at the end of 1923 and in early 1924, the peasant detachments of Pomerania and East Prussia were organized according to the same schema as the Proletarian Hundreds in the towns: squads of between ten and fifteen men; sections made up of three or four squads; hundreds made up of two or three sections.

It is hard to judge how effective this structure was, since the organization of the German Proletarian Hundreds did not develop very far; the Party only began to constitute them at the moment when the revolutionary wave began to ebb, and they quickly fragmented. However, since these Hundreds in essence reproduced the structure of the companies in the imperial army (with which the masses were familiar from the experience of the war), and since moreover the Proletarian Hundreds in the towns won widespread popularity during 1923 (and even before that), one may presume that this organization by hundreds was the form which best suited German conditions.

In Russia during the civil war, the guerrilla movement generally took on the same form as the smaller units of the regular army: sections, companies, squadrons, battalions, cavalry and infantry regiments. Subsequently, when the Red Army attacking from in front and the guerrillas attacking from the rear combined to drive the enemy from the positions he held, the guerrilla detachments either merged into the Red Army units or, as often happened, continued to exist as independent units of the Red Army – receiving their commanding officers and their *matériel* from the latter's general reserve, and operating under the orders of its high command.

The above-mentioned examples of the guerrilla movement's structure in various countries show that, essentially, the same principles apply here as with the basic units of the regular army – *but that it is also necessary to take into account the specific features of each country, the aims of the guerrilla movement in each period, the arms available (or which can be acquired in the course of the struggle), and lastly the need to preserve secrecy.* If all these conditions are observed, we shall arrive at the specific structure of guerrilla detachments: in the initial period, small more or less conspiratorial combat groups of five, eight or ten men, formed village by village and subordinated, via their commanders, to the commune and district military committees and their representatives in the villages. As the movement develops (with the sharpening of the struggle of the poor peasants), these small groups join together into larger detachments (sections, *druzhiny,* battalions). These in their turn can be combined into yet larger units.

In this process whereby small guerrilla detachments are grouped into larger units, it is necessary to observe the established principle of military science which lays down that during operations no single leader must have more than four or five units under his command; for if he has a greater number than this, the task of leadership will be far more difficult and the final outcome will be adversely affected. This principle should be all the more closely adhered to in the case of guerrilla detachments, since their specific character and the inevitable lack of good leaders among the guerrillas themselves will always make the question of leadership one of the hardest for them to resolve.

As for supervising the formation of detachments, their military training, and their operations in a commune, district, province or throughout an entire country – this must naturally be the responsibility of the military commission of the appropriate committee of the Communist Party, for these commissions are in charge of all the Party's military work. Comrades specialized in work among the peasants must be included on these commissions. The district and commune commissions will necessarily have their own military representatives among the peasants in each village or group of villages; their task will be to direct the formation of the detachments and their military training on the spot, through the intermediary of the respective leaders (commanders) of the lower-level guerrilla units and other peasant organizations, where such exist.

Training the guerrillas for military operations, above all teaching them to handle arms, will be one of the main tasks of the organizers and leaders – above all in countries in which the peasants do not have the possibility of learning the art of war in the regular army (i.e. countries with professional armies or arms limitations; countries which did not participate in the last world war, or in other wars). It is not enough to teach the guerrillas to use the arms which they possess at that particular moment; they also need as far as possible to know how to use any arms which they may subsequently capture from the enemy. The key principle here must be that each guerrilla must learn to shoot well with a rifle, to handle various types of revolver, to throw a hand-grenade, and to become proficient in hand-to-hand fighting (pikes, sabres, etc.).

It is also very important that each unit should possess a sufficient number of properly-trained scouts, machine-gunners, couriers, engineers, and nurses. The formation of an adequate number of these specialists is part of the responsibility of the leadership of the guerrilla detachments.

How can weapons be procured with which to arm the new guerrilla organization initially? This is a problem as difficult to resolve as that of arming the red guard. It can nevertheless be resolved, in spite of the difficulties, at least sufficiently to be able to begin a struggle to obtain arms. In general, it should be made clear that it will never be possible to accumulate stocks of arms in advance. It will be necessary to make use of whatever comes to hand: the arms normally available to peasants (hunting guns, revolvers, axes, iron bars, etc.), plus grenades and bombs, pikes, sabres, etc. In certain cases it may be possible to purchase firearms. But the main source of the guerrillas' armament will be raids on arms depots and the disarming of police and groups of soldiers – all this carried out with the primitive weapons available initially. It must be stressed that, for every serious guerrilla movement, adding to its reserves of arms and ammunition will be a constant and ever-pressing task.

The history of the guerrilla movement in Russia, China, and elsewhere shows that detachments which began the struggle against the authorities and the army without at first having anything other than axes, iron bars, pitchforks, scythes or simple sticks, subsequently, in the course of their struggle, captured all the modern arms they needed (rifles, machine-guns, cannon, etc., with the necessary ammunition).

Guerrilla struggle, just like red guard operations in the city, must be waged in accordance with the fundamental principles of military science and tactics. Nevertheless, at each given moment, it is necessary to take into account the specific features of the time and the conditions in which the detachment has to operate.

Just like the combat organization in the city, the guerrilla detachment can only count on succeeding if each of its members, and particularly its leaders, displays the maximum of energy; if, in preparing operations, the 'time' factor is strictly observed; if a plan of action has been carefully worked out in advance; if the forces assigned to each specific mission have been deployed in accordance with the prevailing circumstances; if a meticulous reconnaissance of the enemy and the locality has been carried out; if the principle of surprise attack has been observed, and etc. The shortage of arms, the absence of large units (dispersal of forces), the difficulty of obtaining a good command system over an entire province or even an entire district – these weaknesses must and can be compensated for by the advantages of surprise, audacity, and decision in the guerrilla operations.

To confirm these ideas, let us cite one of the numerous examples provided by the history of the red guerrillas in Russia.

At the end of July 1918, the white guards had surrounded the Sal district Soviet. The village of Platovskaya was occupied by the Gnilorybov Detachment, with a hundred officers and some two hundred forcibly recruited Kalmyks. They began to shoot the peasants who were sympathetic to the Bolsheviks. Budënny formed a group of four men in the hamlet of Kuzorino, and decided to attack Platovksaya to free the prisoners. During the night of 27/28 July, this group carried out a daring attack, freed the prisoners, disarmed the astonished Kalmyks and at once armed the freed prisoners. After bitter hand-to-hand fighting, the company of officers withdrew, leaving Budënny the following booty: 2 cannon, 4 machine-guns, 300 rifles, 60,000 rounds of ammunition and 150 horses with all their harness.[2]

The guerrilla detachments, as long as they are not grouped into a more or less strong peasant army, are not capable of waging a serious struggle against the regular army in pitched battles or on open ground. Thus, in the event of these detachments being attacked by the regular troops, the best course for them to follow is to *avoid the battle* rather than set about defending themselves like regular troops. For, in view of their relative weakness, the guerrillas cannot hope for any success in defensive action. *The strength of guerrillas does not lie in defence, but in their daring and sudden offensive actions. Guerrilla fighters are not strong enough militarily for defensive action. They must in all places and at all times be intent on manoeuvring; deal rapid and unexpected blows at the enemy at the moment and the place in which he is least expecting it; and withdraw quickly and avoid a decisive encounter if the circumstances and the balance of forces in that particular place at that particular time are not in their favour, so as to surprise the foe in another quarter.*

In the organization of large-scale attacks against towns, bodies of troops, etc., the commanders of the guerrilla detachments must pay great attention to the problem of choosing *the main direction in which to strike*. Any attempt to strike with equal strength at every point means dispersing the forces available. The commanders must con-

[2] *The Proletarian Revolution on the Don*, Miscellany no. 1, Moscow, 1922.

centrate their efforts and attention upon the main line of attack, where they can hope to win a rapid and decisive success, and should only keep back minimal resources or men for secondary missions. Furthermore, in the organization of combined operations *by several detachments* with the aim of capturing such and such an objective by surprise, it must be borne in mind that the 'time' factor is enormously important. Non-observation of these two tactical principles frequently leads to failure, and even to the wiping out of the attacking units.

In these combined operations, *unity of command* also plays a very great role. The absence of good leadership, or the presence of several leaderships (with each detachment operating independently), are impermissible. The plan of operation must be worked out collectively, and during the fighting a collective leadership must give all orders to the units taking part in the operation. This is the essential condition for combined operations to have any hope of succeeding.

The need for a unified command in guerrilla actions is a commonplace of guerrilla combat tactics – indeed of all combat in general. Nevertheless, the experience of past guerrilla warfare, especially in China, shows that this elementary requirement is not always observed or put into practice. There have been frequent cases in which a number of guerrilla detachments with a common objective but without a unified command have dispersed their efforts and for that reason been defeated.

No operation should be undertaken without careful prior reconnaissance. Accurate information about the enemy, about his positions, about his strong and weak points, about the terrain, roads, means of transport, the population, etc. – all this should be obtained from scout patrols and should serve as the basis for the plan of operation. A constant flow of intelligence about the enemy is a fundamental requirement in guerrilla warfare. Before each operation, the guerrillas must carry out a special reconnaissance of their targets, paying attention to every tiniest detail.

Appendix

Some Prefatory Remarks
by the Publishers*

The question dealt with in this book has hitherto been largely ignored by world literature. Neuberg's book is thus intended to fill a gap of which every worker has long been aware.

The book is of particular importance in that it is one of the few works to be written by an author who is at once a Marxist and a direct participant in the revolutionary armed struggle of the proletariat. A highly serious work from every point of view, it is notable for the thoroughness with which it treats its subject. The author has brought together a wealth of factual material. Thanks to his linguistic abilities, he has also been able to make use of the extremely rich Russian source-materials on this question.

A further circumstance which confers particular importance on Neuberg's book is its extraordinary actuality, in view of the exceptionally sharp class contradictions and class struggles now rending the entire capitalist world; these have long since become transformed into open guerrilla struggle and civil war – we need only cite events in India and China.[1]

* As Erich Wollenberg explains in his introduction, when Neuberg's book first appeared (in German) in 1928, it was not presented as a communist publication, but carried an apparently innocent 'publisher's name'. It was prefaced by this 'publisher's note' – which in fact represented a Comintern judgement on the book, warning against certain 'incorrect' views expressed in it. When the French edition appeared in 1931, substantially the same introduction (the changes are indicated in this edition in the footnotes) was signed by the Central Committee of the French Communist Party. [Translator's note.]

[1] In the 1931 French edition, the foregoing three paragraphs were replaced by the following: 'The publishers consider this book to be of the greatest theoretical and practical importance; they see it as responding to an ever-growing interest in such questions on the part of the revolutionary proletariat in the present period. It is for this reason that they are bringing it out rapidly, without waiting for such additions or corrections as the author might have made.

'Neuberg's book is valuable for two reasons. It is one of the few works to be written by an author who is both a Marxist and a militant who as fought gun in hand against the capitalist world. It is a highly serious work, rich in facts. Secondly, this book is of extra-ordinary actuality in the present historical situation.'

The programme of the Communist International, adopted at the Sixth World Congress, states:

When the revolutionary tide is rising, when the ruling classes are disorganized, the masses are in a state of revolutionary ferment, the intermediary strata are inclining towards the proletariat and the masses are ready for action and for sacrifice, the Party of the proletariat is confronted with the task of leading the masses to a direct attack upon the bourgeois State. This it does by carrying on propaganda in favour of increasingly radical transitional slogans (for Soviets, workers' control of industry, for peasant committees, for the seizure of the big landed properties, for disarming the bourgeoisie and arming the proletariat, etc.), and by organizing mass action, upon which all branches of Party agitation and propaganda, including parliamentary activity, must be concentrated. This mass action includes: strikes; a combination of strikes and demonstrations; a combination of strikes and armed demonstrations and finally, the general strike conjointly with armed insurrection against the state power of the bourgeoisie. The latter form of struggle, which is the supreme form, must be conducted according to the rules of war; it presupposes a plan of campaign, offensive fighting operations and unbounded devotion and heroism on the part of the proletariat.

The programme goes on notably to add that to miss the peak of the revolutionary situation, when it is the duty of the proletarian party to attack the enemy with courage and determination, 'to allow that opportunity to slip by and to fail to start rebellion at that point, means to allow the initiative to pass to the enemy and to doom the revolution to defeat'.

The Communist International's Sixth World Congress which adopted this programme mentioned in its political resolution the certain and imminent approach of a new revolutionary upsurge. The Tenth Plenum of the Executive Committee of the Communist International, which was held a year after the Sixth Congress, in July 1929, acknowledged that 'a new feature in the situation since the Sixth World Congress is the sharply marked radicalization of the international working class and the rising of the new tide of the revolutionary labour movement'. On the basis of this evaluation of the international situation, the Tenth Plenum defined the main task of the epoch, both for the International as a whole and for each communist party individually, as the conquest of a majority of the working class. It also indicated the decisive means whereby this task could be accomplished – namely, large-scale political strikes. The organization of such strikes, according to the theses adopted at the Plenum, 'will enable the Communist Parties to introduce greater unity into the scattered economic actions of the working class, to carry out an extensive mobilization of the proletarian masses, to increase their political experience in every way and to lead them up to the direct struggle for the dictatorship of the proletariat'.

Events since the Tenth Plenum have confirmed these conclusions entirely. In general, they herald the approach of the moment indicated in the Plenum's resolutions – the moment of direct struggle for the dictatorship of the proletariat.

The direct struggle for the dictatorship of the proletariat is necessarily an armed struggle, an armed insurrection by the proletarian masses. According to the programme of the Communist International, this must be based on the principles of military science and requires a military plan. The communist parties and the entire international proletariat must prepare for this insurrection. They must study military science, and thoroughly absorb the experience and the lessons of past armed uprisings – while bearing in mind the concrete conditions and specific features of their own countries. This, of course, applies above all to the communist parties and proletariat in those countries where the new revolutionary upsurge is today advancing most rapidly – i.e. Germany, Poland and France. But in other countries too, communists cannot and must not, in present conditions, postpone studying the problem of armed insurrection.

Neuberg set out to examine questions concerning the military, tactical and technical side of insurrection. Thus in certain passages there will be found a certain 'military bias' which expresses itself in the insufficient attention devoted to elucidating political factors. Armed insurrection is a special branch of military science, and for this reason it obeys special rules – which were laid down in detail by Lenin in his day and which every proletarian revolutionary absolutely must know.

The programme of the International, resuming the immense international experience of past proletarian insurrections, shows how these developed from ordinary strikes or demonstrations into combinations of large-scale political strikes with armed demonstrations. This international experience, translated in the programme into a general directive, shows that one thing is central in preparing for armed insurrection: the readiness and ability of the Party to bring the proletarian masses onto the streets by means of a strike and, once they are there, to fire them with the will to fight and organize them to make a bid for power. Hence, it is necessary to pay the greatest attention to the way in which insurrectionary situations matured in the past: how the parties reacted; how the proletariat reacted; how events unfolded; what positive or negative conclusions were drawn for the future. *These are the key problems for the coming period. It is necessary to give the parties and the proletarian masses an exhaustive analysis of the experience which has been accumulated; to teach them how to raise strikes and demonstrations to a higher level, and transform them into a general strike combined with an armed insurrection against the state power of the bourgeoisie.*

In the chapter on work in the army, insufficient attention was paid to the new developments in bourgeois military policy and to the most recent experience of the proletariat in that respect. Neuberg writes: 'If an army and police-force with good military training . . . supported by the armed fascist detachments which exist in every country today, *fight effectively against the revolution*, they are capable of rendering the latter's victory singularly difficult even if all the other conditions are favourable.'

Neuberg draws the absolutely correct conclusion from this that it is necessary to make the most persistent efforts to subvert the armed forces of the bourgeoisie. He quotes the following passage from Lenin's article on the lessons of the Moscow uprising: 'Of course, unless the revolution assumes a mass character and affects the troops, there can be no question of serious struggle.' But to give a fuller and more accurate picture of Lenin's ideas, the following lines from the same article should also be quoted: 'The masses must know that they are entering upon an armed, bloody and desperate struggle. Contempt for death must become widespread among them and will ensure victory. The onslaught on the enemy must be pressed with the greatest vigour; attack, not defence, must be the slogan of the masses; the ruthless extermination of the enemy will be their task; the organization of the struggle will become mobile and flexible; the wavering elements among the troops will be drawn into active participation.' The entire experience of past revolutions show that *the conquest of the troops will be achieved in the actual course of the fighting, through direct contact between the revolutionary masses and the wavering elements of the army, who are already demoralized. This will be the physical struggle for the army of which Lenin speaks, involving extermination of the officers – but modified in accordance with the new features of bourgeois military policy since the war*. This recommendation of Lenin's is of particular relevance today. One of the most remarkable features of the new military policy of the bourgeoisie is in fact its orientation towards *the formation of a politically reliable army*. This is a phenomenon which can be observed in all the bourgeois countries, and which involves *the creation of mercenary armies, and volunteer military organizations of the bourgeoisie*, side by side with (or even in place of) the old 'national' armies formed by means of compulsory military service. In many countries this tendency has already had the result that these detachments recruited for civil war against the proletariat *have become the decisive armed force of the bourgeoisie*. This is true not only in Germany, Austria and England, where compulsory military service does not exist, but even in France where, under the new laws, the army in peacetime is made up mainly of volunteers. In Finland, the conscript army is a mere 30,000 strong, whereas the bourgeoisie's volunteer organization the *Schützkorps*, has some 100,000 men and is better armed.

But it would be a big mistake to give up trying to subvert these mercenary armies. It is essential to disrupt by every means the efforts of the ruling classes to endow themselves with obedient and wholly dependable armed forces. This is extremely difficult, but by no means impossible, in view of the fact that these volunteer formations of the bourgeoisie contain proletarian and semi-proletarian elements, and that it is not impossible to send revolutionary elements into them *with the specific mission* of subverting and disrupting them. This merely requires a great deal of determination; for the least waverings or signs of demoralization *among these troops*, who represent their *last line of defence*, will be felt more keenly by the bourgeoisie.

Nevertheless, it is not to be hoped that such work, however bold and persistent, will enable the majority of these troops to be won over to the revolution. The proletariat must expect and be prepared for these troops '*to fight against the revolution*'. On the other hand, however, even if in 1923 there was no hope of winning over a sizeable portion of the Reichswehr and the police, it by no means followed that a victory of the German proletariat was excluded.

In the event of *a large-scale war*, whether among themselves or against the USSR, the imperialist states will find that their highly-trained mercenary armies and fascist organizations are not sufficient. The ruling classes will be obliged to *mobilize large masses of workers and peasants* around these 'reliable' units, and to arm them. More favourable conditions will then prevail for winning over the mass of the troops – above all in a revolutionary situation such as is bound to arise in the event of new imperialist wars. However, this is no way supports the views of the rightists in the Communist International[2] who claim that *the victory of the proletarian revolution is only possible after a war.* Neuberg is absolutely right to differentiate himself sharply from this viewpoint. He very correctly remarks that *a revolutionary situation can mature* in 'peacetime' conditions as well as in the aftermath of a war.

As early as 1906, at a time when Russia had compulsory military service and there was therefore considerable hope of subverting the army, Lenin was already stressing the need for a bitter physical struggle to win over the troops, and for a war to the death against the units loyal to Tsarism. Obviously today, with mercenary armies and fascist organizations, this is all the more true. Today it must be stressed even more strongly that the proletariat must prepare in advance not only to fight for the troops, but also to *fight against them with arms,* to 'exterminate the enemy' in Lenin's words.

But exterminate him with what? How can the proletariat possibly be armed, given the increasing difficulty of subverting the army?

On the arming of the proletariat during the 1905 revolution, Lenin gave the following advice: 'The contingents . . . must arm themselves as best they can (rifles, revolvers, bombs, knives, knuckle-dusters, sticks, rags soaked in kerosene for starting fires, ropes or rope ladders, shovels for building barricades, pyroxylin cartridges, barbed-wire, nails against cavalry, etc., etc.). Under no circumstances should they wait for help from other sources, from above, from the outside; they must procure everything themselves.' ('Tasks of Revolutionary Army Contingents', October 1905).

Although the bourgeoisie of the advanced capitalist countries today possesses means of oppression superior to those of the Russian bourgeoisie in 1905, *the proletariat too has greater possibilities for obtaining arms than it did then.* The workers employed in the arms industry, in metallurgy and in chemicals handle explosives, manufacture weapons, load bullets, *transport* all this *matériel* by rail or inland waterway, etc.

Under these conditions, it is perfectly possible to envisage a serious and victorious struggle against the mercenary armies and the fascist units, even in 'peacetime'. Naturally, this struggle will only be possible if 'the

[2] In the 1931 French edition, the foregoing five words were replaced by the words 'right opportunists'.

other conditions are favourable'; *above all*, the decisive elements of the working population must be ready to take up arms, and must display the maximum energy, adaptability and inventiveness in arming themselves 'as best they can'.

The decisive factor governing the outcome of an armed insurrection is not merely a good military training and technique, but also the will of the masses to fight and make sacrifices, and the existence of a Bolshevik Party to lead the insurrection both politically and organizationally. *In many cases, it is these last factors which are decisive.*

Discussing Germany, Neuberg says that in 1923, although Proletarian Hundreds containing 250,000 men were formed in the course of a few months, their fighting value left much to be desired, since their commanders were ignorant of the tactics of street fighting and of insurrection in general. That the organization of the German red guard left much to be desired is certain; but it is essential to avoid the erroneous conclusion which the opportunists draw from this. The red guards of the insurgent proletariat will be most effective in combat, and will suffer the minimum of losses, if their best-trained soldiers and commanders are properly armed and have a good knowledge of military science – i.e. handling arms, the tactics of street fighting and field warfare, etc. *But it would be a grave opportunist error to wait for the creation of such well-trained and well-armed red guard detachments before launching the insurrection, despite the existence of a favourable and politically well-prepared revolutionary situation.* When the Russian proletariat came out armed onto the streets in February 1917 to overthrow the autocracy, and in October 1917 to overthrow the bourgeoisie, their armament and military organization were notoriously very defective – especially in February. But (just as the Cracow workers were to do in 1923) in the course of the fighting they succeeded in finding arms, allies among the soldiers and military commanders who led them to victory, through all the hardships of the civil war, against an enemy who was well-armed and supported by the whole state machine. Neuberg includes among the essential preconditions for the victory of any proletarian insurrection 'the military superiority of the insurgent forces over the enemy's armed forces', and 'the participation of the masses in the fighting at the same time as the combat organization'. In reality, however, this participation of the masses is not merely one of the key objectives in preparing for armed insurrection; it is the main objective, to which all other objectives must be subordinated. Otherwise, sectarian or grossly opportunist deviations are absolutely inevitable.

At the same time, we must welcome the insistence with which Neuberg stresses the importance of factors of military technique in the preparation of the armed uprising. In all parties there exist strong tendencies to underestimate these factors. *The proletariat must realize once and for all that mere enthusiasm and determination on their own will not suffice to overthrow the power of the bourgeoisie:* arms are needed, and a good military organization which relies on military science and on a plan of operations. Neuberg's great merit here is manifest, and must be acknowledged without reservation.

On the subject of the struggle for the ruling-class armed forces, Neuberg writes: 'The main objective of work in the army, navy and police (or gendarmerie) is to bring the mass of soldiers, sailors and police into the common front of the proletarian class struggle.'

Here, however, *a careful distinction must be made between the various formations which make up the bourgeoisie's armed forces.* An example of the way in which this question should be treated can be found in a manifesto posted up in the streets of Moscow before the insurrection of December 1905. The advice given to the insurgent workers included the following:

Carefully distinguish your conscious enemies from your unconscious and accidental enemies: annihilate the former, spare the latter. As far as possible, do not attack the infantry. The soldiers are children of the people, and they will never willingly march against the people. It is the officers and the high command who urge them on. It is against these officers and against the high command that you must direct your forces. Any officer leading soldiers to massacre workers is an enemy of the people and must be declared an outlaw. Kill him without mercy. No pity for the cossacks. They are drenched in the people's blood and are the sworn enemies of the workers. . . . Attack the dragoons and patrols and annihilate them. When you come up against the police do as follows: seize every opportunity to kill the commanding officers, down to the rank of superintendent; disarm and arrest the lower-ranking officers, and kill those of them who are known for their cruelty and spite; as for the rank-and-file policemen, merely take their arms and oblige them to serve you instead of the police.

This question has lost nothing of its importance since the revolution of 1905. On the contrary, in view of recent developments in the military apparatus of the bourgeois countries – where the system of ultra-reliable armed units and of special forces for civil war is combined with the most varied and extensive forms of general militarization of the population, culminating in the social-fascist 'workers'' military organizations like the National Flag association in Germany and the Defence League in Austria – this question demands the most serious study.

Neuberg's book does not deal adequately with the problem of *direct subversion of the army during the insurrection* – i.e. the struggle for the troops, the direction of their revolutionary actions, and *the organization of revolt inside the army*. It the chapter which should deal with this (Chapter 7) is almost exclusively devoted to work in the army in 'peacetime', and moreover, as its title shows, to the work of *the Communist Party*. It hardly discusses at all the action to be undertaken by the *proletariat in general vis-à-vis* the soldiers, *fraternization* between the working population and the soldiers, or liaison between the barracks and the factories. Yet this problem becomes crucial whenever the struggle grows sharper, and especially in an armed insurrection. A brilliant example of the way in which the subversion of the army should be carried out is provided by the activity of the Russian Bolsheviks during the imperialist war, and also, in the era of Soviet power, during the civil war. Moreover, the lessons of the mutiny of the French Black Sea fleet at Odessa in 1919 must also be studied seriously by the communist parties of all capitalist countries. For it is absolutely necessary to find a wide application for them in their own countries, if analogous conditions should arise.

Neuberg discusses the Bolshevik Party's role in preparing for armed insurrection exclusively in connection with the practical questions involved in the organization and operation of the Party's military detachments. The well-planned operation of these detachments is in fact one of the key preconditions for preparing the armed insurrection successfully. And yet we find that in all parties, right up to the present day, the military detachments are far from being up to their task, and that adequate attention is not generally paid to their work by the Party authorities (in spite of the fact that the twenty-one conditions for joining the Communist International include a special article requiring that all communist parties should carry out military work). Moreover, if it is necessary to discuss the work of the military detachments, it is even more so to discuss that of the special bodies created to prepare and direct the insurrection itself, i.e. *the revolutionary military committees*. A chapter should have been devoted specifically to these, but this was not done.

One should above all put the rich experience of the October Revolution to good use here. The immediate preparation of the insurrection is the essential factor for success in the proletarian armed struggle. This cannot be treated as normal military staff work, since it involves combined action by the armed forces of the revolution and by the broad proletarian masses and their allies among the working population. It involves leading the armed struggle and *the political mass strike*; coordinating and leading the revolutionary activity of all mass organizations, while destroying and annihilating the political influence of all social-fascist or openly fascist parties or groupings; and making the most extensive use of the trade unions, and above all of the factory committees, to elevate the partial struggles of the proletariat onto the level of open armed struggle to establish the dictatorship. It will be particularly important to show, by concrete examples, how essential it is in this phase to be quite unrelenting: once the insurrection has begun, it must be carried through without flinching before any obstacle, however serious. How many times would the October Revolution have perished, if the Communist Party had been swayed by the opportunistic and conciliatory arguments of Zinoviev and Kamenev!

It is extremely important for the Party cadres (and the proletarian masses) to understand the distinction between the functions of the revolutionary military committees and those of the Party organizations. The military committees, set up on the eve of the insurrection, prepare the military attack upon the old régime. The Party organizations continue their work of revolutionary mass mobilization, and of exposing the political adversaries of the plan for an armed insurrection; at the same time, they give instructions to the communist members of the revolutionary military committees, recall any of them who waver or prove unfit for the task, reinforce the committees with new members, etc.

Particular stress must be laid on the role of the Party in the period of open preparation for armed insurrection. As is well known, the Bolshevik Party brought the question of preparing for armed insurrection before the entire proletariat (in meetings, pamphlets, newspapers etc.) several months prior to the October Revolution. This was indispensable, since the armed insurrection being prepared by the Bolsheviks was no Blanquist plot hatched in the deepest secrecy by a handful of revolutionaries. The military plans for the insurrection must indeed be worked out in the closest secrecy; but as far as its political side and the preparation of the masses for armed struggle are concerned, it is necessary for the broad mass of the proletariat to be consulted. The indispensable precondition for success is the dissemination of the idea of armed insurrection among the masses. The mass of ordinary workers must know how events are developing; what the ever more frequent armed demonstrations and political mass strikes mean; and in what consist the duties incumbent on every worker in the event of combat between the armed forces of the revolution and those of the ruling classes.

The reader should pay particularly critical attention to those parts of Neuberg's book which deal with the participation of the peasant masses in the preparation and execution of armed uprisings. Here, it is absolutely essential to make more extensive use of the rich experience of the guerrilla movements in the USSR and China. This experience furnishes practical lessons of the first importance, especially with respect to the structure of revolutionary peasant armies: 1. Revolutionary peasant armies should be formed on a territorial basis; 2. Each village contingent should appoint a command subordinated to the political leadership of the local Communist Party committee (or Peasant League committee – once again, to the latter's communist fraction); 3. The village command *a*) must organize the provisioning of the army, by imposing set taxes on all the inhabitants, *b*) must appoint, from among the old people, a guard for the village and its surrounding region, *c*) must recruit, from among the youth, reserves for the mobile detachments, who are progressively made available to the active units of the peasant army, *d*) must organize intelligence work within the army and in the surrounding region, and constant liaison between the active units; 4. The indispensable preconditions for success in the organization and operations of the revolutionary peasant armies are: *a*) the proletarian and semi-proletarian composition of these armies, *b*) the presence of a nucleus of industrial workers and communists who form their military and political cadre, *c*) the coordination of their operations with the revolutionary struggle of the urban proletariat.

With respect to the volunteer military organizations of the ruling classes, Neuberg, quoting the decisions of the Sixth World Congress of the Communist International, writes: 'Every effort must be made to rouse a passionate hatred among the people towards these forces and to expose their real character.' But this advice requires amplification: it is necessary not only to arouse the hatred of the people, but also to organize a struggle to eliminate the activity and indeed the very existence of these detachments. The praxis of the class struggle has already forged the appropriate weapon for the present 'peacetime' conditions: the various organizations of proletarian defence. But for the most part these organizations are fighting fascism very inadequately; it is thus all the more essential to assist them with concrete advice, and to show them how, under present conditions, the attack on fascism should be organized.

It is impossible to accept Neuberg's assertion that the insurrections of the Paris Commune, of Canton, and of Moscow in 1905, were objectively doomed to failure because they took place when the revolutionary wave was no longer rising. This assertion contradicts the Marxist judgement already adopted by history. Particularly in the case of insurrections representing rearguard struggles in periods when the tide of revolution is on the ebb, it must be remembered that if successful they can serve as a starting-point for a new revolutionary upsurge.

Finally, a word must be said about the chapters devoted to the Canton and Shanghai insurrections. Neuberg gives some extremely valuable material on these, never previously published. But unfortunately his explanation of these insurrections is wholly unsatisfactory and[3] does not coincide with the line of the Communist International.

Characterizing the situation in Canton at the end of 1927, on the eve of the insurrection, Neuberg speaks of an 'upsurge of the proletarian class struggle', etc.; at the end of the chapter, he writes that it was only subsequently established by the Communist International that the Canton insurrection was a rearguard action. It is clear that the writer should have begun from there: should have explained the decision of the Eighth Plenum of the ECCI qualifying the Canton insurrection as a rearguard action, and shown in detail what a rearguard action is. It is not true that a rearguard action is necessarily doomed to failure. As was mentioned above, it can serve as the starting-point for a new phase of the struggle. But Neuberg, on the basis of this evaluation of the Canton insurrection as a rearguard action, draws the false conclusion that 'the indispensable social conditions,

[3] The last four words were omitted in the French edition of 1931.

without which the victory of armed insurrection is impossible, were not present to a sufficient degree in Canton'.

In the chapter on the Shanghai insurrection of April 1927, we find several incorrect formulations which might give the impression that in Neuberg's view the entry of the Chinese Communist Party into the Kuomintang was an error. As is well known, the Communist International decided at the time against the Chinese Party leaving the Kuomintang. The subsequent course of events fully confirmed the correctness of this stand. Neuberg should have shown how the Communist Party ought to have acted, while remaining in the Kuomintang; how it ought to have used its influence inside the latter to form a powerful revolutionary worker and peasant bloc, which, in Shanghai and elswhere, could have taken the leadership of a successful armed struggle of the masses to establish the revolutionary workers' and peasants' dictatorship.

The chapters on the Canton and Shanghai insurrections therefore require particularly critical scrutiny.

The publishers are distributing this book in the certainty that, despite all the defects alluded to above, it will be of the greatest use to every communist and revolutionary worker. Every revolutionary worker should consider it his duty to study this book with the greatest care.